Arturo Barea

The Forging of a Rebel

The Track

translated by
Ilsa Barea

FLAMINGO
Published by Fontana Paperbacks

The Track first published in English
by Faber and Faber Limited 1943

Published in an omnibus edition
(with *The Forge* and *The Clash*)
under the title *The Forging of a Rebel*
by Davis-Poynter Limited 1972

This Flamingo edition first published
in 1984 by Fontana Paperbacks,
8 Grafton Street, London W1X 3LA

Copyright in the English translation
Ilsa Barea 1943

Set in 10 on 12pt Plantin
Reproduced, printed and bound in Great Britain
by Hazell, Watson and Viney Limited,
member of the BPCC Group,
Aylesbury, Bucks.

Contents

Author's Foreword

It does not seem easy to me, the author, to classify this book and *The Forge*, of which it is a kind of continuation. In *The Forge* I tried to show the world of my childhood in Madrid and Castile, and therefore it had to be called an autobiography. The present book describes the world of the Spanish Army, which I had known as a young man, and my own reactions to it, and therefore it also must be called an autobiography. But neither of these two books is meant to be autobiographical in the strict sense of the term, for neither has been written with the intention of telling the public about the author's private life.

It is true – and this constitutes the autobiographical character of what I have written – that in *The Forge* and *The Track* I have tried to put down life as I have seen, lived, and imagined it at the time, as well as the history of my own adjustment to this life – to put down with as much sincerity, detachment, and ruthlessness towards myself and others as I could summon. Yet, in another sense, these two books are novels written in the first person: the child of *The Forge*, the young man of *The Track*, whom you may learn to know through my writing, no longer exist. A great deal of them may live on in me, transformed but still active; yet they are no longer 'I', not my self of today. I have tried to present them as they were, uncoloured by the glasses through which I see things today, as I might wish to write with truth about somebody other than myself. Neither of these two autobiographical books of mine embodies my present state of mind, imagination, and opinions otherwise than indirectly, through the pattern of what my memory has selected or rejected.

In attempting to resurrect myself as a child and a young man I had a very personal objective: I wanted to discover how and why I became what I am, to understand the forces and emotions behind my present reactions. I tried to find them, not through a psychological analysis, but by calling up the images and sensations I had once seen and felt, and later on absorbed and re-edited.

I also had a general objective. In taking and exploring my past self as a member of the Spanish generation, which was the core of the Civil War, I hoped to expose some of the roots of that war. I wanted to describe the shocks which had scarred my mind, because I am convinced that these shocks, in different individual forms but from the same collective causes, scarred and shaped the minds of other Spaniards too. I wanted to expose my own reactions, because I believed that the others' reactions were determined by kindred forces, and that the world they saw was the same as mine, even though seen through different lenses.

What I have recorded in this book of the Spanish War in Morocco and the military dictatorship of the 1920s, prelude to the fall of the Spanish Monarchy, is historically as strictly true as any individual experiences can be. I have checked the objective facts with my limited resources as a counter-check on my memory. It has become clear to me that what I witnessed was the embryonic stage in the development of military fascism in Spain, more particularly the beginnings of General Franco's political career. But I have constantly endeavoured not to let my present knowledge and conviction impinge upon the picture I formed at that time, because only the picture is historically relevant.

A very distinguished critic of *The Forge* pointed out that 'the experiences chronicled by the author' are not 'at all singular', and that 'the conversation . . ., the discoveries . . . and the disillusionments of experience are such as could be described by millions . . .'. This is perfectly true of the present book too, and it is as I think it should be. (It is, incidentally, also the reason why I cannot consider these books of mine as straight autobiographies.) The millions who shared the same experiences and disappointments do not usually write, but it is they who are the rank and file in wars, revolutions and 'New Orders', they who carry on in the Old Order, helpless, restless, and disillusioned. Some of them defended Madrid, some evacuated Dunkirk; others died for General Franco; some of them in this country wonder just what the war is about. They are usually called the common people or the 'little men' or the 'lower orders'. As I was one of them, I have attempted to be vocal on their behalf, not in the form of propaganda, but simply by giving my own truth.

There are stories, true stories, which I love to tell to my friends, but have not included in this book, such as 'How I entered the Sacred City in Disguise together with the General', or 'How I leapt Naked from a Bedroom into a Moorish Café'. These would have been suitable tales for an anecdotal autobiography which puts the highlights on the spectacular and amusing; but to me they carried no deeper association, either personal or general, and so left them out. Yet the filth of the hospital, the gory nightmare of the massacres, the technique of petty graft, the boredom of endless marches, the boredom of night life, the noise of taverns, the unquestioning comradeship of the army, the smell of the sea at dawn, and the glare of the African sun – all this made us what we are, and this I have chronicled.

I am working on a third autobiographical book – autobiographical in the same sense as this and *The Forge* – in which I deal with the crash towards which we travelled along this track: the Civil War. I could not have embarked on that third book without having laid bare the roots of the catastrophe, such as they existed in my own life. But I want to say frankly that I already mean the present book, *The Track*, just like *The Forge*, to illuminate to the public of this country the dark psychological and social under-currents of the Spanish War and its aftermath, which are so palpably still an integral part of this greater war.

And after all, the Spain which I would like to show to the British public must needs be a part of the greater peace.

It would be fatuous for me to give the usual thanks to the translator, because in this case the translator is my wife. But I want to acknowledge the great debt of gratitude we both owe to our friends Olive Corthorn Renier and Margaret Rink, who revised the English version of this book.

ARTURO BAREA

Fladbury, Worcestershire,
April 1943

Part I

1. Under Canvas

I am sitting on a stone, polished by millions of raindrops, smooth like a bare skull. It is a whitish stone, full of pores. It burns in the sun and sweats in the dampness. Thirty yards from me stands the old fig tree, its roots twisted like the veins of a robust old man, its contorted branches hung with the trefoil of its fleshy leaves. On the other bank of the stream, beyond the ravine, the remains of the *kabila* straggle up the hillside.

A few months ago a group of huts stood there, built of straw and twigs. Inside, mats of plaited straw. One mat in the doorway, where you left your heelless slippers, the babouches, on entering; another inside, on which you squatted down round the tea cups. A few bigger ones lined up along the wall for sleeping. The *kabila* was nothing but straw huts and straw mats. Its bread was a kind of cake baked on hot stones and made of grain pounded between stones, a blackish cake bristling with bits of singed straw. The sharp hairs of the dry wheat ears stuck in your throat and bit you there with their hundreds of teeth.

The *kabila* would wake up in the morning and its men would come out of the huts, each beating his pitiful little donkey. Then he would mount it and his babouches would flap on the ground, so small was the donkey. Behind him came his wife, burdened, everlastingly burdened. The three would go to the flatter part of the hillside and the man would dismount. The woman would unstrap the wooden plough from her shoulders and harness it to the donkey. Then she would meekly yoke herself to the plough and the man would inspect the knots in the harness of donkey and woman. He would take hold of the plough, and the woman and the donkey would begin to walk, slowly, in step, the donkey pulling the ropes with his collar, the woman pulling the rope crossed over her flaccid breasts, both working slowly, planting their feet deep in the soil and sinking into their knees at each stop.

The lords of the *kabila* would begin their mounting on horseback, on nervous little horses with thick manes. Their rifles slung on a bandolier, they would disappear into the hills. Nothing remained in the *kabila* but the chickens, the sheep, and the children, all playing about between the huts, pecking, browsing, tumbling in the dust; all smeared with dirt and slime, all toasted and bleached by the sun.

A few months ago the *kabila* was razed to the ground. It was done from so short a distance that the artillery had no need of range finders. The captain of the battery had said:

'What for? You simply fire, just as you throw a stone at a dog.'

At the first shell, everything had come tumbling down. The straw of the huts burst into blazing chips. The children fled uphill among the rocks. The chickens and the sheep scattered as their instinct drove them. The women gave piercing shrieks which resounded throughout the valley. The lords of the *kabila* made their horses caracole, brandishing their rifles in the air. When a few shells had been fired, the infantry marched up the hill and occupied the hamlet. The soldiers rounded up the scattered chickens and sheep which returned to their homestead at sunset. They lit their campfires and ate their evening meal. The air was full of the breast feathers of chickens, which drifted slowly around, sometimes settling gently in a bowl. The operations had gone according to plan. At nightfall there was nothing but some heaps of smoking straw and two or three children mangled by the first shell, chicken feathers drifting in the air, and sheepskins, a banquet for flies, stuck on crossed poles. The place where the *kabila* had been smelled of jute from the thousand sandbags which formed the parapet; it smelled of roast meat, of horses, and of soldiers, of sweaty soldiers with lice in every fold of their uniforms.

The General who had conquered the *kabila* was sitting in his tent. On his table was a burning candle end, a tray, two bottles of wine, and several glasses. The officers of the units which had taken part in the conquest entered his tent one by one, each reporting his casualties in dead and wounded. Every officer had two or three dead, ten or twelve wounded to his credit. The General's adjutant noted them down. The General offered each officer a glass of wine. They went away dreaming of the decorations which the list of dead would bring them. During the night the General snored the snores of an old drunkard who sleeps with his mouth open and his teeth swimming in a glass of water.

The next morning the notables of the *kabila* arrived. They brought a bull and cut its throat before the General whose eyes were still puffed with sleep and wine. The bull bellowed to all the valleys and all the rocks on the hills. The General made a speech, though he wanted to go back to sleep. 'Why must this rabble come so early in the morning?' he thought. Afterwards his adjutant gave the notables a bag of silver coins.

Months have gone by since this glorious battle in which a heroic army gained a great victory over the *kabila*. The *kabila* no longer exists except for a few smoke-blackened patches. Now I am here. The valley is like an ant heap. Hundreds of men are breaking up and levelling the ground for a broad track which is to lead past the foot of the hill and which will be very useful for the *kabila*. Well, the *kabila* will not be able to make use of it, because it exists no longer. But people say there is iron and coal in these hills. Perhaps a mining town will soon spring up where the *kabila* stood, or perhaps a blast furnace. Along the road, a train will run laden with ore and pit-coal. The Moors from the old *kabila* will come back; they will eat white bread without harsh straw. They will travel in the train, grimed with coal dust. They will go to the town and amuse themselves at the fair. They will ride on the merry-go-round and visit the booth with the Negro at whose face they can throw balls. They will shriek with laughter at the Negro's grimaces and will go back to the mines happy.

In the hills there will be a house built of cement, full of soldiers. When the Moors are no longer happy with the mine and with the bruised Negro, the soldiers will set up their machine guns.

But all this will come later, and perhaps I shall never see it. Yet the track for the road must pass here at the foot of the *kabila* and through the place where the old fig tree stands. As its roots go very deep we shall blow up the tree with half a dynamite charge tomorrow. Underneath the trunk we are boring a hole which will reach to its very heart.

And we have eaten its last figs. They were sweet as old honey.

Córcoles and I went right up to the Zoco del Arbaa in one of the four lorries which we had to take to Hamara Hill loaded with material. In the Zoco a group of soldiers was waiting for us under the command of Herrero, a re-enlisted sergeant, a veteran of Africa, dry and bony, with a good-natured face and sun-bitten but finely drawn features. We made friends on a few bottles of German beer, cheaper in Morocco than beer from Spain. The twenty soldiers of the group began to unload the lorry and to load the mule team which was to carry the material to the Hamara position. It was astonishing to see, as the pile on the ground mounted, what a load the four vehicles had contained: plaster and lime, cement and bricks, iron bars, wooden planks, and sandbags. The soldiers came and went. Those on the top of the lorries played at stoning the others, throwing the bricks from hand to hand in a chain. Time and again they furtively turned to take a look at me.

They wanted to look at the new sergeant with the silver stripes on his cuff, all new and shiny, sewn on a fortnight ago. 'What will he be like?' they whispered to each other.

Córcoles and I left with the first convoy of mules which was loaded up, while Herrero stayed behind with two soldiers to see to the rest. Córcoles took the head of the column and asked me to bring up the rear so that nobody should straggle. Thus I went behind all the others, absolutely alone. I looked curiously at the landscape. The men in front talked about me. I felt it almost like a physical impact, but it produced no reaction in me. I looked at the landscape.

To the left there was the endless chain of bald granite mountains which follow the coast of Africa from Rio Martin to Alhucemas. To the right marched the distant green mountains of the Jebel Alam. We rode through a valley which was nothing but a wide, sand-filled bed into which the torrents poured from the mountains during the great rains. The grey-white granite and the yellow sand shimmered in the sun, glittering with sharp points of light, but the green mountains were soft and restful to the eye. Before us, tawny hills enclosed the bottom of the sandy waste. One of them was Hamara.

We reached its foot after two hours of march choked by the heat and the dust which the hoofs of the mules kicked up. A stream traced a semi-circle round the hill whose steep slope rose abruptly from the water. On the edge of the stream the bridle path was slushy where men's feet and horses' hoofs, wet from crossing the ford, had heaped up the mud. The crest of the hill was level as though its

The Forging of a Rebel

The Track

Born in Madrid in 1897, Arturo Barea
lived in England from 1939 until his
death in 1957. The story of his years in
Spain is the subject matter of his
remarkable autobiographical trilogy,
The Forging of a Rebel. The first volume,
The Forge, describes his childhood and
youth. *The Track* takes him from the
age of twenty to twenty-eight – years
spent as a conscript soldier in Spanish
Morocco, as a businessman and as a
husband and father. *The Clash*
describes the Spanish Civil War and his
own part in that struggle.

Forced to leave Spain, he and Ilsa,
the Austrian socialist and journalist who
became his second wife, settled in the
village of Eaton Hastings near
Faringdon in Berkshire. He worked for
the BBC during the war, and
contributed articles to journals such as
Horizon, *London Forum* and *The Times
Literary Supplement*. Barea published
novels and short stories as well as books
of criticism, including *Lorca, the Poet
and his People* (1944) and *Unamuno*
(1952). *The Forge*, *The Track* and *The
Clash* (published simultaneously in
Flamingo) were first published in
English translation and appeared in
eight other languages before the first
edition in Spanish came out in Buenos
Aires in 1951

summit had been sliced off with a knife. Our position was there, on the round plateau: a circle of stone, three feet high, behind a circle of rusty wire bristling with spikes; inside, dirty canvas tents and two small wooden hutments. This was my first sight of Hamara.

Córcoles stayed with the soldiers who unloaded the mules, and I went to report to the Captain. As I did not know the ground I stumbled over tent ropes half hidden by the weeds and made two or three unnecessary detours. The soldiers behind my back tittered as they watched me, and I entered the Captain's tent in a state of irritation.

'All right,' he said, 'go to the sergeants' tent and rest until dinner time. Then I will introduce you to the company.'

In the tent there was another sergeant.

'You're the new one, aren't you? . . . Manzanares, this is Sergeant Barea.'

The orderly was a tiny little man with rapid movements, his features mobile as though his face were made of soft rubber. He spoke with the purest Madrid accent:

'Everything's in order. Here's your bed, good as a king's. And just let me know if you want anything.'

'What about something to drink, then?'

'Poof! Heaps and heaps. Whatever you like: wine, beer, eau-de-vie, brandy, everything except water. Water gives you marsh-fever. Prohibited. The only thing it's any good for is washing.'

'Bring me the coolest stuff you have.'

He brought a bottle of wine which was instantly covered with a grey film of condensed moisture. The wine was almost ice cold.

'Have you got ice here?'

'No, indeed, sir, it's cooled by the sun.'

I laughed in my ignorance. At five in the afternoon the sun was scorching hot and the tent like an oven. The sergeant asked me the obligatory questions and told me the obvious things. Anything new in Tetuan? I did not know, I had come fresh from Ceuta. He had not been to Ceuta for two years. There were four sergeants: Córcoles, and Herrero whom I had met, another one called Julian out on the track, and he himself, acting as orderly sergeant this week, besides being mess sergeant. His name was Castillo. Dinner time was at six in the afternoon. And then the orderly came to tell Castillo that the

Captain wanted to see him. I was left alone and stared at the tent which was to be my home.

In the centre, a pole about thirteen feet high supporting the canvas which stretched cone-shaped, with a diameter of twenty feet at the base. The rifles and knapsacks of the four sergeants leaning against the pole. The door, a gap in the canvas. Opposite the opening a folding-table and half a dozen seats hewn roughly out of branches. Seven beds, like the spokes of a wheel, head ends pressing against the sloping canvas wall of the tent, feet ends towards the centre. Each bed made of six stout branches rammed into the ground, their upper ends in the shape of a fork, carrying a framework of four other branches to which a piece of wire netting had been nailed. Over the wire netting a mattress and bolster of sacking filled with straw, two sheets, and a blanket. Beside every bed a box or suitcase. But there were seven beds and we were five.

The bugle sounded for the meal parade. I buttoned up my coat and went out. Two enormous cauldrons were set up in the open space outside the encampment. A double file was slowly forming up, headed by the corporals. On the other side, beyond the file, was a huge wooden structure, obviously a storehouse, and a few straw huts no more than six feet high. Moors in filthy, tattered burnouses crawled through the low openings and clustered round the huts.

Herrero began the roll-call, standing in front of the double file formed by about one hundred men. When he had finished he waited until Captain Blanco, accompanied by a lieutenant and an ensign, came out of his tent. Herrero shouted:

'Atten-tion! Nothing to report, sir.'

The Captain called me to his side in front of the double file.

'Sergeant Barea has been detailed to the Company and has joined us today.' He turned to me: 'Stand the company at ease.'

'Company – stand at ease!'

I was presented. Afterwards, the Captain introduced me to Lieutenant Arriaga and Ensign Mayorga.

While the food was handed out, Córcoles introduced me to the last of the four sergeants, Julian. They made a good pair. Córcoles was tall, a gypsy type, with frizzy hair, nervy and lively; Julian was short and very plump, with the voice of a soubrette, smooth, apple-red cheeks and lanky hair.

The soldiers took their tins away and sat on the ground to eat. Then the Moors lined up, some carrying rusty, dented old mess bowls, others empty tin cans. The cook had doled out a ladleful to each of them; the Moors went and squatted round their huts, most of them eating with their fingers, and a few with the short army spoons.

I looked at everyone and everyone looked at me. They whispered their impressions to each other, and I felt that some of them would have liked to come and finger me to find out more. The stare of the crowd annoyed me. It was a stare which hid distrust.

After the meal, the Captain sent for me to his tent.

'As from tomorrow you will be in charge of the works. These are the instructions I have received from Tetuan. Apparently you know topography. That's correct, isn't it?' He talked somewhat haughtily, squinting at me. The Captain was terribly cross-eyed.

'I know something of topography, sir.'

'And of accountancy?'

'Yes, sir. More, really.'

'All right. As from tomorrow you will take charge of the material and wages account and of the construction work. As my adjutant, of course.'

'Of course, sir.'

'You can go.'

'But I would like to . . .'

'You can go.'

'At your orders, sir.'

When I left the tent I felt dazed. Ten months before I had been a civilian in Madrid. In the interval I had been a private and then a corporal; I had gone from a civilian to a military office, continuing to work among papers and figures. From one day to the next I found myself in the heart of the Lesser Atlas, in a front-line position, in charge of the construction of a road of which I did not even know the destination, and with the accountancy of works which I did not understand. Moreover, I was a sergeant, that is to say, a vertebra in the spine of the army, or rather – so much I did know – a member of the group which is kicked from above by the officers, and from below by the men.

In civilian life you weigh up difficulties and pit yourself against them, or else you avoid them. If you fail, it is bad luck; if you win, it is your merit; if you avoid the fight, you stay where you are and nothing happens. But in the army it is different. They confront you with the difficulties and you must tackle them. If you fail, they punish you; if you win, you have done your duty. In my civilian life I would never have dreamed of applying for the post of surveyor and accountant of road works. In the army the Captain had cut short my expostulations: 'You can go.' What the devil was I going to do next morning?

I went back to our tent. On one of the seven beds lay a civilian who raised himself on his elbow when I entered. A massive man, rather stout, his trousers unbuttoned, wearing only a singlet which showed the thick, dark mat of hair on his chest. Square hands folded over his paunch; sausage-like fingers with black tufts of hair on their backs; his shoe soles studded with thick, square nails; loosely hanging red socks. He pointed to a case of beer bottles at the foot of the bed: 'Help yourself, but it isn't very cold.' I poured out a glass of beer and gulped it down. Who was this fellow, this civilian in the sergeants' tent? He sat up on the bed, his belly folding in three rolls of fat.

'I believe we don't know each other yet. I'm José Suarez. Everybody calls me Señor Pepe. The stone contractor. I'm sure you and I will get on well together.'

'I suppose so. Why not?' I introduced myself.

But the man was expansive. He got off the bed, holding up his trousers with both hands, and sat down opposite me at the folding table. He fumbled in an enormous cigar case and selected a cigar after crunching one or two between his fingers.

'Smoke this one. It's excellent.'

'I'm sorry. I only smoke cigarettes.'

'Me too. But these cigars are necessary for business.' He grinned a knowing little grin.

We lit our cigarettes and fell silent, looking at each other. In the end he said:

'I suppose you know all about everything.'

I started laughing, somewhat artificially. 'Heavens, man, I don't know anything. As they say in Madrid, I've just come here from my village. The day before yesterday I was in Ceuta, today I'm here, without ever having served as a sergeant in a field company before, to say nothing of all this business of road making. To make things worse, I don't know anyone here. So I just don't know anything about anything.'

The orderly entered with a snack and another of his moisture-filmed bottles of wine. Behind the fat man's back he gave me a wink.

The other said: 'That's what I thought. And that's why I'm glad we've met here alone. We don't need more than five minutes, and everything will be settled. I told you I'm the stone contractor. I've got a gang of Moors working, some quarrying and some crushing stone. The Company supplies the dynamite and I pay for it. And then the Company pays me for the stone per cubic metre. You've got to book the dynamite I use and the cubic metres of stone I deliver. At the end of the month we clear accounts. Sometimes my Moors help your people to level the ground, and it's the same thing: so-and-so many cubic metres of earth, so-and-so many pesetas.'

'It doesn't sound very difficult to me. I don't think we shall have any quarrel.'

'Certainly not. There's enough for both. It's my custom to give a third of the benefits.'

'To whom?'

He gave me a look of blank surprise: 'To whom d'you think? To you in this case.'

'You mean the accounts won't be straight?'

'The accounts will be as straight as anything. No one can find any fault in them. Of course, you must pass them. The Captain takes the other third.'

'The Captain is in it, then?'

'We couldn't do anything without him. You go and ask him.'

'I won't ask him. If he wants to tell me something he can come to me.'

I must have answered rather sharply. Señor Pepe shut up. We talked about anything and nothing. After a short while he buttoned up his trousers and left. 'I must see how the boy's getting on,' he said. Who the devil was the boy? Ten minutes later the Captain sent for me.

'At your orders, sir.'

'Shut the tent flap and sit down a moment.' He looked at me with each of his eyes separately.

'I assume you've settled things with Pepe.'

'He has spoken to me, sir. But I didn't really understand him. I don't know anything yet, as you will realize.'

'All right, all right. That's why I sent for you. I'll explain. You know, the Spanish State carries out all its public works either by contract or by direct management. If it's contracts, tenders are invited and the contractor is paid the agreed sum. If it's direct management, the amount of costs is budgeted, the administration takes sole charge of the work, and pays for wages and materials. Now it is quite obvious that this road here cannot be given in contract since it leads through hostile territory. It is built under direct management. We pay the wages and buy the materials. We map out the project and we carry out the work. The Army Works Department in Tetuan is responsible for the technical and administrative sides. Everyone here gets paid for this work. The soldiers earn two and a half pesetas per day, the sergeants six, and we twelve. It means a great benefit for all. The soldiers get one and a half in cash and the rest goes to improve their food. So there is no need to pinch anything from their mess or equipment. It is easy.'

He made a pause and took a bottle of brandy and two glasses from a box.

'I didn't want to call the orderly. To continue. I am going to speak very openly to you so that we really understand each other. The Company has a particular fund into which goes what we save on our budget. For instance: the Company has one hundred and eleven men but not all of them are working. Some are sick, others on leave, still others are detailed on this or that duty. But since the budget provides for one hundred and eleven men, we get the cash for their wages. Those who don't work don't get paid, and the wage surplus goes into the Company Fund. It's the same with the Moors. According to the budget, there are four hundred of them, but in fact they're never complete. We have about three hundred and fifty here. Now four hundred simply must be accounted for: we put approximately fifty Arab names on the list and everything is fine. Who's going to count them here? The Moors earn five pesetas a day, and they get as much bread on credit as they like. But that's your business. As regards Pepe, it is more or less the same story. He supplies stone to us and we pay for it. Every kilometre of the road requires so-and-so many cubic metres of stone. But if the road has five centimetres less in width, it means in stone . . . Well, work it out for yourself. Five centimetres less are two hundred cubic metres of stone per kilometre. As a matter of fact we put something more to account. In addition the Moors help us in levelling the ground and we pay them per cubic metre. It does not matter if we put some of the work done by our men to the account of the Moors.'

He drank his glass of brandy.

'There are a great many more details which I'll teach you in due course. Now, we're agreed, aren't we?'

I found nothing to say, and I left.

After supper, Señor Pepe took a pack of cards from his pocket and started to deal for baccarat, putting two hundred and fifty pesetas in the bank. I refused to play and threw myself down on my bed.

'Here, all of us play,' he said.

'All right. But I can't gamble with my first pay before I've even got it.'

'Don't worry about money. How much do you need?'

'I? Nothing. I told you I don't play.'

'I'll give you one hundred pesetas as a present. Sit down with us.' I sat down. He dealt the cards, and I put the one hundred pesetas on the first cards he offered me.

'Now look here, that's no way to play. If you lose I'll have to give you another hundred pesetas.'

I won the hundred pesetas and two thousand more. Señor Pepe stopped the game.

'Let's leave it for today. We must talk business.'

Pepe's son, Pepito, who occupied the seventh bed – a large-boned youth with the face of a stone mason in his Sunday best – applauded:

'Cheers, Father.'

He looked the perfect idiot: he looked like a double-dyed rascal shamming the idiot.

Señor Pepe addressed my comrades:

'Barea has heard about our custom. And we agree. I think he's had a talk with the Captain, haven't you?'

'Yes, I've heard about everything. But I am not sure that we have agreed. Señor Pepe is to give me one third of the price of the surplus stone I'm to put to account.'

Córcoles exclaimed:

'One half!'

'You agree, Don José?' I asked.

'Well, one half for all of you, of course.'

'Good. Now the Captain. He explained to me how it works with the wages and with Señor Pepe, but he didn't offer me anything. Apparently he gets it all.'

Córcoles spoke up.

'The Captain won't offer you anything, of course. But it's all very simple. You can't ever pay wages to exactly four hundred Moors and one hundred and eleven men. The figures must always be less; if they were complete it would look funny. We keep, say, a day's wages of ten Moors, and it means fifty pesetas per day for the five of us. The same happens with Señor Pepe's stone and earth. That's where our profit comes in.'

'And the Lieutenant and the Ensign?'

'The Lieutenant is a millionaire and has no idea of the whole game. Just imagine: he's a man who doesn't draw his pay and gives it to the soldiers' mess. The Ensign has a share of our part and a share of the Captain's too. He's a sharp one.'

'So the Captain keeps all the savings of the Company for himself?'

'Don't be an ass. The Company savings are what can be saved on the military budget of the Company. The savings from works and buildings are shared out between the Captain and the Works Department in Tetuan.'

'Then the Major is in it too?'

'Now listen, without him we couldn't do a thing. Don't be stupid.'

None of us spoke. It seemed to me that I was playing the fool. The cards were scattered on the table; I began to gather them mechanically.

'It seems robbery to me.'

'So it is,' said Córcoles. 'We're robbing the State.'

'And suppose I don't feel like stealing, what then?'

Còrcoles looked at me, shrugged his shoulders and began to laugh. But my face was taut and serious. He stood up and took my arm.

'It's damned hot here. Come along, let's go outside for a bit.'

We went out together and leaned against the stone parapet. It exuded moisture. The fields lay silent, furrowed by the moonlight.

'Did you seriously mean what you said?'

'Yes. This is a foul business. It's stealing.'

'Listen. Stealing is when you take somebody's money. But this is quite different. It's the State. If we rob anybody it's the State – and the State is fleecing us anyhow. Do you think you can live on a sergeant's pay, ninety pesetas a month? Do you think you can live on the pay plus the war bonus in Africa, one hundred and forty pesetas? You've got the right to marry. But just you try marrying on a hundred and forty per month.'

He looked at the distant hills and continued more softly:

'Come closer. Listen. There's something else, too. It's like when your hand gets caught in the cogs, and then your arm, and then the whole of you. You can't escape. And if you don't agree to steal for the others and for yourself, they'll take away your job and transfer you. They'll send you where you starve to death and where a bullet is waiting for you. If you want to talk and to protest there are simpler ways and means. They'll deprive you of your stripes for some blunder which can be made to look bad. And there's another thing too' – his voice was very low – 'anyone can have an accident. There are snipers every day on the way to El Zoco. Now think it over. Maybe you haven't heard what they say: behind the door of every barracks is a nail; when we enter the service we've got to hang our manhood on that nail; afterwards, when we get out, we may collect what's left, if any.'

We returned to the tent. Señor Pepe held the bank once more. We played until two in the morning. I lost everything. We went to sleep in our beds, the spokes of the wheel. The pole in the centre, the rifles leaning against it. One after the other began to snore. Señor Pepe snored, it sounded like a pig guzzling watery potatoes in a trough. I thought of Córcoles and his advice, of the journey from Ceuta to Hamara, of the money I had lost.

That was in the first days of June 1920.

2. The Road

The bugle sounded at six in the morning. The camp, where nothing had been moving but the grey shapes of the night sentries, burst into noisy life. Soldiers shouted at each other, their tin plates clattering against the tin mugs. They lined up beside the huge coffee cauldron and the basket heaped with bread and waited, shuffling their feet in the chill of the mountain morning, until the mess sergeant gave the signal for distributing the coffee. At seven, when the general clean-up of men, horses and tents was finished, the working gangs were formed. After the roll-call the men marched downhill, each armed with a spade and pickaxe. Then the Moors began to turn up, some drowsily leaving their huts, others coming from nearby settlements. Many of them preferred to sleep at the camp because their homes were far away or no longer existed, but also because they could count on the abundant left-overs from the mess for their food. Others lived somewhere in the neighbourhood and arrived with their leather bags strapped on crosswise, stuffed with dried figs. These figs and the bread ration – about two pounds – which was given to every man who claimed it, constituted their meal for the day. They never returned to their tribe before nightfall.

The Moors were under the command of a headman, the *Capataz*, who passed orders on to them, saw to discipline during work, held the roll-call and occasionally punished an offender or a recalcitrant sluggard with his stick. They feared the heavy hand of their *Capataz* and never stopped working, but each of their movements was so slow and measured that lifting and bringing down a pickaxe or shifting a shovelful of earth seemed a matter of minutes rather than of seconds.

Señor Pepe was in despair and would sometimes use his horsewhip on the ribs of one of his Moors to make him speed up. To us, and to me, the pace of the men hardly mattered. Nobody had an interest in the rapid progress of the work. The sooner it ended the sooner the pay would stop. The soldiers showed their resentment at being used as labourers with spade and pickaxe. The six hundred men scattered over four kilometres of track and over the granite cliffs of the quarry, a sluggish mass moving slowly under the African sun, did not look as though they were busy building a road.

The orderly sergeant never went down to the track. One of the other sergeants usually went 'shopping' to the Zoco del Arbaa. The Captain slept off the brandy of the night before. The Lieutenant slept. The Ensign slept. At seven in the morning, only three sergeants marched downhill at the head of the soldiers and the Moors. Hours later the Captain or one of the two officers would come down on horseback and inspect the track. Afterwards they would go shooting. And frequently one of them would go to Tetuan or Tangier.

Thus the road building fell automatically to my share. I had to take charge not only of the accountancy but also of the topographical work. Major Castelo in Tetuan had sent an order that I should prepare a map of the terrain from Xarca-Xeruta to the Zoco del Arbaa and suggested the tracing of the road to the best of my knowledge. Previously, the men had worked in the plain and the level ground had ruled out the possibility of blunders. But from Hamara onwards the track had to skirt hills and to lead down into the vale of the river Lau. It was necessary to plan the track carefully. This took me about three weeks, during which I adapted myself to the daily routine without being aware of it. But after this period I found myself at leisure. There was nothing for me to do but to keep watch during the eight hours of work.

I would sit down on a smooth stone between the roots of an ancient fig tree, at the foot of Hamara Hill, from where I was able to survey the whole stretch under work. Sometimes the other two sergeants or the headman of the Moors joined me for a brief consultation, but for the greater part of the day I was alone, except for the little company bugler who sat near by. He had to accompany me wherever I went; he had to give the signal for the hours of rest, to blow the bugle for any general order and to carry messages to the men. If we were to escape boredom in those empty hours of watch, we could not help talking to each other.

I could tell from his age and his size that he had volunteered for our corps, because only tall men, and men with special qualifications, are officially selected for the Engineers. This one was a plump little fellow of about thirty-two years of age, with a grave and quiet countenance but with agile movements. And he was past master in the rogue's wisdom of buglers and drummer boys. For buglers, drummer boys and batmen are in the army what the servants are in an aristocratic residential quarter: they have masonic signs and a secret language of their own. If one of them tells you that you'd better not speak to the Captain, the only thing to do is to follow his advice.

Our company bugler, Martin, was almost illiterate in so far as he was incapable of understanding anything he read, but he was full of what he called 'African Science'. This ranged from the ability to tie tent ropes in scientific knots to the knack of keeping a fire burning under the most violent torrential rain: it included an extraordinary skill in mending clothes and shoes and in manufacturing watch-chains, bracelets and rings from horsehair which he would plait into minute ringlets and links and weave into fantastic patterns. But above all he knew every single piece of news, public or private, from the organization of the next military operations against the Raisuni to the hidden diseases of any private and any general.

From Tetuan, I had carried with me a great number of French novels, most of them with engravings; I usually took a couple or so down to the track to kill time. My first long talk with the bugler arose from this habit of mine. One day he approached me:

'Could you let me have a look at the saints, sir?'

He turned the pages eagerly. The illustrations of those novels mostly showed women who would necessarily seem seductive in the eyes of a primitive Spaniard. But by chance the novel I was reading just then was *Aphrodite* by Pierre Louys. The edition was sprinkled with steel engravings of Greek scenes showing nudes. At every new page the bugler exploded:

'What a wench! *Mi Madre!* What breasts, what thighs!'

Then he contemplated for a while the printed pages innocent of pictures, and said in the end:

'The things they must tell here . . . You understand them, sir?'

'What do you think they are?'

'Well now, you can see what it is. With these painted women here and in French – well, hot stuff. What they call pornography, about all the things they're doing in bed and about how to do them. Once I bought a book like this in Tetuan, it cost me pesetas, and it was stolen from me later on. But it explained all the postures. And there are post-cards too, but they sell them for one peseta each. Now here am I telling you, sir, and you know much more about these things than me.'

Abdella, the headman of the Moors, was coming towards us just at that moment. He was a strong man of Berber type, with a short black beard, wide open eyes, his very regular features disfigured by smallpox. He wore, not a burnous, but a uniform with the badge of the Engineers, a silver tower, on the collar. Before he could speak to me in his usual perfect Spanish, slowly choosing his words, the bugler called him:

'I say, you. A damn' fine woman!' He held one of the illustrations under the other's eyes. The Moor looked at the book and addressed me in French:

'You speak French, then, sir?'

'Where have you learned to speak it?'

'In Tangier, with the French. I served in the *Goumiers* and afterwards in the Spanish *Regulares* and now I have been with the Engineers for the last ten years. That's all.'

Martin looked in surprise from one to the other.

'God save us! Do you speak Arabic, sir?'

'Don't be stupid. That was French, the same as the writing in those books.'

This incident had various unexpected results. Martin spread the news that I spoke French among the soldiers, and their resentment against me – the natural resentment against the new sergeant – increased. Abdella made friends with me and came to seek me in the shade of the fig tree, with one excuse or the other. The bugler saw his opportunity for chats reduced and resented Abdella's intrusion; he made desperate efforts to capture my friendship and to turn me away from the Moor. My comrades, the sergeants, grew curious; their visits to the fig tree became more frequent. In the end a little circle met regularly under the fig tree. And from there I began to establish contact with the world which surrounded me. I began to see it.

Every four or five minutes I saw that Moor repeat the same procedure: he would drop his pickaxe and scratch all accessible parts of his body, furiously, with both hands. Then he would shake himself within the folds of his burnous like a dog coming out of the water. Sometimes he rubbed his back against the edge of the fresh cut in the earth, before he resumed work. I went to him.

'What's the matter with you?'

'I'm ill. The whole body itches. The whole body is very ill.'

His hands were knotty, reddened, covered with dry scales – scab, but a horrible scab. I pointed to his hands:

'Is your whole body like this?'

'Yes, sir, and worse.'

He was a pitiful figure: tall, bony, black, hairy, with the smell of a goat from the innumerable layers of sweat which had dried on his skin; bare-foot and bare-legged, with feet like an old hen, scaly, incrusted with filth, encased in a horny covering. His shaven head was jagged with scars from the scab and from the cuts which his savage barber must have bestowed on him. His eyes were bleary. This man was not ill. He was only dirty. He carried a horrible load of dirt, accumulated on his skin in the misery of all his miserable life.

I asked him: 'Do you want me to cure you?'

He stared aghast.

'Yes.'

'I'll hurt you, I'll hurt you very much. But if you want me to, I'll cure you.'

'Yes.'

His 'yes' sounded like the humble bark of a frightened dog.

We had in store great quantities of sulphur ointment and of what we called 'dog soap'. This was an English soap, red, with a penetrating smell of carbolic acid. I armed myself with ointment and soap, and that afternoon after work we went down to the stream, the Moor, two neighbours of his and me.

I told him to strip. The two others then started to rub him down with soap and with sand from the stream. They rubbed him so brutally that blood gushed from his scab-corroded skin. Afterwards they smeared him from head to toe with the ointment. We buttoned him into an old pair of uniform trousers and a blouse. The old burnous was burned. Within two weeks he was cured.

One day he brought me a basketful of figs and two chickens. He seemed a different man; he had even put on fat. He dug the earth more quickly and whenever I looked at him he laughed like a child. Then other Moors began to turn up, timidly. They would show me the scab marks between their fingers and beg for a bit of ointment. Sometimes they would bring the best within their poor reach, and leave a few eggs or a chicken and always some dried figs between the roots of the fig tree. Sometimes one of them would stop working and come to the fig tree to talk to me in secret. He would stand before me, twisting the edge of his burnous between his fingers. And finally he would say:

'Sergeant, I'm going. I'll work no more. I've had enough.'

'What are you going to do?'

Again he would twist the folds of his burnous in embarrassment.

'Listen, I'll tell the truth to you. I have thirty *duros*. I will buy a rifle. But I will never come here to kill the sergeant. None of us will kill the sergeant.'

'Who's going to sell you the rifle?'

'The French. Don't you know? A good rifle, with bullets as thick as this.' He would show the whole length of his thumb. 'Good rifles. Then I shall get a horse and a woman.'

They would go away, smiling happily like naughty children and assuring me that they would not kill me. But the rifle was the whole future to them: a rifle to kill Spanish soldiers. Their technique was simple. Towards dawn they used to hide in a gully with their rifles loaded, and wait for the first lonely soldier. They would kill him, rob him, and disappear. The old Remington rifles which the French Government was selling to unscrupulous contractors found their way here. The fat leaden bullet made a peculiar noise when it left the barrel, a noise which resounded in the hills: pa . . .cooo! For this reason the snipers were called the *Pacos*. Early in the morning, soldiers of the cavalry used to ride in pairs on reconnaissance between the positions; they were the most coveted prize for the *Pacos*. One lucky shot would win them a rifle and a horse.

One morning at the end of my first month in the position of Hamara, Major Castelo arrived at the foot of the hill. He came in a Ford, in one of those legendary old Ford cars which ran even better on a ploughed field than on a road. Soon afterwards a soldier came for me to the fig tree.

'At your orders, sir. Order from the Major, you are to go to him.'

The Major and the three officers of our company were standing beside the car. On its black roof they had spread out my plan of terrain. Major Castelo looked me up and down. We had never seen each other. He was a corpulent, stocky man, with the attractive child-like agility of some fat men who seem at each step to sit down on their bottoms. His small eyes were alive, his hands very fine, his feet tiny and his boots unbelievably shiny in all this dust.

He pointed to the plan:

'It's you who made this?'

'Yes, sir.'

'Good. Come along with us.'

I took the seat beside the driver, the Major and Don José, our Captain, sitting in the back. We crossed the plain and drove up to the Zoco. On the summit we left the car and went to the edge of the cliff. Castelo sent his driver to the Company of Engineers stationed in the Zoco to borrow the necessary topographical instruments and four soldiers with poles. We looked out over the plain and waited. In the distance the peak of Hamara burgeoned from the level ground like a woman's breast. Its green, fed by the stream, was sharply outlined on the yellow earth. Don José said:

'The sun's stinging. We ought to have taken some refreshment first.'

Castelo gave no reply. He addressed me:

'You've traced the road in an almost straight line but it seems too much of a slope to me.' He turned back to Don José. 'I beg your pardon. You have traced the track in an almost straight line. But since it was Barea who made the sketch . . .'

'Yes, yes. It doesn't matter. Personally, I find it better like this. You know, Castelo, the shortest line between two points is a straight line.'

He laughed a foolish little laugh which Castelo cut short with a look.

'Don't you think, Barea, that it would have been better to make it descend with an angle here, following the hillside?'

'Possibly, sir, but it was a problem of levelling. The trench I've sketched is about one hundred metres long, as you see. An angle would mean a track of more than four hundred metres to get to the same place. There would be more earth to clear away, more firm track to construct, and more wages to pay. By my calculations we would save approximately five thousand pesetas. . . .'

The car with the instruments had arrived. Castelo handed Don José the case with the theodolite:

'Set it up in station here and adjust the levels, please.' He pointed to a spot at the edge of the cliff. A soldier set up the tripod. The Major explained to each of the men where he was to stay with the sights and the poles. Don José had taken the theodolite from the case and stood there holding it. One of the men took the instrument and screwed it on. The Captain made it gyrate and looked through the sight, curious. Castelo asked him. 'Ready?'

'As soon as you wish, Major.'

Castelo went to the instrument and then turned round:

'But I told you to adjust the levels, Captain Blanco.'

'That's right. You can see Hamara perfectly.'

Castelo asked me like an accomplice:

'Would you test it, Sergeant?'

I corrected levels and reticles. Castelo turned to me again:

'Take the clinometer.'

We worked together the whole afternoon, the Major and I. Don José walked up and down beside us, smoking cigarettes. From time to time he asked: 'How're things going? All right?'

We returned to our position. After dinner the Major sent for me. I went to the Captain's tent. They were in shirt sleeves, sitting opposite each other at the table, between them the plan, a case with bottles of beer at their feet.

'Help yourself to a bottle if you like,' said the Major. 'Let Barea sit there,' he ordered the Captain.

I sat down opposite the Major. He began:

'There's a mistake here, but it is a small matter. . . .'

We entangled ourselves in a long discussion of the terrain. Don José sat on his bed and contemplated us for a while with his cross-eyed stare. Then he leaned his head on the pillow and fell asleep. He began to snore gently, like a kettle about to boil.

Castelo was a most intelligent man. His explanations were clear and plain. Time and again he easily settled my doubt. He knew every foot of the ground. The lesson he gave me was admirable. We corrected the plan in pencil. Finally he folded it up and took his coat from the back of the chair.

'I'll send you a blueprint from Tetuan.'

He glanced at Don José.

'I'm going.' Outside the tent he jerked his head towards it: 'For God's sake, don't let that man put his fingers in it. If you meet with any difficulty, ring me up. I'll fix it for you. Where is the telephonist?'

He gave orders to put the telephone at my disposal whenever I wanted to speak to him. I accompanied him to his car and asked him half-way down the slope:

'And, sir, what about the Lieutenant and the Ensign? It seems to me that you have put me in a most awkward position.'

'Don't worry. The Lieutenant is leaving the company in the course of next month. He's joining the Air Force. The Ensign – poof! It took him twenty years to become an ensign. What should he understand of such matters?'

When Don José awoke from his siesta he asked me:

'How did you like the Major?'

'Very much, sir.'

'Good. I suppose you'll have got everything clear in your mind. Do as you like. The plain truth is that I don't understand a word of it. I've forgotten everything. And, anyhow, what's the good of it?' He made a pause. 'Tomorrow I'm going to Tangier .'

Martin the bugler told me his story in instalments. When he was born he was sent to the Orphanage in Madrid. A few days later he was handed over to a foster mother in a little village somewhere in the mountains of Leon. He was lucky. Charity usually entrusted foundlings to foster mothers in the country, who applied, tempted by the pittance which in their villages represented wealth. They would stuff the children with bread soaked in water and come back to fetch another baby if their charge was carried off by dysentery. But Martin's foster mother was a woman from the mountains who had had a miscarriage. The child died and she was left unfit to bear any more children. She nursed the foundling at her own breast, and she and her husband loved him like a son. Their relatives hated the intruder and the whole village called him *El Hospiciano*, 'The one from the Hospice'. When he was fifteen years old, both his foster parents died within a few months of each other. The relatives took possession of the plot of ground, the two mules, and the old cottage where they had lived, and sent *El Hospiciano* to the Hospice. Nobody wanted him there, and he could not adapt himself to life behind closed gates. He applied for the post of bugler in a regiment, and there, a boy among the men of the barracks, he became once more the spoiled child. When he had reached the age of eighteen, he volunteered for Africa. He had never left it since. By now he had served in the regiment for almost twenty years. The things he had seen!

'And what are your plans? Are you going to stay here all your life?'

'Oh, no, sir. I've got the right to retire in three years. I'll have a pension of about five *reales* per day and that, together with my savings, well – it will be enough to set up a little tavern in Madrid. And I'll marry.'

'Have you saved much?'

'Just imagine. All the bonuses for volunteering. When I leave the army it'll be more than six thousand pesetas in all. The only thing is, if I'd been able to read well, they would have made me a corporal in the band, and by now I'd be a sergeant in the band and would not leave.'

'Why didn't you learn to read?'

'I can't. The figures and the letters get all mixed up in my head, and I just can't. It's here. I've got a very hard head.' And he knocked against his skull to convince me that nothing could penetrate there.

Each tent held twenty men. They slept on straw-filled sacks laid out on the bare soil like the spokes of a wheel. Sometimes they lighted a candle and put it in the centre, stuck to the tent pole. Then they would take off their blouses and shirts and stay naked from the belt upwards. They would scan the folds of their clothes and pick out the lice one by one. The louse was lord and master of the camp. Nothing in Morocco was free from lice. There was a tale that on the day of the capture of Xauen, General Dámaso Berenguer had complained because there was no meat with the meal. General Castro Girona said: 'Meat?' He stuck his hand in his armpit and when he took it out there were two or three lice between his fingers. 'This is the only cattle hereabouts, if that's any help to you. . . .'

It was as though the louse were a sacred animal among the Arabs of the hills. They dug their hands into the folds of their burnouses and extracted lice for hours, but let them fall to the ground without ever killing them. To sit down meant to incur the danger of being assailed by a swarm of voracious insects. A pool of the stream had been widened, and the men were made to take a bath there every Sunday. Afterwards they would wash their clothes which dried quickly in the sun. On Sunday mornings Hamara was inhabited by a tribe of naked savages. At meal time the soldiers put on their sun-warmed clothes. In the evening they were infested with lice. It was a silent battle in which there would be no victory.

One evening our orderly, Manzanares, got hold of me.

'You're from Madrid, aren't you?'

'Yes. Why?'

'Nothing. Just curiosity. Hot times I've had in Madrid!' He assumed a thoughtful pose which was comic because he was such an insignificant creature, and added: 'Do you know who I am?'

'Who are you then?' I asked without showing my smile.

'First, they called me the Manzanares but then they gave me the nickname 'Little Marquess', because I married three girls by telling them I was the son of a Marquess. Two in Barcelona and one in Madrid.'

I looked at our orderly; either he had megalomania or he had drunk too much wine. 'All right, go and leave me in peace.'

When the other sergeants arrived I told them about it. Córcoles said:

'I don't know whether the story about his marriages is true. But it is true that Manzanares was a famous pickpocket. It's funny how he came to be here. The Madrid police never caught him with the stuff and one of the inspectors decided he would put an end to his career in another way. One day they arrested Manzanares in the street and took him to the station. They asked for his name, age, residence, and so on, until they came to his profession. Manzanares had money, paid his rent punctually, spent much on women and wine, but he could not explain where the money came from. "No profession, what?" said the Inspector. "According to the Law of Vagrancy, fifteen days' arrest." They could not give him more. Manzanares went to prison, was given one of the cells for those who pay, had his meals brought to him from outside and lived like a prince for a fortnight. One night they opened the gates and put him out into the street. Ten minutes later the police detained him and took him to the same station. Fifteen days again. And so on for months, until Manzanares got tired and asked the Inspector: "Well now, what's the big idea?" "To finish you off." They sent him back to prison, and there he thought it out. He wrote a letter to the Inspector and offered to volunteer for Morocco if they would leave him in peace. And they brought him to us direct from the Model Prison.'

'And here?' I asked.

'Pooh – apparently he has learned how to pick the pockets of the Moors on their market days. But he's making money with the cards now. He's wonderful with them.'

'I don't understand why you've made him our orderly.'

'Now, look here, Manzanares has got his philosophy. He says that as he is the only accredited thief here he will be made responsible if anything's missing. And since he's been with the Company nobody has missed a button.'

Julian told me about himself.

'You know my father?'

'I don't know. I don't suppose I do.'

'No, boy, you must know him. He's Captain Beleno. Master in the Workshops at Ceuta.'

I grinned. Of course I knew him. Who would not know him in Ceuta? Resentful of the grin, Julian said:

'Of course you know him. Everybody does. Well, I'm his son.'

'I would never have guessed it. He's thin and bony and you are a round little ball. Don't be angry, but you really are fat.'

'They call me Sergeant Dumpling, anyhow. I take after my mother who's like the plug of a barrel. Well, if I'm here it's because of my father.'

Julian's father, Captain Beleno, had been a boat maker in Malaga when he was a strong young man of twenty. With a saw, an axe, and an adze, he built fishing boats with the same primitive craftsmanship and the same rules as the Greek and the Phoenicians had used two thousand years ago. By reason of his craft he was put into the Pontoon Regiment of the Engineers after being called up. At the end of his military term, his Captain suggested that he should join the army as a craftsman. In the Spanish Army various artisans are attached to every regiment, such as blacksmiths, carpenters, and harness makers. They do not serve as soldiers in the ranks but are workers employed under contract by the State and subjected to military discipline. In their capacity of persons attached to the army they are given army promotion. Workers who have just joined have the rank of sergeant; in the course of the years they are promoted in pay and rank and finally made captain. They have the right to wear a captain's uniform but in practice they dress as civilians and go to their work in the barracks at fixed hours.

However, Captain Beleno never took off his uniform unless his task in the workshops forced him to do so. He was famous for the military sternness which he, the honorary captain, showed towards soldiers. For more than twenty years he had lived in Ceuta. His dream was that his son should do what he himself had never achieved: command a company of real soldiers. Julian grew up in the discipline of the barracks. When he was taught how to spell, he was at the same time taught the first principles of military science, seen through the mind of his father. When he was seventeen years old, his father took him to the barracks, made him sign some papers in the office of the regiment, and then told him solemnly:

'My son: today your life has been decided. Work hard, and in thirty years' time you'll be a captain in the Spanish Army like your father. More than your father, because you'll be a real captain, not a poor worker such as I am.'

The officers who respected the old man put the boy to office work and kept him there until he was made a sergeant.

'But now I'm a sergeant it's all come to an end. I'm studying for the Postal Service. I'll apply, and as soon as there are exams, I'll quit. To hell with my father and the captain's pips. I wish I'd seen the last of them.'

Herrero protested angrily:

'You're an idiot. If it had cost you what it cost me to become a sergeant! But of course you've never gone hungry.'

I said: 'I think it's quite right that he wants to get a job and leave the barracks. When I've finished my three years, I'll leave too.'

'Then why did you become a sergeant?'

'Why did you?'

'I? To get my food. When I entered the barracks twelve years ago I was starved and my back was beaten blue. When the sergeants in those days boxed your ears you saw stars; and I got plenty of knocks. I couldn't read or write anything. But they told me that by learning things I'd become a sergeant and wouldn't have to go back to digging and ploughing behind the mules. Listen: it cost me twelve years, but I'm proud of it. And if God grants me the health, I'll have my pension when I'm old and I won't have to go to the Home.'

Pepito, the son of Señor Pepe, looked on while I packed my suitcase to go to Tetuan. I had to clear the accounts of the month and to come back with the payroll.

'You'll paint the town red,' he said.

'I don't think so. The whores of Tetuan don't interest me.'

'You don't know them. With money there's something for every taste. Every kind of woman . . . You tell me when you come back. But while we're talking of Tetuan, my father asked me to give you this.' He gave me an envelope. There were five hundred pesetas inside.

'What's this for?'

'Now what do you think? For you to enjoy yourself with.'

Córcoles and I went together. On the way to the Zoco I told him of the incident. He waxed indignant.

'The old bastard. A lousy trick, five hundred pesetas. If he had given them to me. . . .'

We caught a lorry in the Zoco, which took us to Tetuan. Castelo received me with great kindness and glanced through the pile of papers bearing the Captain's signature.

'Everything in order?'

'Everything, sir.'

He signed the papers quickly and handed them to me:

'Go and see the Paymaster, he'll pay you. Come back here before you go.'

I took the money and returned to his room. The Major had spread the plan of the road on the table. He pointed to a spot at the foot of Hamara Hill, between the two parallel lines which indicated the track of the road.

'What's this here?'

'An old fig tree, sir. A wonderful tree. It would cost us hard work to get rid of it. It is at least five hundred years old.'

'A borehole and a dynamite cartridge, that's all.'

He lit a cigarette, and put his hand in the drawer of the desk. He brought it out with a paper and an envelope.

'Now go and amuse yourself. You've got forty-eight hours free. Leave the money here with the cashier if you want to and go anywhere you like. I recommend Luisa'a establishment. That's for yourself and your pleasure.'

The envelope contained one thousand pesetas.

3. Tetuan

For the first twenty-five years of this century Morocco was a battlefield, a brothel, and an immense tavern.

Córcoles and I left the *Comandancia* together. I was to be introduced to life in Tetuan.

'Let's go to El Segoviano's,' said Córcoles.

'What is it?'

'The first tavern of Tetuan. Later we'll go to the House of Luisa.'

'And who is Luisa?'

'The owner of the most elegant brothel in Tetuan.'

'And where are we going to eat?'

'Never mind, you can get good grub anywhere. The Calle de la Luneta is full of restaurants.'

We entered the huge tap-room of El Segoviano's from the street. Opposite the open door was the zinc bar, water running from the open tap in its centre. Three barmen handled hundreds of glasses which were being filled with wine, emptied, rinsed under the tap, lined up with noisy clatter and filled with wine again, ceaselessly. A long shelf spanned the wall behind the barman. On its left it bore a row of square flagons filled with wine, a column whose head alternately retreated or advanced towards the barmen. On its right it carried an ever growing row of emptied flagons. At one end a boy put full flagons in the gap, ceaselessly. At the other end another boy cleared away empty flagons, ceaselessly.

Soldiers hustled each other along the bar. Their shouts were louder than the multiple noise of clattering glasses, splashing water, clink of flagons, and the scratching of coins on zinc. People yelled hoarsely at one another. Beyond the part of the room occupied by the bar and the customers there was a chaotic medley: barrels, cases of beer and wine bottles, demijohns of eau-de-vie, paunchy goatskins swollen with wine, three-legged stools painted red, open and half-open packing cases with straw straggling from them, tin mugs for measuring liquid, full and empty flagons and sausages of all sizes and shapes. Smoked and dried sausages and hams were hanging from the ceiling. The floor was slippery with froth kneaded into a thick paste by the dusty soles of hundreds of people. And everything was swarming with flies, with millions of flies whose drone fused into a single, persistent, intense note as though everything was vibrating. The only clean thing in this infinite dirt were the glasses emerging from the running water. The room smelled like breath from the mouth of a hiccoughing drunkard.

Córcoles pushed me forward through the crowd. 'We go inside.' He went through a little door into the second room.

The dark room, with its door to the street blocked by barrels, and its stone flagged floor, was unbelievably cool. A few dozen people were scattered among the maze of boxes, cases, bottles, demijohns, barrels, and goatskins. Each barrel served as a table, each box as a seat. One of the barrels carried a big tray with glasses full of Manzanilla, and another a bottle inside a circle of coarse beakers brimming over with red wine.

There was not a single private in the room. Nobody was allowed to pass through the little door who was not at least a sergeant. The noisy groups were composed of all ranks from sergeants to majors. Several boys attended to the customers and carried their pewter trays with glasses and bottles from one corner to the other in fantastic meanderings.

Carrasco, the Company Sergeant-Major, called us to one of the barrel-tables. He was an Andalusian who had seen twenty years of service in Africa, somewhat bald, somewhat paunchy, a tireless drinker. He was with a lieutenant of the *Regulares* and a sergeant of the Telegraph Company, and invited us to join them.

'Well, how are you getting on?' he asked me.

'Not too badly.'

He gave me a friendly blow in the midriff.

'Not too badly, eh? You'll grow a belly like a prelate.' He gave his friends a short description of my career. The officer of the *Regulares* manoeuvred until he came to sit beside me.

'Your sort of work must be very interesting. What do you think of it?'

Without transition, without waiting for my reply, he continued: 'The thing for you is a watch like this one' – he produced from somewhere a gold wrist watch.

Rather flustered and believing the Lieutenant to be drunk, I took the watch and examined it. It must have been worth a good five hundred pesetas.

'It's magnificent,' I said when I gave it back.

'You like it?'

'Very much indeed.'

'Then keep it.'

'Who? Me?'

'Yes, yes. Keep it. Pay for it whenever and however you like.'

'But I don't want to buy a gold watch,' I exclaimed.

'What a pity. This is a watch for a man of taste, not for these yokels of the infantry. It's a watch for an officer. Guaranteed for five years. But of course, if you don't want it, that's that.'

From somewhere or other he produced a fountain pen.

'But you'll want this. It's made for you. Fifty pesetas. A real Waterman. You can pay for it now or in monthly instalments of five pesetas or as you like.'

'Are you a living trinket store, or what?'

'Store for everything, for everything.' He gave me a business card. Pablo Revuelta, Lt. in the *Regulares*. Fine jewellery of all kinds. Cash or instalment. 'One has to make a living somehow. With this and the pay one can manage.'

The fountain pen was good. I kept it for forty pesetas cash down, and Revuelta went on explaining.

'At home I've got everything, and it's all first class. Whatever you like: a gold watch and diamond earrings for your girl. Payment as it suits you. You sign a contract and the regiment deducts it from your pay in instalments.'

'The regiment? But debts are prohibited. . . .'

'This is not a debt, it's a purchase. All regiments in the zone accept my receipts.' When we left he whispered confidentially:

'If you are in a fix some day, come to see me at home, as a friend.'

In the street I asked Córcoles: 'What kind of a bird is that?'

'I really don't know how he came to be what he is. An officer in the *Regulares*, but never in the firing line. Officially he has a job in the regimental office but he never goes there. His house is a regular warehouse for jewellery and he sells by instalments to the whole garrison, sergeants and generals alike, anything from fountain pens to jewellery worth ten thousand pesetas. But that isn't his real profit. You go there and buy a trinket or whatever you like. But you don't take it with you, and he pays you what it's worth minus a discount of 20 per cent. That is to say, if you need money he gives you eight hundred pesetas and you sign a contract according to which you've bought a diamond ring for one thousand. You pay it back in instalments and you can't escape because the regiment accepts his rceipts and also because you have the ring in trust as long as it isn't paid in full, and he has the right to prosecute you for theft if you try to get out of it.'

'Still, I don't quite understand how the army can tolerate it.'

'Ta ta ta. If that man opened his "secret draw", as he calls it, not even the generals would escape a scandal. Eighty-five per cent of the garrison owe him money. And apart from that he's a necessary institution. Without him half of us would be in prison. Now look here. You know, we play our game of baccarat every night. One day Herrero played and lost. Señor Pepe lent him five hundred pesetas. He lost them. Then he took five hundred pesetas out of the mess fund, and lost them. Señor Pepe told him that he would not give him a *céntimo* more. And Herrero had no money to feed the soldiers. He asked for a permit to go to Tetuan, and came back with one thousand pesetas. They deduct fifty pesetas from his pay every month now.'

We had reached the end of the Calle de la Luneta and Córcoles turned round.

'Where are we going?' I asked.

'We are just taking a little walk.'

'All right, but let's go over there. I'd like to see the town.'

'There isn't any other walk here but this street. After supper we'll go to the Alcazaba. But now there is nowhere to go. Here you see all the people and here you can get a drink if you like.'

In the Calle de la Luneta everybody was clearly doing what we were doing: walking up and down the street from one end to the other, and from time to time entering or leaving one of the taverns or bars. The street was an ant heap, but you met the same faces over again the second time you walked down it.

The entire trade, both of Europeans and of Europeanized Jews, is installed in the Calle de la Luneta. Away from it there are silent, solitary alleys. The street itself begins at the railway station and ends in the 'Square of Spain', the Plaza de España. In a stretch of five hundred yards the whole life of the town is concentrated. Off the pavement to the left yawn the gates of the former ghetto and pour forth a flock of squalid little children who, with equally squalid Christian and Moorish children, indefatigably pursue the passers-by.

There is an odd mixture of colours in the street. The khaki of uniforms is predominant, but it is spattered with the showy white capes, burnouses, and puffed trousers of the Moorish units, the *Regulares* and the *Mehalla*, with the red stripes of the General Staff and of a few generals, with the gold braid of the aides-de-camp and with the blue of the Transport Corps. Then there are Moors, dirty, barefoot, in grey woollen *chilabas*, and Moors from Tetuan in burnouses of white and blue silk, in shining babouches of plain or multi-coloured leather. There are Jews in loose, dirty frock coats, and Jews in kaftans of fine wool and silk, with snow-white shirts. There are gypsies who sell everything under the sun, beggars of all three races, bootblacks in hundreds who assail your feet even while you walk. And there are few women.

When I saw it first, there were so few women in the Calle de la Luneta that the passing of every one of them, except for some old and obese Jewess, raised a murmur along the entire length of the street. A fine dust permeated the air, the dust of innumerable ceaseless steps. The whole street was thirsty and fed the open, ever-full taverns on both sides.

At nightfall Córcoles took me to the Sergeants' Casino and entered me as a member. The casino consisted of a lounge with divans and chairs, a bar, and another room for games and gambling, with a few billiard tables, some tables for people who wanted to play cards in a foursome, and a big table for baccarat, trente-et-quarante or rouge-et-noir. A crowd of sergeants and sergeant-majors were playing; we looked on for a while, risked some money, lost a few pesetas, and then went to supper. After the meal Córcoles was planning to go to the House of Luisa.

'Don't you believe that just anybody can go there. They admit only those of us sergeants whom they know. But I am somebody there.'

'To tell the truth, I ought to sleep.' I said.

'You take a wench to bed there and sleep afterwards.'

'I don't exactly like brothels.'

'I tell you it's the best place for sleeping. All the inns here make you sick. You get full of bugs and can't sleep a wink. There you pay twenty-five pesetas, and get a woman and a clean bed.'

'All right, let's go wherever you like.'

We crossed the Plaza de España, entered the Moorish quarter, and went up a steep little street with low houses and a pavement of round pebbles, sloping from both sides towards the middle, so as to form a dirty and evil-smelling gutter.

'This is the Alcazaba,' said Córcoles. 'All the whores of Tetuan live here.'

I saw nothing but miserable little houses and long whitewashed walls pierced by large iron-studded gates.

Before one of these gates Córcoles stopped, and a grill was opened. Somebody scanned us; a door in the gate was unlatched. An old woman met us and took us to a lounge, brilliantly lighted, over-decorated with mirrors, a table in the centre and a piano in the background. She clapped her hands and from behind us entered a group of women, most of them in dressing-gowns and almost naked beneath them.

Four sergeants were in the lounge, drinking and joking. The chilly repugnance of a brothel drove me to join the men and chat with them, avoiding the invitation of the women. We talked, we laughed, we sang, we made a bit of a row. And one after the other discreetly disappeared. Córcoles and I were left, he with a girl who claimed to be from Marseilles, with a strident voice and very guttural 'r's', and who was fat and heavy like a cow. I was still the centre of attention of three girls.

Córcoles was rather drunk by now. 'If you don't know which one you want, I'll take this girl,' he said, and smacked the massive naked shoulders of the French woman. They sounded spongy.

'I'll wait for you here, if you are not too long, and if you are I'll go away. I don't feel like sleeping with anyone.'

I ordered a bottle of wine for my spell of waiting. The girls looked at me with contempt. Two drifted away, one stayed with me.

'You don't want to sleep with me?'

'No.'

'Do I bore you?'

'No, do stay. Drink!'

She filled two glasses and gave me one. We both drank. She sat down meekly at my side.

'Let me stay here. One gets so tired, it's always the same – the whole day long. You know . . . this is a miserable life.' And she started telling me the sentimental story which I had heard hundreds of times. I did not listen. I was bored, drinking the wine in little sips and lighting one cigarette after the other. She shut up in the end.

'I'm boring you. I'll leave you – I'm so sorry!'

Noiselessly, she shut the door and I was left quite alone. I went to the piano and began to poke it with one finger. In the little street outside sounded the steps of a few passers-by, and sometimes the hoofs of a donkey or a horse clattered on the round pebbles. A voice behind me said:

'Poor boy. You've been deserted.'

Another of them had entered, more elegant than the rest. She wore a cream-coloured dress of heavy silk which fitted her body tightly. You could see that she was naked underneath and the dress seemed to make her more naked.

'They did not want me because I am too thin.' I said.

'Poor boy,' she repeated, sat down on the divan and looked at me. 'Don't you like our girls?'

'No.'

'Do you like me?'

'No.'

She went stiff as though I had slapped her face. 'There are many who like me.'

'No doubt. Taste is free.'

'Don't you like women?'

'Yes.' And I added like an idiot: 'But the others.'

She laughed and said:

'Nonsense – we're all alike.'

She left the divan, sat down at the piano and began to play. She played well, with a nervous touch. After a heavy chord she slammed down the lid. At that moment Córcoles came back, somewhat redder in the face than before. He filled a glass with wine and drank it down.

'You're in good company,' he said.

'Not so bad. Shall we go?'

She intervened:

'What is the matter with your friend? He can't leave the house like this. Who would you like to sleep with?' She said it mockingly.

'I? Well – with Madame. Let her come.'

The woman turned to Córcoles.

'This boy does not know me?'

'My dear girl, he's only just arrived in Tetuan.'

She took me by the arm.

'Come. You shall sleep with Madame.' And she laughed.

I was so tired in spirit that I did not resist. What did it matter? You must take a joke as it comes. Madame was sure to be a dropsical old woman, tied to an armchair, with a cat in her lap. We would have a good laugh. I followed her through the labyrinth of corridors and doors, rubbing elbows with girls and with homosexuals who turned round to stare at us.

We entered a bedroom, filled with cutglass and beautiful skins. She shut the door, I stood in the middle of the room and looked. I had never seen a room like this in a brothel. When I turned round, she had stripped off her dress and was naked.

'You know, here I am the mistress.'

So she is the mistress. All my instincts rose. The mistress! She might be the mistress of this brothel. She would never be mistress over me, my mistress. She was nothing but a whore like the others with the privilege of being mistress over the other whores. But I had not gone there to sleep with anyone, even less to submit to anyone. If a woman had pleased me I would have accepted it and gone to bed with her. But how could I accept it as a foregone conclusion that if I pleased Madame I must go to bed with her?

Luisa was beautiful, and I slept with her. But I was actor and spectator at the same time. As a male I was completely delivered to the woman. With my brain I looked on, and made use of all my senses to check on my sensations. I watched the woman, I heard her, I felt her, I smelled her, I sampled her mouth, as one may sample a spectacle. She must have sensed it, for she tried to carry me down to the depths of lust and to make herself mistress of me. I came to understand the power of a pimp, the power of a mentally frigid male over a female.

In the small hours of the night we ate a cold supper, Luisa and I, in a little hall beside the bedroom. Many times she put her hand on one of my thighs, and many times my hand touched one of hers. Her skin burned. When we had finished, she sat down at the piano – how many pianos were there in that house? – and I stood beside her watching her pointed fingers wandering lazily over the keys. She leaned her head against me and I looked down on the changing planes of her powerful chin, her long eyelashes and the waves in her hair.

There was a glittering emerald on her little finger. When she stopped playing the stone was quenched, almost dead, with a little subdued funereal glow. She had a blood red ruby hanging between her breasts and when she breathed, the stone sent a flash into my eyes, like a signal. She let her hands lie on the keys like two dead birds, turned her head and leaned more heavily against me.

'You know that I am a Jewess? My real name is Miriam. My father is a silversmith. He embosses silver with a little hammer. My grandfather was a silversmith, and his grandfather too. My fingers are the heritage of generations of men who handled gold and silver.' She caressed the ruby and the emerald with the tips of her fingers, crossing her hands over her breast as though in a gesture of supplication or shame. 'And stones. There is no gold now. In his house father keeps his old gold coins, very old ones, wrapped in a silken cloth together with a big rusty iron key. The forefather of my forefathers was thrown out of Spain, expelled from Imperial Toledo, and he came here with those coins and that key. When the key is returned to its old lock, the old coins will be exchanged for new money. Father dreams of returning to Toledo. They say it is a city with very narrow streets where we own a house built of stone. For they tell me that all the houses which once belonged to the Jews still exist in Toledo. You've seen Toledo?'

She did not wait for my answer but went on:

'And meanwhile we were starving. Father hammered his silver and I went begging in the Luneta, here in Tetuan.'

She stopped and stroked the keys. Then she threw her head back again and laughed the shrill, dry laugh of a drunk, hysterical woman.

'Gold! Do you know that I am perhaps the richest person in Tetuan? I've got thousands and thousands, perhaps a million. It all belongs to me. To Miriam the Jewess.'

She rose and turned to me, full face.

'Do you want money? Much money?'

'No. What for?' I was tired and somnolent. 'Does everybody think of nothing but money here in Africa?' I asked myself dully.

'You're right. What for?'

She dropped her hands on the keys and made them jingle.

'Ask for coffee, will you?' I said.

'Do you love me? Do I please you?' she asked, pushing her face close to mine.

'I don't love you. You please me.'

Her face contracted in rage.

'Why do you say that you don't love me? They all say they love me. They all are willing to do what I tell them. All are my slaves and I am their mistress, and not you? Why?'

'Because it isn't so, quite simply.'

'Didn't you say that I pleased you?'

'Yes.'

'Well then: wouldn't you fight for me? Would you not kill a man for my sake?'

'No. Why?'

Why should I kill anybody for the sake of this woman?

She laughed softly and watched me. After a long and painful pause she said: 'How funny!' and left the room.

Shortly afterwards one of the homosexuals who acted as servants in the house came in with coffee and brandy. I let the sugar dissolve in my cup, with a feeling of unreality at the back of my mind as though I were reading a cheap French novel.

When Luisa returned, she was wearing once more the heavy cream-coloured silk on her golden skin. Her eyes had an absent look. She walked rhythmically, like the Queen of Sheba, and her mouth was taut with arrogant disdain. Suddenly I saw her in a series of fugitive pictures, as a ragged little Jewish girl in the streets of Tetuan, brushing against the immaculate trousers of the officers, stepping on the silken burnouses of the Moorish notables, spitting at the silk kaftans of the rich Jewish bankers, deeply vindictive. I could sense her revengeful hatred now.

For a second I felt afraid and would have liked to go, but she said:

'Give me the brandy. I think I want to get drunk tonight.'

'You are feeling tragic?' I filled her glass.

She caught the glass and looked through it, holding it against the light. Slowly she lifted it to her mouth and stopped when it almost touched her lips.

'Tragic? I? Boy, you don't know what you're saying. Others make tragedy so that I may laugh.'

It sounded like good acting. And then her face underwent a sudden madly violent change and she called out. At once the homosexual who had brought me the coffee appeared.

'Has he arrived?'

'No, Luisa, it's not his hour yet. You've got time.'

'Time for what?'

The homosexual stammered: 'For nothing. . . . For nothing . . .'

Luisa had sprung at him and shook him furiously. He trembled under her hands and looked as if he were about to break out into sobs like a frightened child.

'For what?' she screamed.

'I thought you wanted to stay alone for a while . . . before he comes.'

She pushed him through the door and shut the bolt.

'If he only could, he and the others would like to kill me. But they have not got the courage. They're all cowards. Those because they're pansies, and the others just the same. All men are cowards.'

She stared into my face in naked insult. I took a cigarette out of my pocket, with deliberation, and lighted it while I watched her eyes. Weren't those eyes somewhat dilated? Was she mad?

'You're a coward too, like all the others!'

Quickly she lifted her hand to slap my face. I caught it in the air and twisted her fingers in a jiu-jitsu grip. She bit her lip so as not to cry out. But I increased the twist, coldly and intentionally, and felt a savage pleasure in hurting her. She fell on her knees and cried even while she attempted to bite me with her pointed teeth. I hit with her own hand against them. When I loosed her fingers, she stayed on the floor and bit her arm in fury. I drank some coffee, waiting for her next reaction. She rose, filled another glass with brandy, drank it and looked at me with deep, softened eyes from which the madness had gone. Then she said slowly:

'You're a brute. You've hurt me.'

'I know it. I don't hit women, but I don't let a woman hit me either. You wanted to slap my face. It's better you shouldn't have done it.'

She changed again.

'What would you have done? Tell me. Would you have dared to hit back?' She beat against her breast so that the ruby jumped.

'Hit you? No. I would have spat into your face and left.'

'I would have killed you,' she said after a silence. 'It would have been better to beat me. Do you know that I'd enjoy being beaten?'

'Get a pimp to do it. I'm no good.'

For the last few minutes there had been an unusual commotion outside. Now somebody knocked at the door and Luisa opened it. The homosexual stood there again, his eyes filled with fright. He whispered something and Luisa said:

'I'll come back in a minute.'

How tired I was. My eyelids were heavy as lead after the supper. I drank another glass of brandy. I would have liked to leave but I was dominated by a lazy dislike of going back to the town at this hour of the night, and looking for an inn. I would stay here in one of the bedrooms, alone, and I would sleep.

Luisa was back: 'Come along, some friends have come and I want them to meet you.'

She led me to the officers' lounge. The room was filled with women who laughed and made a noise, the table was burdened with bottles and glasses. When we entered, all fell silent. Luisa, still hanging on my arm, dragged me to the table. Officers and prostitutes gave way in silence. She stopped before the General.

'My boy friend,' she said.

I stuttered under the glare, caught by surprise:

'At your orders, *mi general*.'

The General straightened himself, his face suddenly flushed.

'None of that, my boy. There are no generals here. In this house we are all equals as soon as the doors shut behind us. Take a drink with us.' And he fell back on the seat, as though crumpling up.

In a very low voice he said to himself:

'That girl! That girl!'

An officer of the *Regulares* sought me out. Instinctively I stood to attention.

'So you're Luisa's boy friend?'

I must have laughed with a stupid grin:

'Just a joke of hers, *mi capitán.*' Was he Captain? The folds of his burnous covered the insignia.

He steered me away from the table and said softly:

'Do you know that this is an insult to the General?'

'An insult – why?'

'But don't you know? Where have you sprung from?'

'From out in the country. I've never been in Tetuan. I went straight there from Ceuta, and I don't know anybody here.'

'But man alive . . . Luisa is the old man's whimsy, and he'll make you pay for it. Get away before anybody asks your name.'

But the General had risen:

'Let us leave, gentlemen.'

In passing he stroked Luisa's chin. The officers went with him as his escort. Most of the bottles were left on the table, full. While the patter of the group still sounded in the corridor, Luisa turned round and laughed. Rage choked me. I could have taken that woman by the throat, which was swelling at each trill of laughter, and I could have knocked her head against the wall. I walked out into the street and nobody held me back. Asking my way, I found the Sergeants' Casino. It was four o'clock in the morning. Córcoles was playing baccarat. He rose when he saw me.

'Is it true that you've slept with Luisa?'

The game was interrupted and all looked at me with curiosity.

'Yes. And what of it? Let's go to bed.'

'Wait a moment, it's nearly finished.'

I sat down on one of the divans and fell asleep. I awoke there the next day when the morning was well advanced. Soldiers were sweeping the room. I went in search of coffee or something else to revive me. All the sergeants I met on the way seemed to have known me all my life and all asked me:

'Is it true that you've slept with Luisa?'

4. The Fig Tree

A bore-hole is nothing but a hole in the rock, a tube hollowed out by the three-cornered point of a steel bar driven in by hammer blows. At the bottom of this tunnel in the stone you put a dynamite cartridge, a percussion cap and a fuse. Then you block the tube with earth, rammed in tightly. You light the fuse, and the dynamite explodes. The stone opens as an over-ripe fruit bursts open, spattering its juice.

'What's this spot?' the Major had asked. 'An old fig tree,' I had answered. 'A bore-hole and a dynamite cartridge.' And now Jimenez, an Asturian miner, together with two soldiers, made a bore-hole into the heart of the fig tree. Jimenez cursed and swore. At each blow the steel bar caught in the wood and he had to twist it round, withdraw it and insert it again. And again it would get stuck.

'It's easier to bore granite, God knows.'

The soldiers laughed: 'But this is better!'

Their effort was small indeed. A single strong blow would have driven the steel bar like a nail into the green wood. But Jimenez had to twist the bar loose at each blow, and he sweated. The others waited for him, leaning on the shafts of their sledge hammers.

I was sitting on one of the roots of the fig tree. I was sorry for the tree; I would have liked to save it.

Further down the track a small crowd collected. Jimenez and the soldiers stopped and looked. 'We've got visitors,' they said.

A group was walking along the cut of the earth at a leisurely pace, stopping here and there.

'How is it going?' asked the Major when they had reached us.

'It's a very slow job, sir. It's difficult to bore the wood. The borer gets stuck.'

The Major slapped his little whip against the tree trunk.

'A good tree. What a pity we have to get rid of it. . . . Come along with us. We'll see how we can set up the bridge.'

I went uphill with them. Behind us sounded the intermittent blows, dully, as though the entrails of the earth were being beaten and not those of the tree.

It was in the Captain's tent, while I was studying the blueprint of the track, that I had an idea. We were just discussing how wide a curve eight-ton lorries would need. The fig tree was a speck on the paper, a cluster of tiny white lines on blue ground.

'I've got it,' I said. 'There is water here.'

The Major gave me a highly surprised look.

'*Caramba*, what's the matter with you?'

'I beg your pardon, sir. I was thinking of the fig tree. There is no need to clear it away.'

'How d'you propose to arrange it? With a bridge to pass over it?'

'No, sir. Something better. A spring.'

'All right. Take some refreshment. Drink a glass of beer and let's continue.'

'But I'm sure I'm right, sir, there is water here.'

'Wine, wine – don't drink water or you'll get marsh fever.' The Major lit a cigarette and looked me up and down. I must have been red in the face.

'All right, tell us your story about the spring and the fig tree.'

The Captain laughed and winked with his squinting little eyes. I could have kicked him. Annoyed, I began to explain.

'I believe, sir, that here at the base of the slope there is water almost under the surface. There is a corner which is always damp and overgrown with grass and palmetto. If we found the source we could make a spring. And then we could make a watering-place for the horses and a little square with the fig tree in the middle. After all, between here and Tetuan there is no drinking water anywhere; if you could give permission, we could bore for water. It would cost us no more than a few blows with the pickaxe.'

The Major thought it over for a moment and said:

'All right, try it out. There's time enough to blow up the fig tree.'

When I returned to the tree after the Major had left, Jimenez was swearing more violently than ever. The deeper the steel bar penetrated, the more the sappy roots caught hold of its three-cornered point which by now shone like silver.

'Stop. We're not going to blow up the fig tree.'

With childish pride I explained my idea to Jimenez and the two soldiers. At once we found a working gang of Moors and started to dig into the foot of the hillside. A short way below the surface, water gushed out, and we went on to search for the source. That afternoon we found a water vein. By the evening it was trickling gently over the slope, flooding the roots of the fig tree.

'And now, mother,' I wrote in my letter to her, 'we have got hold of an iron tube and made a spout thicker than my arm. We are going to make a trough where the horses will drink, and a little square round the tree.'

The iron tube existed only in my imagination. But I could not tell my mother that the spring was there, spouting its water day and night, creating a marshy hollow in the ground and flooding it slowly while nobody cared.

For the story of the fig tree was to be the *leitmotif* of the letter to my mother. I had promised her a letter every week, but God alone knows what labour it cost me to write it: to find a subject. That day the subject was the fig tree, 'my fig tree', and of course it had to have a happy ending. An iron spout and a watering trough. A multitude of horses drinking with all the thirst of Africa. We, too, would no longer suffer thirst.

For my mother was a simple woman with scanty book knowledge. She read but labouriously and wrote even more labouriously. She was sixty-four years old, and she was worn out by work and sorrow. Africa was to her a horrifying nightmare, a desert land with a few lonely palm trees where Spaniards were mercilessly slaughtered. My descriptions would never sound convincing to her. How could she believe that Ceuta was nothing but a little Andalusian town on the other side of the Straits? Her mind was crammed with a hotchpotch of memories and traditions: Berber pirates, captives redeemed by friars, captives aboard a galley, rowing under the cruel whip of a big Moor who went to and fro between the benches of slaves. Oh, she never said it, afraid that people would laugh at her. She only thought it. Her brain was full of stories from old books, which had been read aloud before the fireplace in the big house of the village when she was a little girl.

When I myself was a child I used on many evening to read to her out of *Uncle Tom's Cabin*, and she never tired of it. She herself had still known Negro slaves. She told me stories of the Cuban war. Terrible stories full of corpses of Spaniards who had been murdured with the *machet*, the huge knife used for cutting sugar cane, or killed by the Black Pest. She transplanted all these horrors into the African desert. The crossing from Algeciras to Ceuta meant to her sailing the ocean, braving the raging seas and risking shipwreck on the cliffs.

But that letter – I felt it then, and I learned it later – the letter with the story of the spring and the fig tree, my mother kept among her old papers. She read it again and again, her spectacles balanced on her short nose, and she bathed herself in the fresh coolness of the old tree and of the singing iron tube which poured its water into the deep trough where the horses drank greedily.

And we put a piece of zinc tubing to the source. We made a round trough from stones bound by cement. The Moors came there for their ablutions at sunset; they greeted me:

'Salaam aleicum.'

'Aleicum salaam.'

One day a soldier who was digging cried out: a scorpion had stung him in the sole of his foot through the rope-sole of his canvas shoe. There were many black scorpions in the region, about twelve centimetres long, which hid just under the surface of the soil and were furious at being disturbed. The soldier's foot began to swell almost immediately. We carried him in haste to the position and called for the medical orderly, a stone-deaf young man from Cáceres. I asked him for the surgical case. He gave me a box filled with rusty tools.

'What's this?' I asked.

'The surgical case. Nobody here uses the stuff. But it's all there.'

I slashed the wound open with a razor and washed it thoroughly. Afterwards I took El Sordo – 'The Deaf One' as everybody called him – aside and asked:

'Who made you the medical orderly?'

'Well, it's because I'm deaf, so they put me here and told me to be careful. Everything's there, sir.'

'But don't you know that you must clean the instruments?'

'No, sir. Nobody uses them here. If anybody's got something wrong he gets iodine and that's that.'

'But who made you medical orderly?'

'Eh?'

'Who made you medical orderly?'

'Well, the Captain, sir, because I was no good for anything else, being deaf.'

'If you can't hear, why were you called up? Deaf people are unfit for service.'

'Yes, sir. But they say I'm not deaf. The doctor in my village said so. Because of the proportion you know, sir.'

'What do you mean?'

'Well, sir, it is like this. When a village is so small and has so few people that because of what they call the proportion they haven't got to send up a soldier, well, then the village is put together with another village and between the two of them they've always enough to give up a soldier for the army. Well, that's what happened to my place. In the nearest village the one who was due for the army was the son of the boss, and in my village it was me. We ought to have drawn lots, but because I was deaf the son of the boss would have had to go to the barracks anyhow. So then the doctor came and said I wasn't deaf and that the son of the boss had consumption. And so I had to go. Then out here they made me medical orderly, because I'm deaf, you see.'

I took over the medicine chest. During my school days in Madrid I had picked up a few notions of medicine and surgery. I taught El Sordo how to keep the instruments polished. After some weeks there was a decrease in cases of sickness such as we used to have as a result of scratches and slight wounds, which in that climate became horribly infected within a few hours. Then one evening Manzanares entered our tent just as I had come back from the track.

'We've got visitors. An old man with a big beard and four fellows with rifles, and the old man is speaking to the Captain in his tent. He's the chieftain of the village on the other side of the ravine, and I don't like the look of him one bit.'

Shortly afterwards the Captain sent for me. He had the indispensable bottle of brandy on his table but his face was darker than it used to get from alcohol.

'You've got us into a pretty mess. Now you can settle it yourself with that man there.'

He pointed to an old Moor with a broad, white beard, straight and strong as a tower. The Moor began to speak, rhythmically, as if he were reciting a prayer.

'My son is ill. He is very ill. His belly is hard, very hard. He has great heat and great noise in his head. I want the Sergeant Doctor to come with me. Nothing will happen to him. I leave four Moors with their rifles here. If something happens to him, may they all be killed.'

'Now, Mister Quack, it's up to you.'

I argued with the Moor. I was not a physician and I could not make myself responsible for the cure. He ought to go to El Zoco and fetch the doctor of the hospital there. But monotonously the Moor insisted. To refuse would have meant shooting that night, without fail.

'Look here,' I said finally. 'I'll come along and see your son, I'll do what I can and tomorrow I'll send you the doctor from El Zoco.' If he wants to come, I thought.

'You come and you cure him. Nothing will happen to you. I promise!'

'And what if he dies, what then?' I asked outright.

'The will of God is supreme.'

'Do as you like,' said the Captain, 'but I wash my hands of it. If anything happens to you, I know nothing about it. You've gone without my knowledge.'

I took Manzanares with me and various things from the medicine chest. To judge from the old man's description, the son must have eaten too many figs – or be suffering from an attack of malaria, or something of that kind. Manzanares carefully loaded a pistol.

'I'm coming along, but the first disagreeable face I see will get it.'

The village lay between the chain of hills along which we were building the track, and the granite mountains which extended towards the coast. It was only one of the settlements of a large *kabila* which stretched for about fifty kilometres across the mountains from the foothills of Tetuan to those of Xauen. Theoretically, the *kabila* was friendly, but in practice the friendship of its notables was in strict proportion to the proximity of Spanish forces. Near Tetuan they were intimate friends and received a subsidy from the Spanish Government. In the region of Hamara they waged war not openly but singly, from ambushes. Near Xauen they fought openly at the side of the mountain people.

The village consisted of a number of straw huts and a few clay-built and whitewashed houses, in one of which we found the patient. He lay on a straw mat, wrapped in old army blankets and surrounded by a crowd of neighbours who were smoking *kiffi* and carrying on a shouted discussion without heeding the sick man's eternal litany: 'Ay . . . maa, ay . . . maa!'

His stomach was taut like a drum, he had a high temperature and complained of an intolerable headache, but I felt sure that he had nothing worse than violent indigestion from *kous-kous*. Yet I hardly dared to give even the scanty advice I thought reasonable, and told the father that I would send him the doctor on the following day.

'But what medicine will you give him now?' he asked, glancing at the surgical instruments and the medicine bottles Manzanares had spread out on a low table.

I had to do something. Quinine would not hurt – he had fever – and a glass of castor oil would help him. I decided in favour of both. The patient let me give him an injection in the arm, though he groaned pitifully. Then I gave him the castor oil. He sampled it and then sipped it slowly. I felt my own inside revolt at the spectacle and forced him to drink more quickly. When he returned the cup he asked for more. I refused it.

The father invited us to take tea with him. For the first time I partook of a Moroccan tea, mint leaves floating on top, offered with all the ceremonious ritual of a Moorish notable. And for the first time I smoked *kiffi*. When we wanted to leave, Manzanares went to fetch the medicine chest from the sick-room; he returned with a most bewildered face:

'He's drunk all the castor oil.'

The patient had persuaded one of the small boys to bring him the bottle and both had drunk from it, though the child had not liked it much, to judge from its tear-stained and oil-smeared face. The quart bottle was emptied by half.

I made a row and told the father that whatever might happen would be his fault, but he did not believe in any danger, because of the ancient and primitive idea that you can't have enough of a good medicine.

On the following morning the old man arrived at our position before we went to work. I trembled when I saw him come. But he was more than content and gave me the exact details of the prodigious purge which had saved his son. Then he asked me for advice and help against the patient's extreme weakness. With great seriousness I told him that the young man should not be given any food during the whole day except for a cup of milk every two hours. And two days later the chieftain visited us again, followed by four women carrying baskets heaped with fruit and eggs, and four chickens tied by their legs. It seemed that the old Moor now considered me his friend and that not only I but the whole garrison would henceforward be held inviolable by the members of the *kabila*.

The old man himself, Sidi Jussef, would sometimes come to the fig tree and talk to me for hours; sometimes he would invite me to drink tea with him in his house. The Captain insisted once, when he was rather tight, on making the Moor drink brandy, thus putting us all in a difficult and ridiculous position. Sidi Jussef refused and I was afraid the Captain would be hit by a bullet from somewhere, in retribution for the religious insult. But he never strayed from the position alone; nothing happened to him except the final and complete loss of face among the Moorish workmen, the majority of whom belonged to Sidi Jussef's *kabila*.

In those days we were tracing the track which led down into the valley of Charca-Xeruta. I would leave with a dozen soldiers and three or four mules carrying materials and food, and we would go far down into the valley, unarmed, though it would have been very easy to kill us and to steal the precious mules. Sidi Jussef had asked us not to carry arms on those expeditions.

'Sometimes the Moors of the mountains come down here,' he had said. 'If they see you carrying arms they'll ambush you. But we have undertaken to see that nothing happens to you.' And nothing happened except that we occasionally saw the silhouette of a Moor and his rifle on the crest of a hill.

In the asphyxiating heat of an afternoon, Sidi Jussef talked to me in the shade of the fig tree, and I do not remember how the conversation started.

'The Spaniards are bad conquerors,' he said, 'but they are good colonizers. The Spaniard has a very peculiar adaptability. He is able to adopt all the characteristics of the world which surrounds him and yet to preserve his personality. The result is that in the long run he absorbs the people he has invaded.'

He paused and looked at me, at my surprised face. For though he and I had often discussed the divergences and affinities of Spaniards and Arabs, Sidi Jussef had never expressed his opinion of Spaniards in such dogmatic form.

'Look at the history of the conquest of America. The *conquistadores* were just like the soldiers who are in this country now: adventurers, desperadoes, thieves, drunkards, and women hunters. They conquer by killing and corruption. What else do they use but brute force, bribery or political hypocrisy, the means used by Cortés and Pizarro who sought gold and nobility, money and fame. The military conquest of America is a disgrace to Spain. But its colonization is her glory. Those poor men who went there and clung to the soil and mixed with the Indians and had sons and re-populated the land, they were the real conquerors of America. It was not the Spanish colonies which rebelled against Spain, but the Spaniards in America rebelled against their old country. They were helped by the half-castes and the Indians, but every American revolution had a Spaniard at its head . . .'

I told Córcoles of this conversation because it had impressed me: that Moor knew Spanish history more profoundly than many Spaniards. Córcoles shrugged his shoulders.

'They say that Sidi Jussef is a Spaniard who escaped many years ago from the Penal Colony of Ceuta. It would not surprise me if it were true. My father was a warder there and he knew many prisoners who escaped or were released and afterwards joined the Moors. They usually became chieftains in the *kabilas*. But you're taking Morocco much too seriously.'

'It interests me. I think we could do great work here. If we were less barbarian than we are . . .'

'Listen, you should not take it that way. It's just business.'

'I agree. It's business. We kill Moors and the Moors kill us. Doesn't it matter to you?'

'No. If they shoot me, it's bad luck; if they don't get me, I'll be rich in a few years' time.'

'Yes, with the fortune you're earning . . .'

'Why not? Sergeant-Major Pedrajas has just got his papers. After twenty years' service he gets 80 per cent of the pay as his pension. He's got three or four decorations which entail a pension, without ever having been at the front. He's got 150,000 pesetas in his bank, and a house, a very fine house, in his home town. And in the meantime he has refused himself nothing, neither wine, nor girls, nor a thousand pesetas' gamble at baccarat. You see, he was sergeant-major at Headquarters for eight years, and that did the trick.'

'And how did he get rich?'

'By stealing. By stealing the grain from the horses, the clothes from the soldiers, the food, the electric lamps in the barracks, everything, including brooms.'

'Oh yes, I can imagine how many soldiers have fallen ill because they had to go without the blanket he had filched. And it's all the same to you?'

'No, it isn't, my boy. I have been a soldier and slept under a blanket with more years of service than Sanjurjo. But I can't alter things. Here you must eat or be eaten, there's no third solution. Of course there have been men who tried to put things in order, but all of them have failed. The worst is that even if somebody has not stolen, they still put him down as having done it.'

'But one day the soldiers will rebel as they did in Madrid in '09. Or the Moors.'

'The soldiers? Nothing doing. One or the other may rebel, and then they execute him and that's that. The Moors? Their chieftains are bought, and we've got the guns and the MGs. Don't get all worked up about these problems – you won't solve them. And as to the Moors: don't get too friendly with them. There is only one way to treat the Moors if you want to get anywhere, and that's the stick. And again the stick. As soon as they see you're soft you're done. That's what they're used to. The best chief for them is the man who beats them hardest. They have to be treated rough. Come with me to El Zoco tomorrow, it's market day and I'm going shopping. You'll see how one has to treat that rabble. I was born in Ceuta and I've known the Moors ever since I could crawl on all fours. Come along tomorrow.'

'All right. I'll tell Julian to deputize for me. Let's see your talents as a sergeant in this colonizing and appeasing army.'

'Now then – did you ever think I was here as a missionary?'

5. The Blockhouse

Anywhere in Morocco, at least anywhere in the Morocco of the Moors, you find yourself in the vicinity of a *zoco*. A *zoco* is nothing but a free open-air market. It is usually called after the day of the week on which the actual marketing takes place, and after the name of the district; El Zoco el Jemis of Beni-Aros, El Zoco el Arbaa of Tlazta, and so on.

Before dawn they begin to arrive by all the mountain paths, the women carrying the burden, their lords and masters following them on their donkeys. Sometimes the donkey also carries a sheep or goat slung across its croup, or a string of chickens or rabbits, all tied by their legs and all alive, for the Moors never sell dead meat. At daybreak, the open space destined for the stalls is crowded with traders who are buyers as well.

Córcoles and I went to the Zoco del Arbaa, to give the name its Spanish form, accompanied by four soldiers and three mules. We had to buy fresh meat, eggs and fruit for the whole Company. When we arrived at nine in the morning the market was in full swing.

'We'll buy meat last of all,' said Córcoles. 'Sometimes it turns high within half an hour. Anyhow, it's cheaper later on.'

Aimlessly, we wandered round and strayed into the crowd round one of the snake-charmers. We listened to his tale, which was as usual extremely long, but left when he began his operations, because it made us sick to see the man introducing the body of a reptile into his nostrils and expelling it through his mouth.

I have never been able to resist the lure of a junk-stall, and there was one of particular fascination. Kitchen papers in shrill reds and greens spread on the ground. Boxes with candles and Marseilles soap. A couple of burning oil lamps. Cartridges for hunting rifles of all calibres in a big heap. A basket of eggs. Five chickens tied to a pole. A rusty revolver with a broken hammer, six homeless cartridges beside it, their shells covered with verdigris, their leaden bullets dented and pounded out of shape. A heap of sheep's wool recently shorn and sticky with grease, and a heap of empty petrol drums. In the centre, in the place of honour, a medley of pieces of metal: bits of spurs, cogwheels of watches, big needles for sewing straw mats, pincers with twisted jaws, and so on.

The owner was a Moor wrapped in a coffee-coloured, ragged *chilaba*, who smoked his pipe of *kiffi* and did nothing else. He squatted behind his display, mute while all the others around him shouted their offers. For a moment he lifted his eyes to look at us and then sank back once more into the delights of his hemp seed. Córcoles pointed to the basket of eggs: 'How much?'

'Fifty *céntimos* a dozen.'

'Give me two dozen.'

The Moor stretched out his hand to take the money, without changing his posture. Córcoles gave him a silver coin. The Moor did not take the money but corrected.

'Fifty Spanish *céntimos*.'

Córcoles put the coin back into his pocket, took my arm and left the stall.

'What's the matter?' I asked.

'You know there are two currencies here, ours and what they call *assani*, that of the Sultan. What I gave him was a *duro*, worth half a *duro* of ours. But those beggars never want to take the Arabic currency. Well, he'll call us back, you'll see.'

He did not call us. We walked slowly away but the Moor stayed there motionless, blowing smoke rings. Córcoles murmured:

Let's go back. The eggs are cheap.' He said to the Moor: 'Give me six dozen eggs.'

'Six dozen?'

'Yes, six.'

'Six dozen are a Spanish *duro* – five pesetas.'

'But look here, just now you wanted fifty *céntimos* per dozen . . .?'

'That was then.' He went on smoking his pipe.

Córcoles took a cartridge case from his pocket. The Moor put down his pipe and looked at it.

'You sell it?' he brought himself to ask.

'No,' said Córcoles. And we turned disdainfully away. The Moor rose and came after us. He plucked Córcoles by the sleeve.

'I buy the cartridges.'

'How many eggs are there in the basket?'

'Nine dozen.'

'How much?'

'Fifty *céntimos* the dozen.'

'*Assani céntimos?*'

The Moor swallowed his saliva. '*Assani*, yes.'

'How many cartridges do you want?'

The Moor became obsequious.

'All you want to give me. Hundred, thousand, I buy.'

'They're expensive, you know.'

We went back to the stall. Córcoles took the egg-basket and hung it over my arm. 'Here, give it to the boys; they'll pack the mule,' he winked and I went away.

When I returned Córcoles had a Moor of the Mehalla, the native police, at his side. The three were in a heated discussion. After a short while Córcoles left the two others standing and joined me. 'What was that?' I asked.

'Nothing. We've got the eggs cheap, at twenty *céntimos* a dozen, and it's given that little Moor a scare he won't get out of his system in three months.'

'What have you done to him?'

'Nothing. I simply promised to supply one thousand cartridges at twenty-five *céntimos* apiece. When he accepted the price I called the Mehalla guard. And of course, with the police there, the fellow turned repentant, and – nothing happened at all. Those people are worse than the gypsies. You'll see. Now let's buy a goat.'

The butcher's stall consisted of rows of poles with hooks, from some of which hung the skins of animals already sold. In the background was a pen crowded with sheep, lambs and goats. Córcoles chose a goat.

'How much?'

'Seven *duros*, Sergeant?'

'Five.'

'Six and a half.'

After the interminable bargaining they agreed on five *duros*, the skin to remain with the butcher. 'Now you'll see,' Córcoles whispered.

The butcher killed the goat on the ground and hung it on a hook.

He made a triangular cut in one of its legs, lifted the flap of skin, put his lips to the slit and began to blow. Slowly the skin lifted from the flesh and the goat swelled up to a monstrous shape. Finally he cut a long slit in the belly and stripped off the skin as though it were a coat. He laid the naked animal on the table which was covered with a yellow oilcloth crawling with flies. Córcoles put five *assani duros* beside it. The vendor broke out into violent protest: 'No *assanis*!'

Córcoles left the carcass lying on the table and dragged me away. 'You'll see, the goat is ours.'

The butcher followed us. He shouted, remonstrated and implored. We paid no attention. Finally he accepted four Spanish *duros*, twenty pesetas, for the goat and we took it away, with all the curses of Allah following us.

'It's very simple,' said Córcoles. 'He couldn't have sold this goat. The Moors don't buy meat when they haven't been present at the killing. After an hour in this July sun the goat will no longer be saleable. No Spaniard would give him as much as ten pesetas for it then. Except perhaps a sergeant of the infantry.'

'Why should he do it?'

'Because that's where their graft comes in, my boy. They pay five or ten pesetas for a goat or a sheep which is half rotten. They use it in the soldiers' mess, and in their account it is put down at thirty pesetas. That's their profit. You see, they haven't got extra pay like we have and they can't grow fat on road gravel like we do.'

'But it's a beastly thing to do. What about the men?'

'The men? Why, they get dysentery and fever and typhus. But soldiers are cheap.'

'Really, there are not so many epidemics among us.'

'We're well off. You're all right out here, if you've got money. Have you ever met a general with malaria? But just take a look at the infantry, especially the Chasseurs, and you'll see.'

The butcher turned up again, this time leading a goat with milk dripping from the udders.

'I've sold the kids. I'll sell her to you.'

'What do you think,' Córcoles asked me.

'It would be nice to have milk.'

'How much?'

'Ten *duros*. Spanish.'

'Five.'

We got the goat for five *duros* and took her away tied to the tail of one of the mules. I resumed the discussion.

'Then you think there would be less sickness if the men had better food?'

'Of course. Well, you don't know these things yet, but I'll tell you. Nearly all the officers come here to get rich. As a matter of fact they spend all their money and never get rich – but that's by the way. It's different with the warrant officers and the sergeants. They come here as privates, directly from their villages where they've gone hungry. And one fine day they find themselves with pay they could not have dreamed of while they were labourers, and with a uniform and a rank which gives them a chance for graft. Now these are the men who get rich out here. It's time you got wise to things. Tomorrow I'll take you to the blockhouse.'

Blockhouses, as we knew them, were wooden huts, six to four metres wide, protected up to a height of one and a half metres by sandbags or, very occasionally, by armour plates, and surrounded by barbed wire. In this small space a platoon under the command of a sergeant would be stationed: twenty-one men, isolated from the world. In exceptional cases a signaller from the Engineers would be detailed off with a heliograph and signal lamps to keep in day and night communication with the nearest blockhouse, and through it and a chain of others with the base. But mostly there was no such means of contact.

On a hill overlooking ours, on the other side of the stream of Hamara, was a blockhouse. Day and night we could hear the sound of stray shots over there. It was an outpost facing the valley of Beni-Aros, and the Moors were forever lying in ambush to fire at the outline of a figure or the light of a cigarette. The post was garrisoned by Chasseurs.

When I arrived with Córcoles we were welcomed by a lean and bearded sergeant, his ash-coloured face marked by fever. Our horses carried a few bottles of beer, a string of sausages, and two bottles of brandy, and a dirty little man in a tattered uniform was told to cook rice in our honour. Another little man was walking up and down, a rifle on his shoulder, behind the parapet of sandbags which covered the opening in the barbed wire. The fields below us were infinitely peaceful.

'We'd better go inside,' said our host. 'Here you're never safe, and even less so a group of people as we are now. Those bastards are good shots.'

We went inside. In the right-hand corner beside the door the sergeant had put up boards to make himself a bedroom. Otherwise the hut was a single room with bare soil for its floor. The beds of the men stood in two rows along the side walls, with a narrow passage in the middle. On each bed was a knapsack and a wooden box. Most of the men were lying there smoking. A little group clustered round one of the beds in the background gambling. At head level, the walls were pierced by loop-holes. The sun fell through them in jets of light which threw dazzling rectangles on the floor, dipping everything else in darkness until your eyes were accustomed to the twilight. There was a smell which not only assailed you through the nostrils but seemed to stick to your skin and clothes and deposit layers on them. It was like the stench of dirty linen left for months in a damp corner; only much worse.

We chatted of this and that until I said that I would like to know the details of their existence.

'He's new here,' Córcoles explained. 'And what's more, he's got socialist ideas, or something. He's not one of us, anyhow.'

He grinned the grin of a man in the know, and the bearded sergeant looked at me pityingly.

'He'll change,' he said. 'As for me, you can do what you like. I'll stay here with this beauty.' He patted the neck of one of the beer bottles.

I left the sergeant's bedroom and went into the common room. While I was walking along the beds the men watched me with the eyes of curious dogs. A few got up from their camp beds halfway to salute me. Further down, someone rose obsequiously:

'If you want to make water, Sergeant, the tin is over there.' In a corner at the back there was an oil-drum. Later I was to hear all about it. The men used it for urinating because otherwise they would have to go outside. While the enemy attacks were at times frequent, they used it for all their needs. When the drum was full, the orderly on duty had to empty it outside the barbed wire. This feat usually provoked a shot; sometimes there would be a casualty, and the tin would be lost. The first to feel an urgent need then had the choice between fetching back the tin which was certain to be covered by an enemy marksman, or relieving himself somewhere else outside the barbed wire at his own risk. In a place where only a very few disciplinary measures could be taken, offenders were punished by double time on watch, by having to fetch water or by having to empty the tin for a number of days. Thus the oil-drum had become a symbol of life and death and the main topic of conversation and commentary.

When I reached the camp bed where a game of cards was in progress, the men stopped and kept silent in embarrassment. I produced a packet of tobacco and they rolled their cigarettes, parsimoniously.

'How are things?' I asked.

'All right,' one of them replied after a long pause. 'If they don't hit you and if you don't get fever.'

I sat down on the bed, a piece of sacking stuffed with straw, laid on the naked floor and covered with two ragged blankets.

'But what do you do with yourselves here?' I tried to make them talk. 'Over there in Hamara we are building a track for the road, and we can see you from there. And sometimes we hear the *pacos*.'

'Well, we don't do anything at all,' said the one who had spoken before. 'I've still got three months to go—'

'Then you're a veteran, really.'

'Thirty-three months. I'm the oldest here. All those are just green. The number of lice I've caught! Never since I was a boy (you see, sir, when we were children we all had lice) have I had lice like in this place. They've got their nests in the boards, you know.'

'What will you do when you sign off?'

'What can one do? Work.'

'Then what's your profession?'

'My profession – digging and ploughing with the mules. What profession can you have in a village, if you're not a priest? And the priest has to dig sometimes, too. So it means everybody to the land!'

'Now look here, there must be some shops in your village, and a doctor and a chemist. And a cobbler. They can't all be labourers.'

'Oh, yes, sir. I'm from a little place in the Sierra called Maya, in the province of Salamanca. And there's nothing like what you say. A sort of inn, that's all. If anybody falls ill you've got to call the doctor from Bejar. But we have a healer, an old woman who knows more than a doctor. As soon as the doctor comes somebody dies, that's sure.'

'Have you got a girl?'

'Oh, yes.'

'Do you write to her?'

'I can't write. The only one here who can write is Matías over there.'

He pointed to a soldier with a face of a poor brute who began to laugh foolishly.

'And I write her things,' said the scribe.

'What things?'

'What things do I write? Well, the things like he says: "I want to give you a good squeeze." One day he said a good thing and I wrote it to her just like he said it. And then I wrote the same to the girls of all the other boys, and to my girl too: "When we are married, I'll put my snout between your breasts and I'll burrow there like a pig until I choke ".'

The inventor of the phrase went red, more with pride than with modesty, and explained:

'You know, sir, if you're doing nothing all day long, you think and you think and then you get ideas. And then this chap, who's slept with lots of women, tells us things and – well, you know what I mean.' He paused. 'Not that I'm ashamed, because men are made that way, but then, you see, well, you can't sleep afterwards.'

'So you've had your experiences?' I said to the boy who knew about women, a little town rat in an over-large uniform.

'Just imagine, sir, I was a bootblack in Salamanca, and that's something: The City of Syphilis. You've been there?'

'Oh, yes.'

'Then you'll know how it is. In daytime in the cafés and in the doorways of the Square and at night in the houses. The tarts are good girls and you clean their shoes and the suckers pay. And then you've always a girl of your own. These boys here don't know anything about life.'

'But I slept with my best girl before I came here,' said one of them.

'You say you've slept with her? You're cissies, all of you. When you go to Tetuan you're afraid of taking a woman to bed.'

'Because they're sows. You give me one of the sergeants' tarts and I'll show you. Listen, sir, in Tetuan there are women for fifty *céntimos* but they've got more lice than we have here. The only thing they're good for is when there is an operation on.'

'An operation?'

'Yes, sir. When there's going to be fighting. If you're lucky you get leave to go to Tetuan and you find a bitch who's sick and you sleep with her. Then they send you to hospital for three or four months and you don't have to run about when it's raining bullets. But those lousy bitches know it and ask for double the price.'

We were interrupted by dinner, a huge bucket of beans swimming in a brick-red gritty soup, followed by coffee, faintly tinted water into which the men threw chunks of bread. One of them produced a tin of condensed milk and poured a fine trickle into his coffee.

'*Caramba*, what a luxury!'

'Oh, no, sir. It's only because I've got the tertian ague and they give me a tin of milk every three days.'

'But if you've got tertian fever you ought to be in hospital.'

'Oh, well, that's if you've the ague all day long. But with a little bout of fever every third day you get quinine and milk and you stay on duty. Of course I'm off the day the fever comes.'

We ate with the sergeant, rice enriched by the sausages we had brought along, and drank coffee which was certainly better than that of the soldiers, though it was still infernally bad. Then we chatted, the brandy bottle between us.

'How do you get along?'

'Not too badly. The kitchen yields me about ten pesetas a day. And there's always something to be got out of the clothing, even if I must leave the quartermaster-sergeant his portion. And my food is thrown in gratis: where sixteen eat, seventeen can be fed.'

'It must take a bit of figuring to keep ten pesetas daily and to feed seventeen.'

'Not as much as you think. Beans, chick-peas, potatoes, rice, and dried cod; oil, salt, and pepper. All from the Commissariat and all cheap. I don't spend more than seventy-five *céntimos* per head and sometimes I get a barrel of wine for them at that. I don't like exploiting the poor devils. They know I'm robbing them, but others are worse than me, and they know it too. In Miscrela they had a sergeant who fed them for two months on nothing but beans boiled with water and red pepper. My men look after themselves as much as they can. If one of the Moors in the district is careless they steal some chickens or lambs. They set traps for rabbits and when they get a chance, they shoot birds.' He stopped and thought. 'One earns more money, though, when there is an operation on or when we go on convoy duty. Then every man gets a tin of sardines and biscuits, and that's all for the day.'

'No wonder they crack up and land in hospital.'

'Those who crack up aren't any good. I've been in Africa for twenty years, and nowadays it's fine. You ought to have seen the food when I came here. Biscuits at every meal. Biscuits from the time of the Cuban war, so hard that we had to pound them on a stone with our *machetes* and soak them in water if we wanted to eat them. There are still some left, but they can't risk distributing them because they're full of maggots.'

'How long do you stay in the blockhouse?'

'The rule is a month, but I stay on here. If you go to Tetuan you just spend your money. Here you earn money, and that's the only way to live. I've saved more than ten thousand pesetas already. And apart from that, one's better off in the blockhouse than at the front; it's quieter. But you, you're lucky. If I served in the Engineers, I would be rich.'

Towards evening, Córcoles and I went down the hill from the blockhouse. The fields were still absurdly peaceful. A Moor rode along a field-path on his little donkey, a small dog trotted behind him. From the track, a milling ant-heap in the distance, there came the notes of the bugle calling the cease-work.

'But those men live worse than the Moors in their straw huts,' I said to Córcoles.

'Never mind. Muck that doesn't choke you makes you fat,' he replied.

6. Eve of Battle

It is frighteningly easy for a man to slide back into an animal state.

In the monotony of unvarying days, confined to the narrow circle of the position which was my city and to the even narrower circle of the cone-shaped tent which was my house, I slowly went under in the daily routine and abandoned any effort to break with it. Breakfast, sit in the shade of the fig tree, lunch, sit in the shade of the fig tree, dine, sleep and wake up with the same prospect before you.

At first, I used to read; by and by I forgot to open a book.

At first, I liked to go shooting rabbits and partridge; then I left my rifle leaning against the fig tree for hours; finally it stayed in the tent for days on end.

I had finished the topographical work and had nothing to do but to muster the Moors and sit and keep watch. Keep watch for what? I let the slow hours pass by, like a ruminant beast, with a sluggish nodding of the head, in a doze, telling myself at times that I was thinking, but in truth thinking of nothing, submergd in a lazy mist.

I remember making only a single observation during that time, the observation that what happened to me was happening to all the others. The soldiers, in civilian life simple workers or labourers, were rapidly stultified and turned into eating and digesting machines, possessed by the one thought that work was something to be avoided at all costs. Everybody was degenerating in this existence without action, in the orbit of a radius of one kilometre. We all forgot what day of the week and month it was. We slept, we ate, and we digested.

When I received a telegram ordering me to Tetuan it came as a relief and as a worry. I did not feel like going to Tetuan; I wanted to go. The drowsiness was there, and the desire to break away from it as well.

In the army an order is an order. I left the following day.

Major Castelo said:

'Until the army has crossed the river Lau, we can't do anything. HQ need somebody who knows topography. Report to Major Santiago of the General Staff. I think you'll be all right.'

Major Santiago was a half-breed. The soldiers called him 'The Chink' because he had slanting eyes and a greenish-yellow skin. Apparently he was the son of one of those Spanish officers who had been stationed in the Phillippines and married a native girl. His colour and his almond eyes had given him a very bad inferiority complex; he was in a state of perpetual irritation. But he was a clever man of exceptional mental agility.

He told me to sit down at a draughtsman's table.

'Copy this.' He gave me a topographical sketch of the bay of Rio Martin. When I had finished he examined my work carefully.

'You'll stay here. We have to make a map of the whole region of Beni-Aros.'

'At your orders, sir.'

'My orders! Making a map of Beni-Aros! Do you know how to do it? No? Neither do I. But we haven't any map at all and the French maps of the region are rubbish. They've drawn the line of the frontier and then a few little strokes, and that's all there is. All right, my boy, we have to make a map of Beni-Aros.'

He went out of the room and left me alone with a Chasseur who was bending busily over some tracing paper. After a short silence I asked him:

'The Major doesn't seem to be in a very good temper?'

'How could he be? Berenguer says: "Make me a map of Beni-Aros," when nobody knows Beni-Aros, with the exception of Castro Girona who went there once to a wedding in the Raisuni's family. And there are no maps, no sketches, nothing. Make me a map of Beni-Aros. He might as well tell us to make a map of the North Pole. . . . You've come here as a draughtsman?'

'Yes, I suppose so.'

'Good, then there will be two of us. We'll share our furies fifty-fifty. You don't know this job yet.'

He stood up and I saw that he was a corporal. Finely drawn features, spectacles for near-sightedness, tapering hands.

'Come and have a look.'

The sketch on the transparent paper before him showed part of the Spanish zone of Morocco, with a blank space in the middle.

'This is Tangier, here are Tetuan, Ben-Karrick, El Zoco el Arbaa, Xauen, and here the French frontier passing by Larache. Here's Larache, Alcazarquivir, Arcila. So far, so good. But the whole white space here is Beni-Aros. And we must fill it in. Operations will start in the spring, and the plans are needed.'

'How can we fill it in?'

'That's precisely the question. You'll see. They'll drop in soon.'

The Major came back. 'Well, Montillo, are you explaining the problem?'

'Yes, sir.'

'When the people arrive, give him the necessary instructions. Barea, this is Montillo, topographer at HQ. The two of you will have to work together, and you'll have to follow his orders though he is only a corporal.'

'Very good, sir.'

For a while Montillo showed me maps and more maps. He explained their method of working; they drew on tracing paper and made blueprints. There was a stupefying lack of maps. Not even a complete plan of Tetuan existed.

An hour later a native soldier of the *Regulares* arrived, together with a Moor. 'Where do you come from?' Montillo asked.

'From Tlazta. This man here knows the district.'

Tlazta was an advance post, a speck on the map. Montillo, the soldier and the Moor immersed themselves in a series of questions. 'Here is Tlazta. From here towards Beni-Aros, how would you go?'

'Well, you go down a path and then you turn to the left and then . . .'

Montillo extracted every imaginable piece of information from the Moor. Here a tree, there a stone, a field-path, a stream, a ravine, and so forth.

After the two had gone Montillo exclaimed: 'How easy it could be! An aeroplane and a few photos. Do you know that we have a captain here, Captain Iglesias, who wants to do it and they won't let him? There is a new system, they call it the photogrammetric system. You simply take some pictures with a new German apparatus, and from them you can make a sketch of the ground and get the altitude of all the points.'

'I've never heard of it.'

'Still, it exists. But Iglesias demands I don't know how many thousands of pesetas to carry it out. As he's a decent chap they won't give him the money, and we here must cudgel our brains. What a bloody mess!'

During the morning we did no work at all. We took our meal together and walked up and down the Calle de la Luneta. Late in the evening Montillo said:

'Let's go to the House of Luisa.'

'You go if you like. I'd prefer not to go myself.' Suddenly I asked: 'Do you know that I have slept with Luisa?'

'The devil you have.' He stared at me and added: 'But we've got to go, you'll see why.'

While we were walking up the Alcazaba he explained.

'We must have agents for all kinds of information. But most of them would not be seen entering HQ for anything in the world. Now, everybody can go into the House of Luisa and nobody cares. Why do you go there? To sleep with a woman. It's the best place for a talk.'

The House of Luisa was a centre of Military Intelligence. They led us into a little hall where we were visited by a motley crowd of people entering one by one, at short intervals: Moors from the mountains, sutlers, itinerant tea vendors, a storyteller of the *zocos*. Montillo interrogated and made sketches and entries. Then he shut his notebook. 'Enough for today. Let's get a bottle of wine.'

Luisa entered. When she recognized me, she openly showed her surprise at seeing me involved in such activities: 'How well you've kept it secret. . . . I'm glad you've come. Tonight I shall enjoy myself, I can feel it in my bones.'

'But I can't.'

We emptied the bottle between us and then Montillo left. Luisa and I were alone. She was cajolingly affectionate, like a cat.

'And you'll take part in the operations?'

'I don't know.'

'They'll start in April.'

'So they say. Spring is the best season.'

'Some people say they'll begin from Ben-Karrick and others say from Xauen. Of course you know it better than I . . .'

'Of course.'

I had not an inkling of the plans, but I could not resist the desire to show myself well informed.

'Tell me about it. I bet you're going by Xauen.'

'Of course. Look, the valley of Beni-Aros is shut off by Xauen and by Larache at both ends, and by the French positions and ours on the two sides. We're going to send a column down from Larache and another from Xauen and the Raisuni will be caught in the middle, without an escape.'

But Luisa wanted to know more. Like a perfect armchair strategist I expounded all the operations. And then we went to bed. That night she did not expect the General. But on the following day I told Montillo of Luisa's curious interest in the operational plans.

'You were right to tell her a tale. The bitch is trading with both sides, or rather with three, I think, for it seems to me that she's passing on information to the Moors, and to the French in Tangier. In any case we'll tell the Major.'

The result was that I was asked to cultivate the friendship with Luisa and to give her increasingly detailed information about the operations which were to start via Xauen. I had no more idea of the plans than before. My work was to cull information from agents, to collect notes and to trace a more or less rudimentary map of the valley of Beni-Aros and its communication lines.

Slowly I came to know the commanding officers of the operating forces: General Dámaso Berenguer, High Commissioner of Morocco, fat and heavy, with an unctuous voice; General Marzo, also of the tribe of fat generals, with a corset beneath his uniform, sanguine and apoplectic, prone to anger; Colonel Serrano, a stout, resolute, fatherly man, adored by his soldiers for his good-natured humour and his absolute fearlessness; Lt. Col. Gonzalez Tablas, tall, energetic, an authority to the Moors of the *Regulares* whom he commanded, very much the aristocrat among the high officers who mostly looked like wealthy farmers and who hated him cordially – or so I believed. And finally, there was General Castro Girona, very affable, but outlandish with his deep tan, his clean-shaven head, and his genuine interest in the Moors.

This General, who seemed cast for the Man of Morocco, enjoyed an immense prestige among the Moors, many of whose dialects he spoke very well. An astute politician, he made it possible for us to occupy Xauen without bloodshed, at the cost of a few stray shots; weeks before the action he entered the town disguised as a Moorish charcoal-burner and negotiated the surrender of the city with the notables, threatening them with a bombardment of the town and promising them financial benefit at the same time.

This feat had doubtless saved hundreds of Spanish families from bereavement, for Xauen lies hidden between mountains in an almost unassailable position. But it had earned him the enmity of the Generals who dreamed of a 'conquest' of Xauen, the Sacred City, and of a 'glorious page in history'. In the actions to come, Castro Girona was not given any operational command. Decorations and promotion were to be reserved for the others.

What I saw of the Spanish General Staff at that time makes me wish to do it justice. I saw men who represented what there was of military culture, studious, self-denying, eternally struggling against the envy of their brother officials in other corps and against the antagonism of the Generals, many of whom were unable to read an army map and, being dependent on the General Staff, hated or disparaged its members. The officers of the General Staff were on the whole powerless; whenever a General had an idea, their task was to find the least dangerous way of putting it into practice, since they were unable to quash it. The ideas of the Generals were almost without exception based on what they were pleased to call guts, though they used a cruder word.

Towards the end of March 1921, the preparations at HQ for the impending operations were finished. I went back to my Company at Hamara. They had orders to cease work on the road and to join one of the columns, leaving behind a platoon under Ensign Mayorga, and Señor Pepe with his Moors.

I was to go to war for the first time.

Every soldier who is caught in the machinery of an army asks himself on the eve of going to the front: 'Why?'

The Spanish soldiers in Morocco asked themselves the same question. They could not help trying to understand why they found themselves in Africa and why they were to risk their lives. They had been made soldiers when they were about twenty years old, because they were twenty years old; they had been put into a regiment and sent to Africa to kill Moors. So far theirs was the story of all conscript soldiers who are mobilized by a decree and sent to the battle front. But at this point began their Spanish story.

'Why have we to fight against the Moors? Why must we "civilize" them if they do not want to be civilized? Civilize them – we? We from Castile, from Andalusia, from the mountains of Gerona, who cannot read or write? Nonsense. Who is going to civilize us? Our village has no school, its houses are of clay, we sleep in our clothes on a pallet in the stable beside the mules, to keep warm. We eat an onion and a chunk of bread in the morning and go to work in the fields from sunrise to sunset. At noon we eat the *gazpacho*, a mess of oil, vinegar, salt, water, and bread. At night we eat chick-peas or potatoes with dried cod. We crack up with hunger and misery. The boss robs us, and if we complain we are beaten by the Civil Guard. If I had not reported at the barracks the Civil Guard would have beaten me. They would have carried me off and I would have to be here for three years. And tomorrow they're going to kill me. Or will I do the killing?'

The Spanish soldier accepted Morocco as he accepted inevitable things, with the racial fatalism in face of the inevitable. 'Be it as God wills' – which is not Christian resignation, but subconscious blasphemy. Said like this, it means that you feel powerless in front of reality and must resign yourself to God's will, just as you might have to resign yourself to the will of the usurer when he takes away your land, even though you have paid up three times its value, in the ground that the total sum of the debt was never once in your hands.

This Spanish 'Be it as God wills' does not signify hope in God's kindness but rather the end of any hope, the expectance of worse things to come.

The Spanish soldiers in Morocco had every cause to feel it.

On the eve of our departure three soldiers were on the sick list. One had a high temperature and had to stay in the tent. Another, who had slightly hurt a finger on barbed wire, had his hand badly inflamed. A third had gonorrhea. They were to stay in Hamara until they could be sent to the hospital in the Zoco del Arbaa. The rest of the Company started the march towards Ben-Karrick.

The bugler Martin walked beside my horse. Not only was he thus resuming the intimacy of our conversations beneath the fig tree, but he could also rest part of his equipment against the horse and catch hold of its tail when we had to climb a hill.

'Martinez has a violent temperature,' I said.

'All he has is a dodge.'

'A dodge?'

'It's clear that you don't yet know these people, sir. There's nothing the matter with him. Nor with the other two.'

'Don't tell me that I'm blind and dumb. Martinez had fever. Sotero's hand was as big as my boot. And Mencheta is dripping puss all the time.'

'Yes, yes. And none of them wanted to go where we're going now. Martinez put a head of garlic in his armpit during the night. Sotero put pounded stinging-nettles into his wound. And Mencheta used a poultice.'

'A poultice?'

'Yes, sir. One of those mustard papers you buy at the chemist's. You make a little roll and put it in the urinary passage, and on the following day you've got something awful. Now the three will go to hospital, and when their tricks no longer work the operations will be over. I've done it many times. There are plenty of other things you can do. You eat tobacco, and turn yellow as if you had jaundice. You heat a copper, and get an ulcer on the leg. Now we're here in the country. But I'm sure in Tetuan there were queues before the houses where there are sick women last night. In a fortnight's time dozens of the men will be in the hospitals.'

'You know what it means, though.'

'Yes. But a bullet in the stomach is worse. If you get it in the stomach you're finished. You get peritonitis and you die. For the doctors stay in the rear. You'll see. All these fellows here come along bcause they're dumb, most of them, and because they can't do what they would do in Tetuan. Sometimes there are as many as twenty on the sick list the day before an operation, and after the first few days a dozen more.'

'And you, why do you come? You could have used one of those tricks.'

'I can't do it any longer. Sooner or later they spot you, and then they send you to jug. Nowadays when an operation is on, I tell myself: "Be it as God wills", and start marching.'

Early in the afternoon we reached Ben-Karrick. At that time it was a base. The place was a small settlement with a barracks of the *Regulares*, Infantry and Commissariat units and supply dumps of the army contractors. Various canteens had been set up by sutlers, well stocked with wine, spirits and tinned or pickled food. From time to time two or three women would come from Tetuan and stay for a week.

We pitched our tents outside the position. A column of eight thousand men was being formed under the command of General Marzo. We would have to wait a couple of days until we left, and in the meantime Ben-Karrick became a *fiesta*. It offered nothing except food and drinks, but how we ate and drank!

In the Spanish code of personal relations, drunkenness is considered not only disgusting but also as proving a lack of virility. A group of friends will relentlessly exclude a man who cannot carry his drink or at least restrain himself in accordance with his powers of resistance. They will expel him because he showed himself wanting in manhood. But on certain occasions there is an exception to the rule, as for instance on Christmas Eve and New Year's Eve. And it was the same in Ben-Karrick. The men drank in order to get drunk.

The cabin of El Malagueño was the favourite meeting place of the sergeants, and the owner, proud of his clientèle, drove away any soldier who dared to enter. El Malagueño had begun as a peddler who followed marching columns with a little donkey and four pitchers filled with water. The water pitchers became goat-skins full of wine. Then he set up a little wooden structure in an encampment at Regaia. Now he had a big store in Ben-Karrick, complete with hams, sausages, tins of sardines, German beer, Dutch tinned milk, spirits from everywhere, fine Andalusian wines, and a kitchen which could produce a meal within ten minutes. Close to the stores he had built a hut where he killed lambs and occasionally a cow, and from where he supplied the kitchens of all officers and sergeants in the position with fresh meat.

Julian was in the same situation as I was: he was going into action for the first time. His natural gaiety of a fat young man was clouded by his feelings. He who used to drink wine mixed with water at meals poured down big glasses of Manzanilla.

'You'll get tight,' I told him.

'The more the better. I want to get tight. It's my father's fault: if they hit me tomorrow, what then?'

'We'll bury you, don't worry.'

'Poor fellow, he's so fat that he'd make a good target,' said Herrero.

'They'll hit you right in your tummy.'

'Don't be afraid, just hide behind me,' Córcoles wound up, showing off his slimness.

But Julian was not susceptible to jokes. He became increasingly sulky, and he drank and drank. Suddenly he smashed his glass on the floor and shouted:

'I spit on my father!'

El Malagueño knew Julian and his father and the story of both of them. He opened the flap of the bar, crossed over to us and patted Julian on the back.

'Yes, I spit on my father!'

'Well done. If I were you, I'd do the same. And I'd play him a dirty trick. You know what I would do if I were you?'

'What?'

'Well then, tomorrow or the day after, when you're in front of the Moors, if I were you, I should go ahead and let them hit me. And my father would tear out his hair.'

We shouted with laughter, but Julian turned livid and hit El Malagueño in the face. The other screamed hair-raising blasphemies, then caught up the knife for cutting ham and shouted:

'I'll kill him! Let me kill him! Not even the Almighty may lay hands on me. I'll slit his guts open like a pig's!'

Herrero cut him short:

'First bring us some glasses of Manzanilla. Then you can kill him if you like. But the best thing to do is to give him a double brandy.'

'That's an idea, old man!'

El Malagueño filled our wine cups and then poured eau-de-vie into a glass which he handed to Julian:

'Drink, son, drink this, to get rid of your blues.'

Julian drank the stuff at one gulp. Three seconds later he was lying on the floor like a stuffed sack. El Malagueño lifted him tenderly and laid him on some bales in the warehouse. We drifted into a group of infantry sergeants, all mature men of long service in Africa. One of them, a tiny yellowish fellow, seemed to take a liking to me.

'I've been waiting for operations to begin,' he said.

'So you like a fight?'

'Oh, well, I don't exactly like it, but it's the only chance for a bit of luck.'

'For what, did you say?'

'For promotion, I meant. With us it isn't like with you Engineers. It takes us a good ten to twelve years to become a quartermaster sergeant. The only stroke of luck one of us can have is to get the right sort of wound or to have one's platoon bumped off. It's easier to be promoted for merit in action than for seniority.'

'But how much would you gain? Ten *duros* per month.'

'How much would I gain? Just a little more. As a sergeant you get your fingers in the pie only when you're mess sergeant or when they send you to a blockhouse. But as a quartermaster sergeant, who dresses the whole company, you're on top. At the least a thousand pesetas per month, I bet you. And with a bit of luck during operations . . .'

'What do you mean by luck?'

'You're a fool, my boy. If I'm quartermaster sergeant and I take part in one of those operations where they make it hot for us and half the men get killed, then it's simple. Next day I report the Company's equipment as lost. Just imagine. Two hundred blankets, two hundred pairs of boots, two hundred shirts, two hundred coats, and so on . . .'

7. The Legion

We were among the first to arrive. Only the artillery and the commissariat had come before us. On the crest of the hill we saw the outline of eight guns pointing towards the valley. At the foot of the hill the Commissariat had pitched their tents; there rose a strong smell of straw and horses. We had been allotted the slope by the Captain of the General Staff who organized the encampment. Within half an hour our tents were set up and the kitchen fires burning.

The hill rose from a stubble-covered plain. The barley had just been cut. Far back in the rear we could see the huts of a Moorish village which had surrendered a few weeks before. At this distance the ugliness of its hovels was softened and it looked a homely enough place in the middle of the harvested fields. Our cone-shaped tents, scattered over the hillside, looked as though the village were preparing for a fair.

Our Captain had suggested to the Captain of the General Staff that we should be given the open field for our camping ground. The answer had been: 'It is reserved for the Legion.' Our Captain had pulled a wry face.

The Legion arrived in the afternoon, a whole battalion – they call it *bandera*, Standard – which was to go into action for the first time. Their tents were quickly pitched. At the far end of the camp barrels of wine were lined up beside two square tents: the canteen and the brothel. The soldiers of the Legion began to crowd round the casks and the tents; they started drinking and 'making love'.

Together with the other sergeants I watched the bivouac of the Legion growing below us.

'Those are the new Americans,' said Julian. 'I suppose most of them are here because they've been duped.'

'Duped? Don't tell us that anybody comes here by mistake.'

Córcoles said: 'There are still some saps left in the world. They'll have heard fine words about the Mother Country and her daughter nations in America, and so the grandchildren have come here. Well, they won't find these four years much fun.'

A legionary was coming up the hill towards us. Córcoles pointed to him:

'Where's he going? I think he's got on the wrong floor.'

In those days it was the rule for legionaries and ordinary Spanish soldiers never to mix.

When the man came nearer I recognized him. It was Sanchiz. We waved to each other. Córcoles turned to me:

'So you know him?'

'Yes, he's an old friend of mine.'

'Nice friends you've got.'

Meanwhile, Sanchiz had arrived.

'Hallo, how are things? I've come to fetch you. We've got some first-class wine down there. They told me your Company was here, so if you're free, come along with me.'

We went down the hill together; Sanchiz had taken my arm. The legionaries looked at me askance. We met a sergeant with the face of an old jailbird, and he asked Sanchiz threateningly:

'Where are you off to with that fellow?'

'He's an old friend of mine. Come on and have a glass,' said Sanchiz.

'No, I'm on guard tonight, and if I start drinking, I'm lost.'

The caterer was a thin, yellow-skinned old man with transparent ears and a nose like a beetroot. He was so deaf that we had to shout our orders and point with our fingers at what we wanted. As a rule, the wine which was sold to the forces in Africa contained a shameless dose of water and half a dozen chemicals to prevent quick fermentation. But this wine was excellent, dry and strong, so that you had to smack your tongue against your palate.

'What do you do to stop them putting water in your wine?'

'*El Sordo* takes jolly good care not to play tricks. Otherwise he wouldn't have a sound bone left in his body – to say the least.'

'But how is it you're here? I thought you were doing office work in Ceuta and living like a prince.'

'Wine's to blame for that. I got tight, and the Captain sent me along with these fellows for two months. I've got to teach them. They're a lousy crowd. Sons of Negroes, and Chinks, and Red Indians. To hell with them. They talk to you, all sweetness, and as soon as you turn your back they stick a knife between your ribs. A rotten lot. Just look at their faces. . . . I wonder what Millán Astray will say to them tomorrow.'

'Has he come here, too?'

'Yes, and tomorrow at ten he's going to address them. Come and listen. He's terrific, I'll come and fetch you at your tent.'

The abstemious sergeant joined us: 'You've made me envious. Will you stand me a glass?'

He drank in slow sips, staring at me.

'Is he really a friend of yours, Sanchiz?'

'Yes, he's like a brother to me. Or rather, like a son, for I could be his father.'

The sergeant offered me a huge calloused hand:

'If that's so, I'm glad to meet you.' He took another sip. 'And if you are his friend, why don't you come with us? If I were in his skin,' he said to Sanchiz, 'you'd see – I'd be a lieutenant tomorrow.'

'Don't be a fool. A sergeant-major at the most. But he's no good for us. We scared him stiff in the tavern of *El Licenciado*.'

The din round the wine casks was infernal, it was impossible to understand one another. Sanchiz and I parted at the boundary of the Legion's camp. Walking up the slope, I wrestled with the problem of my old repugnance against the *Tercio*, and remembered the tavern of *El Licenciado* in Ceuta.

Spanish taverns usually paint their doors red. That one in the little square behind the church of Our Lady of Africa had been lavish with red paint. The harsh vermilion of red lead had been daubed on doors, tables, three-legged stools, the bar and the shelves, laden with bottles. The tavern was like a bleeding gash in the whitewashed front wall. Outside the sun had bleached the red colour to a dirty pink. Inside, smoke had blackened it to the shade of dried blood. The landlord was an old convict from the penal colony on Monte Hacho; he went about in a dirty sleeveless vest, with the hairs of his chest sticking through the mesh. His customers were legionaries and whores. His nickname – 'The Licenciate' – was a reference to his convict past and a cheap joke at the same time. The wine was greenish-red and tasted of copper sulphate. To drink it you had to have a thirst such as *El Licenciado* produced by serving chunks of sun-dried tunny along with the glasses of wine. The fish hung in a row from a beam above the long bar. Slit open from head to tail and spread-eagled on bamboo frames, they looked like small kites. The same beam carried two hooks from which two oil lamps hung suspended on twisted bits of wire. At night, *El Licenciado* lighted the lamps, and their smoke licked slowly at the dried fish until they were dyed black and tasted of oily soot.

At noon the tavern was empty. A woman or a legionary would come in for an instant and take away a bottle of wine. Towards nightfall the customers drifted in. I went there some evenings while the bar was still deserted, to wait for Sanchiz. The first to come would be a lonely legionary who sat down near the light, and wrote, nobody ever knew what. Then came an avalanche of men who had finished their duty at the office of the Ceuta delegation of the *Tercio*. They leaned against the bar in a row and argued about who was to stand whom drinks. After a time some started a game of cards, others sat down in small groups round a square flagon of wine, and a few went away. The women came only with the darkness. Their coming coincided with the lighting of the lamps. Mostly, they were accompanied by a casual bed-fellow of theirs who had invited them to a drink afterwards. Other came to look for someone and asked for him from the doorstep. Then they were invited to sit down, and entered. A few regular customers came simply to drink and to find somebody who would pay for their drinks.

The cross-fire of blasphemies, the barbarous language, the smoky light, the red paint, and the metallic wine filled the tavern with a naked brutality which was scarcely disguised – was indeed rather heightened – by the uniforms. The women added the high lights: they were old, corroded by disease, in rags of glaring colours, hoarse from syphilis and alcohol, their eyes red-rimmed. When the women came, the blasphemies tore through the room like the lashing of whips, in a sexual battle between males and females. Sometimes a man slapped the wrinkled cheek of a woman, sometimes someone caught a trestle in his fury and lifted it above another's head.

When the quarrels went beyond the limits of the Licentiate's code, he slowly left his place behind the counter, moving like a boar, and put the adversaries outside into the little square without saying a word. Then he turned and slowly fastened the latch of the door. The door had no bolt and was a simple glass pane with short red muslin curtains. Yet I never saw anybody attempt to force the entry. The tavern keeper was taboo through a mixture of physical fear of his murderous past, and of instinctive dread that the tavern might be closed, since it was one of the few which belonged to the Legion.

That tavern had for me the same fascination which the first visit to a lunatic asylum has for a normal person: repulsion, fear and the attraction of the unknown horror of madness. Through the peculiar code of the lawless, I was a sacrosanct person there, for I did not belong to them and yet was the friend of one of them. But this contact imbued me with a fear, almost a terror, of the *Tercio*, which has lasted all my life.

On the eve of a battle there is always the nervous tension born of the risks to be run. That night I found it difficult to sleep, but my nervous tension, my fear, rose from the stubble field where the barley had been cut, and not from the other side of the hills, where the advance guards were firing at each other in the darkness.

Lieut.-Col. Millán Astray came out of the tent, followed by a couple of officers. The crowd fell silent. The Commander stretched his bony frame, while his hands mangled a glove until it showed the hairs of the fur lining. The whole might of his stentorian voice filled the encampment, and the noises from the bivouacs of the other units died down. Eight thousand men tried to hear him, and they listened.

'*Caballeros legionarios!*'

'Gentlemen of the Legion . . . yes, gentlemen! Gentlemen of the *Tercio* of Spain, offspring of the Flanders *Tercios* of old. Gentlemen! Some people say that before coming here you were I know not what! but anything rather than gentlemen: some murderers, others thieves, and all with your lives finished – dead! And it is true what they say. But here, since you are here, you are gentlemen. You have risen from the dead – for don't forget that you have been dead, that your lives were finished. You have come here to live a new life for which you must pay with death. You have come here to die. It is to die that one joins the Legion.

'What are you? The Betrothed of Death. You are the gentlemen of the Legion. You have washed yourselves clean, for you have come here to die. There is no other life for you than in this Legion. But you must understand that you are Spanish gentlemen, all of you, knights like those other legionaries who, conquering America, begat you. In your veins there are some drops of the blood of Pizarro and Cortés. There are drops of the blood of those adventurers who conquered a world and who, like you, were gentlemen – the Betrothed of Death. Long live Death! . . .'

'*Viva la Muerte!*'

Millán Astray's whole body underwent an hysterical transfiguration. His voice thundered and sobbed and shrieked. Into the faces of these men he spat all their misery, their shame, their ugliness, their crimes, and then he swept them along in fanatical fury to a feeling of chivalry, to a readiness to renounce all hope, beyond that of dying a death which would wash away their stains of cowardice in the splendour of courage.

When the Standard shouted in wild enthusiasm, I shouted with them.

Sanchiz pressed my arm:

'He's a grand fellow, isn't he?'

Millán went round the circle of legionaries, stopping here or there before the most exotic or the most bestial faces. He stopped in front of a mulatto with thick lips, the liverish yellow-white of his rounded eyeballs shot with blood.

'Where do you come from, my lad?'

'What the devil's that to you?' the man answered.

Millán Astray stared straight into the other's eyes.

'You think you're brave, don't you? Listen. Here, I am Chief. If anyone like you speaks to me he stands to attention and says: "At your orders, sir. I don't want to say where I come from." And that's as it should be. You've a perfect right not to name your country, but you have no right to speak to me as if I were the likes of you.'

'And in what are you more than I am?' The man spat it from lips wet with saliva as if they were on heat.

At times men can roar. At times men can pounce as though their muscles were of rubber and their bones steel rods.

'I . . .?' roared the Commander. 'I am more than you, more of a man than you!' He sprang at the other and caught him by the shirt collar. He lifted him almost off the ground, hurled him into the centre of the circle and smacked his face horribly with both hands. It lasted two or three seconds. Then the mulatto recovered from the unexpected assault and jumped. They hit each other as men in the primeval forest must have done before the first stone axe was made. The mulatto was left on the ground nearly unconscious, bleeding.

Millán Astray, more erect, more terrifying than ever, rigid with a furious homicidal madness, burst into the shout:

'Attention!'

The eight hundred legionaries – and I – snapped into it like automatons. The mulatto rose, scraping the earth with his hands and knees. He straightened himself. His nose poured blood mixed with dirt like a child's mucus. The torn lip was more bloated than ever. He brought his heels together and saluted. Millán Astray clapped him on his powerful back:

'I need brave men at my side tomorrow. I suppose I'll see you near me.'

'At your orders, sir.' Those eyes, more bloodshot than ever, more yellow with jaundice, held a fanatical flame.

Dawn was breaking. At the bottom of the vale, where the river ran, the light was pushing against the blue-black of the sky. Suddenly the flame of the sun rose, and its red disc showered crimson stains on the waters. From the height where we were posted, the light seemed to creep up the mountain slopes, and the shadows stretched across the valley, immense and shapeless. The crests were illuminated by the light coming from below, and the tree tops glowed as though the trunks were on fire. The smoke columns from the shelled *kabila* were tainted red as though the flames had flickered up once more.

Our artillery protected the advance. We saw the fast Moorish cavalry riding uphill and the infantry of the *Regulares* running between the shrubs and the dwarf palms. Little white puffs dotted the ground, transient as a photographer's magnesium flare. The shots merged into a continuous crackling noise which grew steadily.

The *Tercio*, in the centre, carried the assault against the summit where, in the middle of a bare, stony clearing, stood the *kabila*, surrounded by a stone wall. Once more shells fell within the enclosure. The machine guns sounded like motorcycles accelerating on many distant roads.

At ten o'clock we sappers were given the order to advance. We were to fortify the hill which the Legion had just stormed. It was to be a position big enough to hold a whole company as well as a battery of field guns, protected by a circle of ten thousand sandbags. When we reached the edge of the summit, we were ordered to lie flat on the ground, load our rifles and scatter. A staff captain came and went. He held a whispered conversation with our commander and galloped away to the hilltop, only to reappear shortly afterwards. Then we were ordered to advance again. And we advanced, slowly; we reached the edge of the clearing and cautiously raised our heads. Behind every stone, every ripple on the bare ground there was a legionary, firing his rifle. Now and then one of them started to rise and collapsed. A few tried to find better shelter by going backwards. It was a slow, individual retreat, but the legionaries were retreating. Again and again, another of them came closer to us as we crouched motionless, fascinated, behind the evergreen oaks. The stone parapet of the *kabila* was ablaze, a single firing-line. The bullets whistled over our heads while we clung to the ground, straining to see.

In the middle of the clearing was a rider on horseback, dashing to and fro; at his side ran a tiny figure: Millán Astray with his bugler. There was a momentary lull in the fighting. The horse stopped, the horseman stood upright in his stirrups:

'To me the Legion! Fix bayonets!'

He raised an arm stained with blood.

The men jumped the stone parapet in clusters.

The handling of explosives was one of my specialities. That afternoon they came to fetch me. A sergeant of the Legion came together with one of our officers. They explained the case to me. They were just burying the dead. A legionary had bayoneted a Moor and stabbed him through the chest, but with such barbaric force that the rifle had penetrated up to the bolt. It was impossible to pull out the weapon except by sawing the corpse in two. But the rifle was still fit for use. So they had thought of introducing explosive into the rifle and blowing it up.

I organized the explosion as best I could. I poured a few percussion caps of mercury fulminate, such as we used for blowing up bore-holes in the quarry, down the rifle barrel which stuck out from the Moor's back. His was a skeleton-like body, wrapped in a torn grey burnous soaked in blood.

The mulatto, his lips still inflamed, his hands idle, watched me with curiosity while I dropped the golden little percussion caps with much care into the barrel. He stood back when I gave the order. I set fire to the fuse in the rifle mouth and ran away. The Moor's stomach burst open.

The mulatto laughed like an animal, with a twist to the lip that still smarted.

Back in my tent, I drank a large glass of brandy and stopped myself from being sick.

Dusk came. On the far side of the mountain, at the bottom of a ravine, the Moors had ceased firing. There was a great silence in the fields. Only in our position the fire crackled on through the din of the victors as they pitched their tents, tied up their horses, sang, complained of their wounds, and shouted orders at each other.

A voice rose from the depth of the ravine, intoning the evening prayer. I saw the distant, earth-coloured figures of the Moors making their salaams to the sound of the savage, wailing psalmody, their rifles at their sides. At the foot of the shadowy mountains the mist began to rise, enveloping the praying figures. Only the chant rose above the swirl of the fog, as though the fog itself were singing. Outside the parapet, on the stony clearing, lay a dead Moor who had fallen face downwards, black arms flung wide, hands clenched, black desiccated legs apart. The big tuft of hair on his shaven head fluttered in the blue night wind.

8. Disaster

It is three o'clock in the afternoon, and we are still waiting for the order to advance and to start with the fortification work.

At dawn the Spanish columns poured into the valley of Beni-Aros like armies of migrant ants; we, the Ben-Karrick column, from the north, the Larache column from the west. The two goups are now converging towards the centre where we can see the huts of the Zoco el Jemis of Beni-Aros, one of the most important markets of the whole region. The French frontier positions close the valley to the south, the hills of the Jebel Alam and a supporting column gathering in Xauen close it to the east. The forces of the Raisuni are shut in from all four sides, and their only way out is to cross the French frontier, or else to flee to the mountains of the Jebel Alam.

The Moors defend themselves furiously behind every stone and every shrub. The attacks of our advance troops, the *Regulares* and the *Tercio*, batter against an impalpable enemy who is everywhere. Now the rebel cavalry is challenging ours. We see the charge of the Spanish cavalry against the Moorish horsemen who gallop away across the green lawn of the *zoco*, leading their pursuers on to where riflemen are lying in ambush between the stones.

We see our cavalry close its broken ranks and withdraw. Somebody must have given the order to shell the enemy guerrillas, for the shells are falling just where our riders are. Heliographs throw sun-sparks in every direction. In front of us, at six miles' distance, the French are sure to be following the spectacle at our feet, just as we do.

The day is so beautiful, the light so violent in a cloudless sky, the land so rich with trees and grass, with rocks and harvested fields, yellow squares in the green, and the men in the battle are so very small, that you lose every thought of the military operation and seem to be looking at a great play performed in a gigantic setting. The crackling of the machine guns and the detonations of the guns, the single aircraft which has dropped three bombs on what from here looks like a white house, wrapping it in smoke, the tiny figures which run about and sometimes fall, all of it is false and artificial against the background of these fields and under this sun.

It is a long time since we have eaten our cold meal. For hours we have been waiting in the shelter of the hill for our turn. The men are nodding with sleep, many have thrown themselves on the ground and are now dozing, bored with the spectacle of a fight which is still undefined and which consists of the same scenes played over and over again for hours.

At long last a captain of the General Staff arrives at a gallop. And we begin our march, suddenly in a great hurry, climbing up and down slopes. Someimes the mules stumble and their drivers swear, but more to keep themselves awake by the sound of their own voices than to curse the girth which has worked itself loose or the pack-saddle which is knocking against the mule's legs.

It takes us an hour to reach our destination, a hill jutting out over the valley, on which we have to set up a blockhouse. The *Tercio* is still fighting on the very hill top, but this makes no difference. We must clear out before nightfall, and the blockhouse must be set up at any price.

On the sheltered side of the hill, our men hastily dig earth and fill sandbags. The wooden parts of the blockhouse frame are laid out on the ground so that the jig-saw puzzle can be fitted together. The rolls of barbed wire are untied and their ends straggle, sharp-clawed whips.

The first thing to do is to build a parapet facing the enemy. Otherwise we cannot work at all. The men crawl up the hill, pushing the sandbags in front of their heads; but once they reach the top they lose their cover. They put the bags into line and crawl back, swifter than any reptile, while the bullets whistle overhead and hit the earth or the bags with a dull thud. The enemy is concentrating his fire on the crest of the hill, and the scattered legionaries, who bump against our legs and our sandbags, curse us in protest. But when the parapet is finished, the legionaries use it as their cover. The thuds on the earth wall sound like the fat rain drops of a thunderstorm falling on the stone flags of a cloister; but the bullets over our heads hum like bees in mad flight. The wooden frame is rising skeleton-like and the sun draws out the scent of freshly sawed pine wood.

There is a lull. The Moors know what is to come, and they wait for it. We know, too. We know that they are taking aim most carefully, waiting until we emerge up there with the zinc sheets of the roof, clearly outlined against the hill, the wooden frame and the shining metal.

These sheets are now lying at our feet like a monstrous book with corrugated pages. We are afraid of opening it, for fear that we might find our fate written on one of its pages, in undulating writing, like a snake stretched across the folds.

History tells a thousand times of heroism in the heat of battle. A warrior or a soldier cuts, hacks, thrusts, smashes skulls with his battle club or rifle butt, and enters the pages of history. There is nothing of this kind here.

We do not fight, we do not even see the enemy. We take a metal sheet, half a metre by two metres in size; we climb a ladder, laboriously; we place the sheet at an angle of forty-five degrees while the sun shines in our eyes; we drive nails one by one into its four edges, taking care not to crush a finger with our hammers. Meanwhile, ten or twenty or a hundred eyes behind rifle sights take aim at the little doll posturing before the sheet mirror. Bullets tear sharp-edged holes into the zinc and sometimes into the flesh. The hole where a bullet entered a man's back is small and neat. The hole on the other side is wide, with bleeding rims lacerated by the metal, plastered with shreds of flesh and cloth.

The blockhouse stands, but we must still set up the barbed wire entanglement. In groups of five our men have to jump over the parapet. One holds the wooden stakes while another hammers them rapidly into the ground. A third unwinds the barbed wire, which bites into his hands, from a reel guided by a fourth. The fifth fastens the wire to the stakes with steel staples. They work under fire.

By seven o'clock we had finished our work. Our casualties were three dead and nine wounded. One more blockhouse rose over the valley of Beni-Aros. We received the order to withdraw; night was beginning to fall, and we had thirteen miles to go back to our base. Two hours later the Company of Engineers was still marching through the darkened fields. The battle noises behind us had long ceased.

Of what did we think? In a war men are saved by the fact they cannot think. In the struggle man reverts to his origins and becomes an animal in a herd, his only instinct that of self-preservation. Muscles which had not been used for centuries come alive. Ears stiffen at the whistle of a bullet close by; the little hairs on the skin bristle in a critical moment. You jump sideways like a monkey or you throw yourself down behind the only wrinkle in the ground, just in time to avoid a projectile you have neither seen nor heard. But think? You do not think.

During those withdrawals in which one man marches behind the other like a sleep-walker your nerves grow calm at last. Nothing is then left but the rhythm of heavy feet – and how heavy they are! – of hands hanging down and swinging like automatons in line with your legs, and of a beating heart that you hear inside yourself, marching, sleep-walking, in step with the heart of the man in front of you, which you cannot hear because your own heart makes too much noise. Drink and sleep. Drink and sleep. Your brain is filled with a longing for a drink and a longing for sleep. In the darkness, thirst and sleep ride on the neck of a hundred soldiers on the march, a hundred empty brains.

By midnight it was obvious that we had lost our way. We found ourselves at the foot of hills which were immense shadows under a starry sky. Where were we? We called a halt, and the Captain consulted the sergeants. We had not a single lamp and not a single compass. Before us, the stone wall of the mountains; behind us, the shadowy fields with dogs or hyenas howling in the distance. We decided to climb the mountain. We might see something from the top, a light, a point which could guide us. And we began the ascent, stumbling in the darkness, bent like pilgrims but muttering blasphemies.

From the top we saw one light, two lights, and very far away a tiny white speck of light blinking rhythmically. The mountain dipped down in a precipitous slope before us. To go down there might mean crashing on the rocks. It was decided to camp on the spot and to wait for the day which would come in two hours. We improvised a parapet, using the material carried by the mules and the mules themselves. In its shelter we lit fires and set out sentries, and within its narrow circle we all slept, men and beasts, wedged against each other, frightened like children.

At dawn we saw before us the sea. The sun rode on ripples of glittering, silvery gold on a ground of green waves tipped with white crescents of foam. Down there to our left was Rio Martin.

We never knew how many miles we had marched that night. Our feet were swollen, all our limbs numb. We had to rest until noon before we were able to start on the slow descent to Rio Martin.

It was there, while the Captain was waiting for his call to Headquarters to come through, that I had the first conscious thought – it had stirred in my brain ever since the night before: not a compass, not a light, not a map! The units of the Spanish Army in Morocco went into action without any means of finding their bearings. Men were sent out, and it was left to their instinct where to advance and, above all, how to return to their bases; unit after unit was lost in the night. Suddenly I understood those tragic Moroccan withdrawals in which, after a victorious operation, hundreds of men perished in ambushes.

Two days later we received orders to march to Xauen, fifty miles to the east. We were to join the column which covered the exit from the valley of Beni-Aros and the slopes of the Jebel-Alam.

Xauen is an infinitely old city in a gorge hemmed in by mountains. You only see it when you enter the gorge itself. The town comes as a surprise. It is not an Arab city, but a town of the Spanish Sierras with the pointed, red-slated roofs on its whitewashed houses, roofs from which the snow slides off in the winter. The Moors call Xauen the 'Sacred' and the 'Mysterious.' When you see the city nestling behind its granite walls, you understand why it was unconquerable for centuries. A small number of men distributed on the surrounding peaks, invisible marksmen hurtling stones, could close the path to any invader.

Xauen's narrow, steep, and twisted streets were a maze. Early during our occupation, it happened not infrequently that a Spanish soldier was pierced by a poignard without ever knowing from where it had struck. The Hebrew quarter was a fortress shut in by iron gates which opened for the first time in centuries when the Spaniards occupied the town. Within its precincts – thick walls, tiny doorways, mere holes for windows – they still spoke Spanish, an archaic Spanish of the sixteenth century. And a few of the Jews still wrote that dusty Castilian in antiquated letters, all curves and arabesques, which made a sheet of paper look like a parchment.

I loved Xauen. Not the Xauen of the military, with its Plaza de España and its General Encampment, with its canteens and brothels, its eternal drunkeness, its pretentious officers and obsequious, false Moors. I loved the other Xauen, Xauen the Mysterious: its tranquil streets, in which echoed the hoofs of the little donkeys; its muezzin intoning his prayers high from the minaret; its white-veiled women with nothing but the sparkle of their eyes alive in their phantom robes; its Moors from the mountains, in rags and tatters or resplendent in milk-white wool, but always haughty. Its silent Jews gliding along the walls, so close that they seemed disembodied shadows, forever running in short, rapid, timorous steps.

On moonlit nights Xauen always evoked Toledo for me with its solitary, crooked little streets. And Toledo on moonlit nights always evoked for me Xauen. They have the same background of sound, the river running swiftly and tumultuously, the wind entangled in the trees and in the crags of the mountains and growling in the depths of the gullies.

Xauen was an industrial town. They washed their wool in the torrents, bleached it in the sun and tinted it with ingenuous reds, blues, and yellows, made from the juice of trees and from pounded stone, following prescriptions handed down from father to son. They tooled their leather with the lost art of Cordova, City of the Caliphs. They ground their grain between pear-shaped stones which the water had made to go round for five hundred years; they were smooth, covered with minute pores, and they turned slowly like the breasts of a woman turning in her sleep. They hammered their iron and tempered it over charcoal made from old oak; they dipped it hissing into the water of their river, and it emerged blue as steel or yellow as sun-toasted straw. The Jews embossed silver with rapid little hammer blows, on pitch plaques which made a soft bed for the figures their tools raised on the metal. They had lime-kilns and potters' wheels for primitive pottery with simple lines and graceful proportions. And they had the Legend of the Burning Stones.

A holy man from one of the great tribes which live in the southern desert went with his disciples on a pilgrimage to the Prophet's Tomb. They marched day and night, for months and months, until they came to the big mountains which shut in Xauen. In winter the nights are cold and snow sleeps on the summits; the men from the desert thought they would have to die in the snow. The holy man withdrew in prayer. They could not light a fire where there were only stones, and the hour had come to die. Then Allah bade him take the black stones which hurt his knees when he prayed, and light a fire. This fire burned with a brighter flame than any wood could kindle. And the pilgrim was saved. At daybreak they wished to extinguish the fire and poured on to it water from a source which gushed forth among the stones. And the fire was so powerful that the water burned in flames higher than a man.

In a hidden corner of the mountains, the legend said, the stones and the water are still burning in honour of Allah. And many eyes look out at night to see the flame which burns, nobody knows where.

The Arabs scanned the night for the miraculous flame. Prospectors from all parts of the world have searched, and are still patiently searching those mountains with their hammers, to find the coal and the petroleum which doubtless gave rise to the legend.

But nobody will find those visions in Xauen now. They were lost many years ago. The Spanish invasion drove out the magic of the old city. Nowadays its wools are dyed with the aniline dyes of the I.G. Farbenindustrie and mixed with cotton. The few looms left are not worked with hands and feet but with engines. The silversmiths closed down their workshops years ago, and stamped plate from Marrakesh and from Pforzheim is shamelessly exhibited in Europeanized shops. Leather is no longer tanned with bark and laboriously fined down by handicraft, its pattern is no longer tooled with hammers and heated irons; it is tanned by a chemical process, cut by machines, stamped in relief with steel plates produced in Paris or God knows where. The Fondak, the old Arab inn for travellers, no longer exists, but there are hotels with French cooking. Xauen is neither mysterious nor sacred any more. There are taverns and brothels. In 1931 it was a show place for tourist traffic, with posters on the walls and a wide road which rich Americans and Englishmen could travel to make the trade in printed silks from Lyons prosper.

But I knew Xauen when it was not yet cheapened and when it meant adventure to walk through its streets. A Moor would look at your silver stripes and salute you: '*Salaam aleicum*'. A Jew would stutter the old Romance greeting: '*Dios os guarde*' – God guard you. A mountaineer would give you a hate-filled glance and clutch the horn handle of the dagger in his belt; he would spit ostentatiously in the middle of the street. The eyes of Moorish women would look at you from the depth of their veils, and you would never be able to guess the age and the thoughts of their owner. The Hebrew girls would lower their eyes and blush. Your feet would slip on the smoothe round pebbles on which horses and donkeys would walk at ease.

When we were there, in the midst of that medley of races and hates, old and new, of rival religious communities enclosed within four city walls – our field in the General Encampment, the muezzin chanting the wonders of Allah and the Jews silently seeking their synagogue, their hands crossed and hidden in their kaftan sleeves – it was as though I saw medieval Spain come alive. If I was not astonished to see an Arab warrior astride his horse, with a silken horse-cloth and silver stirrups, then neither would I have been astonished to see a warrior encased in iron, the double cross of the Crusaders in enamel on his shield.

We were resting in the General Encampment, reorganizing for the coming operations. As usual, conjectures and comments were carried from tent to tent, from canteen to canteen. Manzanares came to me with an air of mystery:

'There's something big on.'

'What is it?'

'I don't know. But all the senior officers are running about from the tent of the General to the tent of all the corps commanders, and all the time they're in conference with Ceuta and Tetuan. One of Colonel Sergano's orderlies says the Moors have taken Ceuta and cut us off, and that they'll hack us all to pieces.'

At nightfall that day – it was the 11th or 12th of July 1921 – the bugles sounded the officers' call and the commanders of all the units gathered before the tent of the C.-in-C. At daybreak we all began the march towards Tetuan, with the exception of a small garrison which was left behind in Xauen.

The miles piled up. The march and the July sun choked our need for comment. But at noon the halt which we so eagerly expected was not called. We went on without rest in a forced march. Some of the men were unable to go on and began to lag. When the first of our Company fell out the Captain gave me the dry order: 'If he cannot go on, let him stay and look after himself.'

At ten o'clock at night we entered Tetuan. We slept on the stone floor of the barracks without time to take off our leather straps. At dawn we left for Ceuta. In Ceuta we went on board a steamer; in Ceuta we learned the news.

The Moors had killed the whole garrison of Melilla and were standing at the gates of the city.

History books call it the Disaster of Melilla, or the Spanish Defeat in Morocco in 1921; they give what is called the historical facts. I do not know them except from those books. What I know is part of the unwritten history, which created a tradition in the masses of the people, more powerful than the official tradition. The newspapers I read later spoke of a relief column which had embarked in the port of Ceuta, filled with patriotic fervour to liberate Melilla.

All I know is that a few thousand exhausted men embarked in Ceuta for an unknown destination, worn to the limit of their endurance after a sixty-mile march through Morocco in the glare of the sun, badly clad, badly equipped, badly fed. They left port and at once began to be seasick and to sully the decks of the ship. They began to swear and to take whatever liberties they could: drinking, gambling, getting drunk and coming to blows over gambling losses, singing and brawling, mocking those who were vomiting, laughing at the pot-bellied colonel with the greenish face and the uniform spattered with half-digested food. The ship was hell.

And Melilla was a besieged town.

Many years afterwards I learned what life means in a besieged town, under the constant threat of entry of an enemy who has promised himself loot, lives, and fresh women. People in the streets walk rapidly, because nobody goes out except for an urgent reason. All public services are stricken; the telephone does not function, the water taps are leaking, there is no coal, the light suddenly fails, shoes are worn through but the shoe shops are shut, men who had not been ill for ten years fall sick, and the doctor must be fetched while the guns are firing; the streets are dark and there is danger at every corner.

Into besieged Melilla a big steamer poured those thousands of sick, drunken, over-tired men who were to be its liberators. We set up camp, I don't know where. We heard guns, machine guns, and rifles firing somewhere outside the town. We invaded the cafés and taverns, we got drunk and rioted in the brothels. We challenged the frightened inhabitants: 'Now you'll see! Now we're here and that's that. Tomorrow not a Moor will be left alive.' The Moors had disappeared from the streets of Melilla; after the ship had anchored alongside the jetty, a legionary had cut off the ears of one of them and the authorities had ordered all Moors to stay indoors. On the following morning we marched to the outskirts of the town; we were to break through the encirclement and to begin the re-conquest of the zone.

During the first few days we Engineers built new positions but returned each time to the camp within the town. The newspaper headlines screamed of horrors which we had not yet seen. Then we went farther afield, away from the city, and we saw horror.

A big house pitted by bullets. The white chalk scooped away from its walls so that the bricks showed like flecks of dry blood. In the courtyard a dead horse, its belly slit open as though gored by a mad bull, the blue entrails clustered with flies, and one of its legs cut away. In the windows of the first floor one, two, three, five dead men, a dead man in every window, some with a neat hole in their foreheads, crumpled up like dolls with the sawdust stuffing gone, some lying in the pool of their own blood. Empty cartridge shells rolling on the floor, sounding like broken rattles, making us stumble comically in face of the dead. In the ground-floor rooms bloody tracks, traces of men dragged away by the shoulder with blood streaming down their boots and tracing two wavering lines as of red chalk on the stone flags.

And then the back room.

A little boy has got hold of a jug of chocolate sauce in his mother's absence. He has painted his face and hands, his legs and his clothes, the table and the chair. He has climbed down from the chair and poured a big blob of chocolate on the floor. He has passed his fingers across the walls and left the print of his hand in every corner, on every piece of furniture, in lines, hooks and hieroglyphs. Jumping up and down in his joy at seeing dark stripes on all the clean things, he has put his foot in the jug and splashed the chocolate on the walls, right up high. It was so beautiful that he has plunged both hands into the jug and spattered big drops and little drops everywhere, even on the ceiling. Right in the middle a big blob has stuck half-dry.

In the back room were five dead men. They were smeared with their own blood, face, hands, uniforms, hair, and boots. The blood had made pools on the floor, stripes on the walls, blobs on the ceiling, sprawling splashes in all the corners. On every clean, white place it had painted hands with five or two or one finger, fingerless palms and shapeless thumbs. A table and a few chairs were turned into scattered kindling wood. Countless flies, droning incessantly, were sucking blood from the thumb printed on the wall and from the lips of the corpse in the left-hand corner.

But I cannot describe the smell. We went into it as we might have gone into the water of a river. We went down in it. There was no bottom, no surface, and no escape. It saturated clothes and skin, it filtered through the nose into throat and lungs, and made us sneeze, cough, and vomit. The smell dissolved our human substance. It tainted it instantaneously and turned it into a viscous mass. To rub one's hand was to rub two hands which did not belong to one, which seemed to be those of a rotting corpse, sticky and impregnated with the smell.

We heaped the dead in the courtyard on top of the horse, poured petrol over them and set fire to the pyre. It stank of roasted flesh, and we vomited. That day we began to vomit and we went on vomiting for days on end.

For the fighting itself was the least of it. The marches through the sandy waste land of Melilla, the outpost of the desert, did not really matter, nor the thirst and the dirty, salty, scanty water, nor the shots and our own dead, warm and flexible, whom we could put on a stretcher and cover with a blanket; nor the wounded who groaned monotonously or screamed shrilly. All that was not important, it lost its force and proportion. But the other dead: those dead we were finding when they had lain for days under the African sun which turned fresh meat putrid within two hours; those mummified dead whose bodies had burst; those mutilated bodies, without eyes and tongues, their genitals defiled, violated with the stakes from the barbed wire, their hands tied up with their bowels, beheaded, armless, legless, sawed in two – oh those dead!

We went on burning the dead in piles sprayed with petrol. We fought on hill tops and in ravines, went hither and thither, slept on the ground, were devoured by lice and tortured by thirst. We constructed new blockhouses, filled thousands of sandbags and lined them up. We did not sleep; we died each day, only to awake the following morning, and in the interval we lived through horrible nightmares. And always we felt the smell. We smelled each other. We smelled of death, of rotting corpses.

I cannot tell the story of Melilla in July 1921. I was there, but I do not know where: somewhere in the midst of shots, shells, and machine-gun rattle, sweating, shouting, running, sleeping on stone and on sand, but above all ceaselessly vomiting, smelling of corpses, finding at every step another dead body, more horrible than any I had known a moment before.

One day at dawn we came back to the city. It was filled with soldiers and with people who were no longer besieged. They lived and laughed. They stopped to speak to each other in the streets and sat down in the shade to take their vermouth. The bootblacks worked their way through the crowds in the cafés. A silvery aeroplane traced circles overhead. A band was playing in the park. That afternoon we embarked.

We went back to Tetuan. After passing through two days, maddened by images and suffering torture from my disordered stomach, I fell in a dead faint on the table of the sergeant on guard in the barracks of Alcazaba.

9. The Aftermath

Somebody pulled me by the arm. I had been asleep. It must have got very late. In front of me I saw a sun-filled window.

'Yes, yes, coming.' But I could not speak. The tongue inside my mouth was a shapeless chunk of flesh. My jaws ached.

'The doctor,' said somebody beside me.

'The doctor?' I answered, but again without speaking. My mouth refused to speak.

At the foot of the bed were an army doctor and a soldier, two blurred figures with the white cross on their collars.

'How do you feel, my boy?' the doctor asked.

'I? What? Well.' But without speaking.

The soldier said something: 'It looks as if he understood. I believe we've pulled him through, sir.'

'All right. Go on with the treatment.'

The two disappeared from the foot of the bed. Slowly I began to take in the details of my surroundings. I was in a bed; opposite there was a row of beds; on my right and on my left there were rows of beds. I felt a nauseous smell rising from my sheets, that is to say, from me. But it was different from the smell of the room. The room? It was a huge wooden hut with a pointed roof on cross beams, a row of windows on each side, and the sun streaming through those in front of me. There was a sticky smell of fever and a ceaseless drone overlaid with panting breath and dull groans. Flies and dying men.

By the side of the bed stood a glazed white jar and a round box of pills. There was milk in the jar and dozens of flies paddled in it. I felt a torturing thirst, with that piece of flesh which was my own tongue between my teeth. I turned away from the fly-pool and saw a livid, emaciated face, laboriously breathing as though at any moment the breath might stop.

I knew where I was: in the hospital in Tetuan, in the ward for infectious diseases. They used to call it the mortuary, for patients would leave it through a back door on a trolley with rubber tyres, wrapped in a sheet. And they would never come back.

Only the sick were in the room, but no nurses or medical orderlies. Nobody. My clothes hung over the foot of my bed. The silver stripes on one of the empty sleeves shone. I thought that another 'I' was waiting there at the foot of the bed. There was tobacco in my coat! An irresistible longing to smoke took hold of me. I crawled over the bed, snatched my uniform from the iron bar and took out my cigarettes and matches. An hour passed before my heart calmed down and the sweat ceased pouring from me. Only then did I light a cigarette. It tasted of nothing and it hurt to suck it; my lips must have been terribly swollen.

A medical orderly came in and went from bed to bed. He put a thermometer into one man's mouth, left it there, took it out, rubbed it with a rag and put it into the next man's mouth. He chalked something up over the head of each bed. Another orderly followed him with one empty and one full pail. He emptied the glazed jars on each night table into one pail and filled them from the other.

The man with the thermometer came to me.

'Are you better?'

'Yes,' I told him by nodding my head.

'Open your mouth.'

'No.' I pointed with the right hand to my left armpit.

'No, it has to go into the mouth.'

'No.'

He put the thermometer into my armpit and bent my arm to cover it. 'Stay quiet now. Do you want milk?'

'No. Water.' But I could not speak and made an effort to show him by gestures what I wanted. He understood in the end.

'Water?'

'Yes.'

'No, milk; only milk. Water is prohibited.' He wanted to give me the jar which was still dripping from having been dipped into the pail.

'No.'

He left the milk on the night table, and flies dived humming down into it. The medical orderly gave me one of the pills from the box. It stuck to my palate until the wafer dissolved and my mouth was filled with a bitter taste. Quinine. Was I down with malaria, then?

When the two men had left I turned round, very painfully, to read the slip at the upper end of my bed. It said 'Typh. Ex.' below my name and a date and above a fever curve traced over four squares. Had I been here four days? And – 'Typh. Ex.'? Exanthematic Typhus.

But I had been inoculated against typhus!

The mind of the very ill is like the mind of a child. It clutches at hope with a faith, or sinks into a despair, which hardly ever has any foundation. I was inoculated against typhus, therefore I would not die of typhus. I could not die. All the medical treatises in the world affirmed it: I would not die. Of course, if I had not been inoculated. . . . An infinite calm pervaded me. I would be ill for a week, or two, or three, but I would not die.

'Give me a cigarette,' said a very weak voice, 'and light it for me.' A skeleton-like hand appeared from under the sheet.

I lit the cigarette and gave it to him. 'What is the matter with you?' I was astonished to hear a hoarse voice, coming out of me, speaking with a swollen tongue.

'Consumption.'

'Then don't smoke. Throw it away.'

'What does it matter? I'll die today.' He said it so flatly that he convinced me he was going to die. At dusk he moved a hand and said something.

'Eh?' I tried to ask him.

'A-d-i-o-s,' he pronounced distinctly and very slowly.

Shortly afterwards the two medical orderlies returned, the one with the thermometer, the other with the pails. They pulled the sheet on my neighbour's bed up to the iron head rest, covering him completely. When they had finished their tasks, they came back pushing one of those high hospital trolleys. One man took him by the feet, the other by the shoulders, without turning back the sheet, but gathering the drooping folds under him, and put him on the trolley. They wheeled him out through the back door.

That night I could not sleep. Drowsy flies kept falling on the whiteness of the sheets and on my face and hands. The heat was suffocating. Electric lamps on the beams shone with a reddish light through their film of dust. Someone at the end of the room began to scream, or rather to howl. He threw himself out of his bed and crawled down between the two rows of beds. But just before he reached me he gripped the iron posts at the foot of a bed, drew himself up, vomited, and crumpled up. Not a single orderly, not a single bell. He stayed there the whole night long on the beaten earth of the floor. In the morning they wrapped him in a sheet and took him away on the trolley.

Then came the doctor. He passed quickly from one bed to the other. 'How are you, my boy?' he asked me.

'Better, sir.'

'By Jove, it's true.' He turned to the next bed.

'And this one?'

'He died yesterday.'

'All right. Well, go on giving the sergeant quinine. Buck up, my boy, that's nothing.'

That day two died. The next night five died. One of them died of smallpox in the first hours of the night. By daybreak he was in full decomposition. Nausea, fear and horror were choking me. In the morning I asked the doctor:

'*Mi capitán*, could I be evacuated to Ceuta?'

'Why, aren't you all right here?'

'Yes, sir. But I've got my family in Ceuta.'

'That's a different matter. All right. This afternoon I'll give you an injection and we'll send you there. I quite understand.'

They gave me an injection in the arm, wrapped me in blankets, and took me on a stretcher to an ambulance car. There were six of us, three on each side. They must have given me morphine. I went under. When the car began to move, it sickened me and I lost consciousness altogether.

I woke up in another bed beside a wide-open window. There were trees nearby, with many noisy birds. I was on the top of a hill and there, in the distance, was the sea. The small hut held six beds, five of them empty. There were three more windows and the sun flooded the hut. 'Morphine is a good thing,' I thought. But it was not the effect of morphine.

I was in Ceuta, in the Docker Hospital for infectious diseases, two miles from the city on a hill overlooking the Straits of Gibraltar. An old man in civilian clothes was sitting near the door reading a newspaper. He turned his head, glanced at me and came limping up:

'Now, my boy, are you better? Do you want a drop of milk?'

He went into a little room beside the door and came back with a glass of cold milk. I drank it greedily.

'All right, stay quiet. The Major will come soon.'

I have forgotten the Major's name, as we are apt to forget those who have helped us, while we remember enemies. He was a tall, slim man with grey hair, a young and sensitive face, and the hands of a conjuror; he was a most able surgeon and a great psychologist.

He sat down at the upper end of my bed, took out his watch and felt my pulse. He auscultated my chest. He turned down the sheet and examined my abdomen with his clever fingers. I felt as though he were singling out each of my entrails and testing it. Then he covered me up and said:

'Where are you from, my boy?'

'From Madrid, sir.'

'Right. Do you smoke?'

'Yes, sir.'

He took out his cigarette case, gave me one, and lit another for himself.

'You like girls, don't you?'

'Rather.'

'All right. I suppose you've been gadding about like everybody else. Have you had any venereal diseases?'

'No, sir.'

'That's good. And what did you have as a child, tell me.'

Within a quarter of an hour he had drawn out a general confession of my sins and of my whole life. In the end he said:

'Do you know what you've got?'

'Typhus, I think. But I've been inoculated.'

'Yes, typhus. And you're very weak. But never mind, we'll pull you through.'

At noon the old man put a bucket of water at the foot of my bed. The Major came back, took my pulse, and told the old man: 'Let's get on with it.'

He soaked a sheet in the water and between the two of them they wrapped me in the wet sheet and several blankets. The chill moisture on my feverish skin hurt; it dried within a few minutes. They took off the steaming wrappings and put me into another cold, wet sheet, gave me a glass of milk and a pill. I fell asleep. In this way a few days passed. The Major came each time to help the old man. My hands on the sheet grew transparent. I had lost all notion of time.

One day the old man wrapped me in a blanket, lifted me and carried me to a chair by the window. There he left me for an hour to look at the sea and the trees and to listen to the birds. I had forgotten how to walk. The old man taught me each day for a short while. Then I went out and sat down under a tree on the hill top breathing deeply. But I was so weak that the fifty steps from the hut to the tree cost me a river of sweat. I weighed thirty-seven and a half kilogrammes, about eighty-three pounds.

Then one day they put me into an ambulance and took me to the Central Hospital of Ceuta. There was a panel of five doctors; they read out my name and the Major gave the necessary explanations; the five whispered among themselves and one of them said:

'Two months.'

A sergeant came to ask: 'Where do you want to go? You have got two months' leave.'

One morning I went to the barracks, packed my suitcase, and embarked for Spain. Before I went Major Tabasco, the chief of the regimental office, told me:

'When you come back I shall have a surprise for you.'

One day when I was seventeen, I took a bad fall while doing gymnastics, and lost consciousness. They carried me to the first-aid station and from there home. I came to in my bed, wrapped in bandages and feeling a sharp pain. It had been a nasty shock which might have cost me my life, but a week later I was already able to leave the house. The gravest scar the accident left me was the shock I had received when I woke up in bed without having consciously gone there, surrounded by the frightened faces of my people – a shock which was repeated when all persons and things looked so utterly different the first time I went out into the streets again.

I had a similar feeling when I arrived in Madrid. I had carried a very clear and well-defined picture of Madrid and of my people in my mind. But when I was welcomed at the station by my mother, sister, and brother, and when beyond the station gates I met Madrid, my Madrid, everything was changed. There was a vacuum of two years between my family and myself, between Madrid and myself. We had broken the threads of daily contact. If we wanted to join our lives together once more, we would have to tie the broken ends into a knot. But a knot is not a continuity, it is the joining of two separate bits with a break between them.

'How are you, son, how are you?'

'Well, Mother. Quite well.'

'Very thin . . . just bones.'

'Yes, I know. But never mind. I'm alive. Others have stayed there.'

'Yes, yes, I know. Many have stayed there.'

'And how are you, Mother?'

'Well.'

'And all the others?'

'We manage. Don't worry. We'll fatten you up here in a couple of weeks.'

We linked arms and left the station, Rafael carrying my luggage.

'Have you brought tobacco?' he asked.

'Yes.'

'And for me, what have you brought for me?' asked my sister.

'A piece of silk. But I've brought nothing for Mother.'

'You've come back.'

'Ah, but I have brought you something, old lady, old granny – I have brought you something!'

She laughed that little, restrained laugh of hers.

The Plaza de Atocha was filled with early morning noises. People were storming the trams. The taxis waiting at the station and the lorries going to market fought each other for their right of way, and the carts laden with vegetables and fruit tried to filter through, their drivers swearing at the tops of their voices. The street was swept by the sound of tramway bells, motor horns and shouts. For two years I had not heard city noise; I felt weak, weaker than I had been at any time since I left hospital.

'Let's take a cup of coffee or something. I slept badly on the train.'

We took coffee, and I drank a small brandy to revive me; but in the end we took a taxi. As soon as we arrived home I went to bed, pausing only to take out the tobacco for Rafael, the silk for Concha and the scarf for my mother. They had prepared my bed for me, my old gilt bed with fine white sheets, and the room smelled of fresh paint.

In the afternoon I reported to the military authorities to get my papers in order, then went home and dressed in mufti. My uniform was left hanging on the clothes-peg of my bedroom, and Rafael and I went out for a walk. When we were already in the doorway my mother pleaded:

'Do go and see So-and-so and So-and-so. They've kept on asking about you.'

'Mother, I won't go and see anybody.'

'Do as you like, my boy.'

But Madrid was still too much for me. My ears could not bear the Puerta de Sol. We took refuge in the silent little streets round the Calle de Segovia, walked round a bit and returned home. We had not spoken much; we did not know how to begin. We commented on street incidents and fell back into silence. At home, mother laid the table for supper. She had prepared steaks and fried potatoes and put them on the table proudly and gaily.

None of us had spoken a word about Morocco yet. I would have wished to spare my mother the pain, I would have liked to be able to eat that meat with an appetite and a happy face. But since those dead of Melilla I could not touch meat. The sight and the smell of it invariably made me see and smell corpses, rotting or burning on a petrol-soaked pyre, and made me vomit. It produced an immediate mental association and reaction against which I was powerless.

I wanted to master myself, and began cutting the meat on my plate. Rosy juice trickled out. I was sick.

The others were alarmed, and I had to explain.

'It's nothing. I'm not ill. It's only nausea.'

In order to escape from myself, I began to speak. I told them what I had seen, in all it's details. I told them of the dead of Melilla, of the dying in the hospital of Tetuan, of hunger and lice, of mouldy beans boiled with red pepper, of the miserable life of Spain's soldiers and

of the shamelessness and corruption of their commanders. And I
began to cry like a small boy, unhappier than ever because of the
pain I was causing, because of the pain I had seen.

'How you've deceived me!' said my mother.

'I?'

'Yes, you with your letters. I knew things were not going well.
They never go well for soldiers. But lately I'd been content. You
were a sergeant. And I believed many things, very many, you told
me in your letters.'

'But, Mother, they were all true.'

'Yes, to be sure, they were true. But you always wrote about
things and never about yourself. Now I see what it meant. A curse
on the war and whoever invented it!'

'But, Mother, we can't do anything about it.'

'I don't know – I don't know.'

On the following morning I felt unable to get out of bed. My mother
sent for the doctor, a kindly old man who examined me from head to
foot. There was nothing the matter with me, I was just extremely
weak and suffering from the sudden change of climate and altitude. I
should gradually accustom myself to the city, go to a park and sit
there in the open, simply breathing. As soon as I felt stronger I
should begin to walk about.

In the meantime I was left alone. My brother went to work. My
sister was in the little fruit shop the family had set up in the Calle
Ancha. My mother pottered about in the flat. I got up and searched
for something to read.

In an odd corner I found a heap of old newspapers, over a hundred
of them, an odd assortment of dates and types; there were morning
and evening papers, illustrated weeklies and literary reviews. The
main theme of their headlines was Morocco. I read them all.

What a soldier sees of a war can be compared with what an actor
sees of a film in which he has a part. The director tells him to stand
in a certain spot, make certain gestures, and say certain words. He
puts him in a field and makes him repeat a sequence of phrases and a
sequence of gestures; ten times he makes him open the door of a
drawing room which has only three walls, and kiss the hand of a
lady. When the actor goes to see the finished film, he hardly recog-

nizes himself, and is forced to reconstruct scenes which he had repeated a number of times. Thus the actor has two sets of impressions. The first is part of his own life and consists of a series of postures, make-ups, lighting effects, rehearsals, decorations and instructions from the stage manager. The other set of impressions comes when he sees the finished picture in which he is no longer himself but quite a different personality, part of a plot, a person with an artificial life which depends on the way in which scenes acted by him are linked up with the scenes of the other actors.

I found myself passing through a similar experience when I read that heap of out-of-date newspapers.

'The vanguard advanced amid a hail of bullets, the soldiers singing patriotic songs. "Give it to them, boys," shouted the Colonel at their head. Ferocious Riff warriors were lurking behind every shrub and stone. The gallant Major X led his *Regulares* in a bayonet attack. A cavalry squadron pursued the fleeing Moors with drawn swords. At the same time the Larache column scattered into small groups on the left flank, over a front more than two kilometres long, and began an enveloping movement.' And so on and so forth.

I had seen the Spanish war correspondents in Morocco, attached to the Staff of a column, clad half in uniform, half in sports clothes, field glasses over their shoulders, observing the front at a distance of five kilometres, taking notes and asking the staff captains to explain things to them. Occasionally one of them would risk his life by joining advanced troops during an operation. In neither case did they see the war as a whole, but they were forced to tell about it as though they did; therefore they created for the benefit of their readers a war as artificial as the plot of a film, and described it as though they had been magically floating in the clouds, taking in the battlefield as a whole and with every minute detail at a single glance.

The war – my war – and the Disaster of Melilla – my disaster – bore no resemblance to the war and to the disaster which those Spanish newspapers unfolded before their public.

One photograph showed 'General X addressing the heroic forces of the Ceuta Relief Column before their embarkation for Melilla'.

There I was, somewhere among the 'heroes'. The report, which accompanied the photograph, stated that the General's address had been listened to with reverence and received with acclamation. As though we were in a state to acclaim anything after our march through Morocco! They had lined us up on parade to be inspected by the General and his Staff. A few soldiers at the back lay down and immediately fell asleep. A few fainted while they were standing at attention after that day of ceaseless marching. The only acclamations I remember were muttered curses. While the old man with the beard was walking up and down the rows we called him 'son of a bitch' and 'bastard'; our feet were swollen, our throats parched, and he forced us to stand at attention with every bone in our bodies aching.

'A fifteen-centimetre howitzer shelling the enemy'.

The photograph showed an enormous gun with smoke pouring from its mouth. Perhaps it was one of those ill-famed batteries sent over from the Canary Islands, which showered shrapnel on our own troops and made us scatter like rabbits.

The descriptions of the Disaster of Melilla were full of the horrible sights in the reconquered positions, sights which enabled the garrison's last hours to be reconstructed. Occasionally the 'sole survivor' was quoted on the tragedy. All accounts agreed on the matchless valour of the officers, which had sustained the morale of the men.

I had met survivors whose officers had torn off their insignia or simply changed uniforms with a soldier, because it gave them a better chance of being spared by the Moors, and had run away from their posts, pursued by the bullets of their own men. And I had known at least one surviving officer who had earned his laurels by wenching in Melilla town during the night of the Disaster, after which there was no one left at his post to testify against him. His superiors were faced with the alternative of decorating him for bravery or court-martialling him for desertion from a front-line post. They had decorated him. He might have been one of the men quoted in the press.

I vented my bitterness to Rafael. 'You don't know any more about Morocco here than about the moon,' I said.

'Don't you believe it,' he answered. 'You've been reading the front pages, but in reality things are far more serious. I believe they'll cost the King his crown. People are demanding an investigation into what happened and of course the whole Opposition has made use of the opportunity to air the Moroccan problem in the

Cortes. It has been said publicly that the King himself gave the order to General Silvestre[1] to advance, even against Berenguer's instructions. And they say that an inquiry will be held.'

'An inquiry? Do you mean a military inquiry directed against the army and the King? Who is supposed to conduct it? You're all crazy. The first Parliamentary Commission to go to Africa and investigate what those fine gentlemen have been and are doing there would be chucked out, or driven out by bullets.'

'I tell you things are getting serious. There is a very important factor in public opinion now, I mean the expeditionary corps. The people who paid up their "quotas" for others to go to Morocco instead of them must now go themselves. All those fathers who've paid cash to keep their sons out of Africa now find that the boys are being sent there all the same, and that they must pay for the equipment on top of everything, and they feel they've been swindled. Oh yes, if it were only the poor people who were affected you would be right. But now the others feel it where it hurts most. Things are moving.'

Slowly, I was absorbed into the atmosphere that reigned in Madrid. My ignorance of past events made things difficult for me. Very few Spanish newspapers, if any, had reached the Moroccan camps. In Ceuta a few Madrid dailies and the local paper, *El Defensor de Ceuta*, were on sale. But everywhere in Morocco, in Ceuta as well as in the outposts, only the most reactionary press had been admitted. A soldier who read *El Liberal* was at once marked as a 'revolutionary'. In the barracks, papers like *El Socialista* were strictly prohibited; to be found in possession of a copy meant immediate arrest and ceaseless persecution. Theoretically, everyone was free to buy whatever periodical he wanted. But in practice the owners of the few newspaper kiosks knew the tricks of the game;

[1] Silvestre was the commanding general of the zone of Melilla, one of the three military zones into which Spanish Morocco was divided. He launched a series of operations against the *kabilas* of the Riff, at a time when operations against the Moorish leader Raisuni were in full swing in the zones of Ceuta and Larache. Silvestre advanced in a straight line from Melilla to Annual, leaving nothing but a thin chain of strong points behind to cover his offensive. Abd-el-Krim roused the Moors in the rear, and Silvestre with his force, as well as the garrisons of all his outposts, were massacred.

when anybody asked for a Leftish paper he was told that it had just sold out or that it had not arrived that day – and he was offered *ABC* or *El Debate*. The civilian population kept up the boycott. The majority depended on the army for their living, directly or indirectly; as there was no industry, there were no skilled workers apart from those attached to the army, and the few fishermen and labourers were nearly all illiterate, and all subservient.

When I had first come to Africa I had tried to keep up my daily reading of the Madrid press. I had been told gently that if I wanted to stay in the Regimental Office (where I was corporal) and not to go to the front line, I would have to become a reader of *ABC* or *El Debate*. For a time I had read nothing but *El Defensor de Ceuta*; I had even sent in a few sentimental poems under a pen name. They were printed, paid for at a rate of five pesetas each and served me as a half-conscious vengeance. Later I had stopped reading newspapers altogether and confined myself to books of which I soon had a small library. But one day, when I was reading in the office, the senior major had happened to see me and asked me the title of the book. It was a cheap and bad edition of Bertha von Suttner's *Lay Down Arms!*

'*Caramba*, you certainly bring a nice kind of book into barracks!'

I had not read more than a few pages, and said ingenuously: 'They've sent me some books from home, including this one. As you can see, sir, I've only just started it, and can't say anything about it, but since the author is an Austrian aristocrat' – I had read the introduction – 'it won't be very revolutionary, I imagine.'

'All right—So they've sent you more books, have they? Let's have a look at them.' He said it, not severely, but paternally. He was a very kind and good man, was Don José Tabasco, but very much the Catholic army officer. He was convinced of the infallibility of all the laws and rulings of the Roman Catholic Church, and of their good effect when put into practice. Thus I lost a number of books by Victor Hugo, Anatole France, Miomandre, and Blasco Ibañez, and of course *Lay Down Arms!*

He had not confiscated the books because he was incapable of violating the letter of the law which entitled me to read all books published in Spain. But he patted me on the back: 'My boy, I'm going to speak to you as if I were your father. We're in barracks here. I know you for a good lad, and I've nothing against your reading these books. But I know how things happen in barracks. Your comrades will want to borrow the books, and you won't say no, of course. Now, once put these books into the hands of poor devils who can hardly read or write and they act as explosives. Look here, do as I tell you and burn them.'

The Major was my direct superior. I had years in barracks before me. The Major was pleased when I burned those books in the fire of the regimental kitchen. Yet I knew that the clandestine sale and purchase of pornographic books was viewed with more than tolerance by the officers in general, both in barracks and in front-line positions. Whenever one of the captains began a campaign to rid his company of filth, his fellow officers would say to him: 'Look here, you fool, you must leave the men something to amuse themselves with. After all, we all like to see a fine woman without her clothes on. You won't change things. You can't search their pockets every day, and anyhow its better they should read that sort of stuff than *El Socialista*.'

After these experiences in Ceuta I had clung to my reading of French books while we built the road at Hamara; and I had wearied of it. I had not seen any newspapers there. In Tetuan I did not even try to break through the laws of military life. And then came the campaigns in Beni-Aros, and Xauen, and Melilla, and the hospital: when I found myself in Madrid I had to begin all over again, to pick up threads, to understand what was going on.

The bar of the 'Portugese' still existed at the corner of the Calle de la Paz. The clerks from the banks and the insurance companies in the neighbourhood continued to meet there as they had done when I was serving my apprenticeship in the bank. At seven o'clock in the evening the bar was overcrowded, but I knew that my old colleague Plá would be in his customary place. I saw him at once when I entered, at the second table to the left in the back room. He was fitter and more short-sighted than ever. It seemed as though his eyeglasses had become bigger, and his nose was glued more closely to the newspaper. He wore his hair cropped and as it was of the stiff, black variety, his head looked like the back of a worn-down nail brush.

I tapped him on the shoulder: 'Hallo, Plá!'

He raised his little pig-eyes, made still smaller by the lenses. Either he could not see me well enough, or he did not recognize me; but it must have been due to his eyesight, for my face had hardly changed since I was sixteen, except for the beard which had begun to sprout in odd places.

'Eh? Hallo. Have a drink and sit down.'

'So we don't remember our friends any more?'

His small eyes seemed to sniff me; for when he tried to see you, moving his head from side to side to find the right focus, his protruding eyes appeared not so much to look at as to scent you. When his face was only a foot from mine he recognized me. He stood up, his short legs shuffling, and embraced me with excited ejaculations.

First I told him about myself, then he poured out his lamentations about the work in the bank, and finally we began to talk about the political situation.

'What do you think of it, Luis?' I asked him.

'I think things are coming to a head now. The racket has just about finished for "Narizotas".' (Narizotas, Long Nose, was the name by which the King of Spain was known among the people during the last years of his reign, the same name which had been given to his great-grandfather Ferdinand VII before him.) 'In a year at the outside we'll have our Republic.'

'You're an optimist, Luis.'

'But it's bound to come.' He waxed confidential. 'All kinds of dirty stories are coming out now about Narizotas. Marquet paid him millions to get a licence to open his gambling houses, the Ice Palace, you know, and the Casino of San Sebastian. People say Narizotas has got his fingers in the *Circulo de Bellas Artes*, too. He's in the Riff Mines together with Romanones, and in the supply business of motor vehicles for the army with Mateu. And now there is the Morocco business on top of it.'

'The Morocco business – and what is the Morocco business?'

'Pooh, a nasty story! Because it's he who's responsible for the Disaster. He wrote to Silvestre behind Berenguers's back and told him to carry on. They say he even sent a telegram to Silvestre after Annual had been taken, in which he said: "Long live your guts!". And when he was told about the catastrophe and that there were thousands of dead, he is supposed to have said: "Chicken-meat is cheap!" Of course, all the reactionaries are defending him in the Cortes, but the Republicans and Socialists are getting very strong. And then there's another thing. Now that the expeditionary forces are sent over and all those fellows who had bought their exemption have got to go too, many of the Liberals want to get to the bottom of things. It smarts when they've got to lose their sons after paying the money. One thing is certain: there will be legal proceedings.'

'Proceedings?' I exclaimed.

'Yes. Proceedings to establish the responsibility for what happened in Africa. The generals themselves are seething with rage. They have threatened to demonstrate in the streets as in the times of Isabella II. But things are different now. Just let them come out! They'll see fireworks all right.'

'And what about Barcelona?'

'Oh, nothing. Only that people in Barcelona go for a walk, and someone comes up and pumps them full of lead. And the other people don't even turn their heads. Sometimes the gunmen are Anarchists and sometimes they are paid by the Government. But the Catalans don't interest me. They can all get killed, for all I care. Mind you, all these things help, of course. The greater the row, the better. Then we'll have a new government every fortnight, and then d'you think the ministers will even have time to sort themselves out?'

He paused, drank his glass of wine, called for the waiter, and ordered more drinks.

'But it's all because of the European war. It's a question of economics, d'you see?'

'Not quite.'

'But it's very simple. Look, during the war our people got sick of earning money. Men who had been going round with their trousers torn suddenly opened fantastic bank accounts; newspapers with no sale at all got paid by some embassy and bought a rotary press over night; ministers got million-peseta tips; old mules, for which a gypsy wouldn't have given fifty pesetas, fetched five thousand; the Catalans manufactured millions of blankets; people in Valencia sold their fruit before the crops were ripe; wheat brought in a double price; sailing boats got a thousand *duros* to sail from Bilbao to St Jean de Luz; they were torpedoed as soon as they left harbour, and got ten thousand *duros* insurance money. And then the war was over, and everything came to an end. The new factories have all been closed and the workers have been turned out into the streets. The railways are ruined, or at least they say they are. While everybody had money Madrid was invaded by taxis; and now taxi owners are starving. And the banks established during the war have suspended payments. . . . From the King down to the last Spaniard everybody needs money now. The King sells a licence to open a casino, or eggs on Silvestre to conquer the Riff so that he can sell a few more mines to Romanones. The railway companies demand State subsidies and threaten to suspend traffic without them. Then they get their subsidies, and the ministers get their commissions. You can go to any ministry with fifty pesetas in your hand, and they'll give you what you ask for. If you have a million they'll give you the whole ministry with all the civil servants and their desks thrown in. And because somebody has to pay for it all, they get rid of workers or reduce their wages. And so we have a strike every ten days. Believe me, it'll all come to a bad end.'

Rafael brought me an invitation to see his boss. Don Manuel Guerrero was at that time managing director of the Madrid Bakeries (in liquidation), but he had been a major in the Engineers and had left the army, as had many of the more cultured and socially more independent officers of the Engineers and Artillery corps, because they found themselves involved in ugly conflicts with the other type of officer, those who were only interested in making a rapid career and doing business in the Moroccan war.

Don Manuel was some fifty years old, grey-haired, short and squarely built, with deep-set eyes, a powerful forehead and a somewhat aggressive jaw. He spoke brusquely, but after a few minutes of conversation all his stiffness vanished, and he took me over his closed factory, telling me his story, which was filling his whole mind.

He had set up a big, modern bread factory in the outskirts of Madrid, near a railway junction, apparently with every prospect of revolutionizing the bread supply of the capital. His organization and the site of his plant permitted him to buy and transport the wheat direct from the Spanish producer or from the ports. He was able to produce bread more cheaply and under far more hygienic conditions than small bakers, many of whom still kneaded the dough with their feet and undercut each other by adulterating the flour and cheating over the weights. There was a single other modern bakery, belonging to Count Romanones. The enterprise was launched as a limited company, financed by the banks. But soon he had found himself pitted against the vested interests of two powerful groups, both profiting from the high price of wheat: the landowners and traders in control of Spanish wheat and the businessmen controlling the wheat imports. He had had to obtain special permits for importing his own cheap wheat, but he was unable to pay the customs duties which were raised as soon as his grain cargoes had arrived. He had tried to fight. And then he had come up against the banks which preferred their bigger and more profitable customers, his adversaries. Now he was ruined.

'My last hope', he said, 'was to get a supply contract with the army; but to come to an agreement with the Commissariat, I should have had to stop being honest. And I've always been honest.'

Between the huge trays of the ovens, the shovels of the kneading gear, the beams of the roofs and the conveyor belts hung spiders' webs.

'Do you realize that this is an object lesson – a very grave symptom of the catastrophe which is overtaking Spain? If God does not avert it. But it does not look as though He would avert it! You see, we are an exporting country, and if we don't import the grain and the raw materials we need, the other countries won't buy our oil and fruit and textiles. I can't import wheat, but the textile plants of Catalonia are lying idle because the Argentine no longer buys cloth in exchange. Then the workers there demonstrate, and it all ends in man-hunts in the streets. And now, to crown it all, Morocco: tell me about it.'

I told him I knew nothing of Morocco but what I had seen; I spoke of the track of Hamara and the expedition to Melilla. He listened, nodding his head sharply from time to time. Then he said:

'It would be best to clear out of Morocco. Let the Powers of the Algeciras Treaty see how they can clear up the mess. But the trouble is that anyone who tries to follow such a course will provoke a revolution from above. Where and on what are all those people to live? They cannot live without their profits. And they are too powerful.'

He stopped, thought it over and fell back, inevitably, into his own story:

'Even this poor factory of mine would have worked if I had liked to take part in shabby deals, or if I had listened to the good advice of the biggest baker of Madrid, Count Romanones.'

But I hardly followed his argument any longer. The name of Romanones sounding through the dusty, deserted hall made me think of another plant in which I had worked years before, as secretry to its managing director: Spanish Motors Ltd, the great factory whose aircraft were to transform Spain's aviation.

I had been a lad of nineteen then. I had seen and taken in things as they came, without understanding them. I had an important and enviable job: the prettiest girls of the small town of Guadalajara were interested in me because I was the secretary of Don Juan de Zaracondegui, and because the thousands of pesetas on the pay roll went through my hands, and because I had to interview and engage workers. I had my adventure and liked it, enjoying myself hugely when I deceived the watchfulness of the girl's parents and the blackmailing brutality of her brothers.

Guadalajara had been the seat of the administration of a small province, a tiny, miserly town under the iron rule of its greatest landowner, political boss and permanent deputy to the Cortes, Count Romanones. It consisted of farmers, tavern keepers, and a Military Academy for Engineers. The girls became engaged to the cadets but married farmers, with the result that at night the students from the Academy and the farmers' sons went in separate groups to play the guitar under the windows of pretty girls and to end up in free fights. Occasionally a captain of the Engineers would come back to Guadalajara and marry one of the girls; this fact kept alive the hopes of the unmarried ones.

When the plant of Spanish Motors had been installed in Guadalajara, it had caused an upheaval. A host of draughtsmen, employees, and mechanics invaded the taverns of the cadets. Farmhands who had earned two or three pesetas a day became workers in Spanish Motors and earned double. Parents and daughters saw unhoped-for vistas beckoning. Their life was changed and to me it had seemed fun to be part of it.

Now, four years later, I saw the other side of the story; I saw the pieces falling into place.

During the Great War, Spanish Motor Engines of Barcelona had produced engines for the Allies in co-operation with French factories, and as a sideline for the Spanish Army which was then going through the first stages of mechanization. Later, the new Service Corps were placed under a separate military department called the Electro-Technical Centre, with a captain of the Engineers, Don Ricardo Goytre, at its head. Perhaps because there were so many commissions to pay, Spanish Motor Engines Ltd began to supply the Spanish Army with material, which failed in the hard test it had to undergo in Morocco from 1918 onwards.

Soon, extraordinary budgets had to be granted to the army to buy new and better cars. Finally the Cortes decided that a big national competition was to be held for motorcars and aircraft. The successful types were to be adopted by the army, but only Spanish factories were admitted.

The only national plant of any importance was Spanish Motor Engines; but too many of its motorcars and lorries were lying dismantled, as scrap-iron, in the military car parks of Spain and Africa. It would not have been popular for Spanish Motor Engines to emerge as the winner in the competition. So Spanish Motors Ltd was created.

Count Romanones supplied a large site near the railway station of Guadalajara, where workshops were constructed as soon as shares had been issued to a value of five million pesetas. Ample room was left for an aerodrome which, by its strategic situation, seemed destined to become the most important in Spain, and indeed, one of the most important in Europe. Don Miguel Mateu became chairman of the Board of Directors; he happened to be the managing director of Spanish Motor Engines Ltd in Barcelona. Don Ricardo Goytre resigned from his post as director of the Army Electro-Technical Centre and became technical director of Spanish Motors; Captain Barrón, the designer of one of the two plane types which were to be entered for the competition, became chief engineer. Don Juan de Zaracondegui, a Basque aristocrat who had been a highly placed official of Spanish Motor Engines, became managing director. And finally, the director of the Madrid branch of Spanish Motor Engines, Don Francisco Aritio, became business manager of Spanish Motors.

'Rich people get everything for nothing' is a saying of the Spanish poor.

Don Miguel Mateu owned one of the biggest iron and machine-tool stores of Spain in Barcelona; he was also the agent of the biggest North American and German tool factories. He supplied all the machine tools to Spanish Motors.

Count Romanones owned extensive waste lands in Guadalajara. He supplied the site for the factory.

Neither of them accepted any money for this. Spanish Motors was a patriotic enterprise which would free Spain from her dependence on foreign countries, and give her her own aviation.

Five million free shares, or rather, shares allocated for a consideration other than cash, were issued. I was ordered to begin the account books of Spanish Motors by entering the following accounts in my best copper-plate letters:

S.M. Don Alfonso XIII	1,000,000
Don Miguel Mateu	2,000,000
El Conde de Romanones	1,000,000
Don Francisco Aritio	500,000

The rest of these shares were entered in the name of the inventor of the engines of Spanish Motor Engines. They were the payment for his patent rights on those very engines which were now to be produced under the name of Spanish Motors Ltd. But I forgot what name I wrote.

The competition was duly held. The contracts for the army were given to Spanish Motors Ltd, while the engineer Lacierva, with his first autogyro models, was ridiculed. The new plant of Spanish Motors was inspected by His Majesty the King. Don Miguel Mateu sent machinery from his stocks in Barcelona, provided by the Allied Machinery Company of Chicago. The shares rose on the Stock Exchange. Green-painted lorries arrived from Barcelona in

Guadalajara and were handed over to the army. The Board of Directors of Spanish Motors arranged for an English firm to construct aircraft for them.

At that stage I left my job because my amorous adventure had led me into deep waters. Since then I had forgotten about the books I had kept there.

Now, with the typhus of Africa still in my bones, in the storm-laden atmosphere of Madrid, I saw that the track from that deal in Guadalajara had led to Africa.

I went back to Africa after two months' leave, deeply afraid for Spain.

Part II

1. The New Game

There was a rough sea in the Straits. The little old steamer rose and
sank, pitched and lurched. Hills and houses were swaying drunkenly
as we entered the port of Ceuta.

I found the town utterly changed.

When you live in a place you build up a mental picture of your
surroundings. It sleeps at the back of your brain while you are there
in the flesh, but when you go away it comes alive and takes the place
of the lost direct vision. Then you return one day, expecting to find
places, things, and people as you have carried them in your mind, as
you have come to believe them to be. But your mental picture and
reality clash, and the shock goes right through you.

The cool silent little street is now filled with people, noise and
glaring light. The crowded café, where your friends had sat in heated
discussions, is half empty and the friendly waiter cannot remember
what you used to order. It is as though an actor were to go to the
theatre at ten in the morning, convinced that he would have to
appear on the scene, only to find charwomen dusting the plush seats
in front of an empty stage strewn with props and flooded with grey
daylight.

Often have I suffered this jarring shock, but when I came to Ceuta
from Madrid, I was conscious of it for the first time. I had known
every corner of Ceuta, each corner in its own moment. Now, time
and place failed to synchronize, and I found myself on strange
ground.

I wanted to breakfast before reporting to barracks, and I went to
my café, that is to say, to the café I had frequented as a corporal. But
in the doorway I realized with a jolt that I was now a sergeant. This
was not the right place for me. I would have to go to the sergeants'
café. So I went to the 'Perla'. A few other sergeants were
breakfasting on coffee and buns; I sat down and ordered coffee. The

waiter did not know me, I did not know the place, and everyone looked at me because I was a stranger to them. I gulped down my coffee and left, bitterly resenting that I had not been able to feel the welcoming warmth of my soldiers' café where the waiter had been a friend and the room had been dirtier and less pretentious, but more human.

To be a sergeant in Ceuta meant to have a social standing. There were three castes in the small town, neatly separated into water-tight compartments. The privates and the corporals, together with the simple workers, dockers, masons, street sweepers and so on, were the proletariat. The non-commissioned officers, sergeants and sergeant-majors, the few skilled workers and minor tradesmen, the lesser clerks and employees, were the middle class. The upper class, or aristocracy, consisted of the officers, businessmen, civil servants, judiciary and clergy. The whole social life of the town was so regulated that these groups could not mix. There were cafés for soldiers, for NCOs, and for officers. There were brothels for each of the three castes. Certain streets and even certain parts of the same street were practically reserved for one or the other group. In the Calle Real, which runs straight through the town from north to south, the soldiers would keep to the middle of the street. On the pavement they would have to make room for women and for all their superiors; and as they could not fail to meet a woman or an officer at every five steps, they preferred not to leap continually from the pavement to the street. On the whole the soldiers fled the streets in the centre of the town where they had eternally to salute; the officers avoided the side streets where they could not exhibit themselves to the public that counted.

As in other Spanish towns, people in Ceuta used to promenade from sunset to dinner time, walking up and down a length of pavement, greeting friends and flirting. Each caste had its own length of street. In one, the soldiers walked out with the servant girls. In another, the officers walked out with young ladies who were accompanied by their mammas and watched over by grave-faced papas. And the sergeants had a promenade of their own, where they courted girls pretending to be well-to-do young ladies, with papas pretending to occupy important posts.

I could no longer go to the soldiers' café.

I would no longer be able to enter the familiar tavern, I would not be able to promenade on that length of pavement, and so on and so forth.

In this frame of mind I reported to barracks; they told me to present myself to the Major who would come at eleven o'clock. For more than an hour I wandered round the Engineers' barracks. A building with two terraces, an enormous wooden hut, outhouses for kitchens, stables, workshops, infirmary, flanking big courtyards and small courtyards, all whitewashed and very clean. Every day a soldier was detailed off to put another layer of whitewash on some of the walls, so that every few days the cycle would begin again.

I was bored with waiting and I was bored with the endless white glare of the barracks, almost deserted at that hour. Well, next morning I would go to Tetuan and from there to the front; there I would be less bored. I would at least know people and find company. In Ceuta I knew hardly anybody. My contact with the soldiers was severed, my contact with the sergeants stationed in the place not yet established on the new level of equality. I felt an outsider with both.

At eleven the Major entered the regimental office. I let a short time go by, and went into his room. 'At your orders, sir.'

'Hallo, Barea – back already? You're still pretty thin. Take care of yourself. Now, Sergeant Cárdenas has been promoted to quartermaster sergeant. I thought that you might take over the office work. Let me know whether you would rather go to the front. Not that I imagine you would.'

I thanked him.

'Take it easy for a few days and get into touch with Cárdenas, to learn about things. But no fooling about, eh?'

You entered the Regimental Office through a small anteroom furnished with two tables and a monkish bench of hard wood, just wide enough for six persons. The two orderlies were forever sitting on that bench, zealously preventing anybody else from occupying their territory. Behind the table sat two scribes, who interrogated arrivals and made everybody fill in a form. Then there was a wooden partition topped by wire netting, and behind it two cubicles separated by a wire screen and joined by a small opening in the wire. The left-hand cubicle was that of Corporal Surribas, the right-hand one that of Sergeant Cárdenas. Surribas was a kind of secretary to

Cárdenas, from whom he received orders through the little window. Cárdenas was a kind of secretary to the CO and had not only a desk of his own but also a smaller desk in front, so that he could dictate to somebody else if he wished.

There was a bigger room at the back, with five desks and four clerks. The shelves that ran along its wall were stacked with paper bundles tied with red tape. These bundles contained the history of all the soldiers who had passed through the regiment within the last twenty years. One book-shelf was bulging with larger folio files which held the history of all the officers throughout the same years.

The room smelled of worm-eaten paper and of insects. For there is an insect smell; it is sweetish and sticks in your nose and throat, inseparably mixed with the finest dust. If you lift a stack of very old papers or a worm-eaten book from its place, there rises a little cloud of dust and powder, and the smell is so strong that even the oldest clerk cannot help sneezing.

And the room was filled with insect sound. In my days as a corporal I worked there and came to know it. While the four of us were busy writing or typing, and chatting in low voices so as not to incense the sergeant, we would not hear the sound. But whenever I sought refuge there on hot African nights, I heard the ceaseless toil of the demolition squad attacking bureaucracy. They were gnawing the paper, boring through it, nesting in it, making love. There were centipedes with a nib-like claw like crayfish, which dug through whole bundles from cover to cover. There were crunching cockroaches, which slowly ate away the edge of the pages. There were caterpillars spinning their cocoons underneath a file, to leave them as butterfly-moths in May. On the highest shelves with the oldest stacks of paper monstrous spiders, wasps, and horseflies had their nests where they slept through the winter. In the lowest files, near the floor, mice were padding their holes with fibres taken from the red tape. Time and again, ants would invade the place, as though they wanted to carry printed and written letters away to their antheaps, like grains of wheat.

While I had worked in the office I had nicknamed Sergeant Cárdenas 'The Parrot', partly on account of his wire cage and partly on account of his shrill voice, which would cut through the silence, always rasping, always angry. Otherwise I knew nothing about him but the outside: a well-built, dark man, meticulously shaved, exceedingly grave and exceedingly irritable, his peasant origin visible only in the uneasiness with which he wore his expensive, correct uniform, as though it belonged to somebody else.

Now I found myself in the parrot's cage, sitting at the desk in front of him and waiting. He wore a brand new uniform of quartermaster sergeant; after his promotion he had not sewed on the new stripes, but simply bought a new outfit.

'Well now, you're going to be my successor. It ought to have been Surribas by the right of seniority, but the poor fellow is quite mad. One couldn't rely on him. This is a post which needs a lot of tact. The work isn't difficult but you must always know where you're treading, and who's who. Keep your eyes skinned, because if they can, they'll try and put a fast one over on you. I'll explain to you how it works, in general terms. You'll grasp the details in time, and anyhow you'll be staying in contact with me because I'll be on HQ duty.'

He made a pause. We lighted cigarettes, and he went on.

'I've been looking after the accounts myself. You'll have to do the same if you want to get on. Surribas keeps the books and will help you in all the auxiliary work, but the accounts are your job. Surribas may write the figures into the ledger and add them up, but it's you who give him the figures and you alone know why they are given. Sometimes you won't know either; for instance, if the Major comes and tells you to enter something or other. Then you put it down and that's that. You may guess at the reason, but keep your mouth shut and don't ask questions. In such cases you're to the Major what Surribas is to you. But those are exceptions. Normally, you simply keep the regimental accounts.

'As you know the State allots a certain sum to every man in the army, from private to colonel. On the basis of this budget, each Company makes out its accounts and presents them to you at the end of each month. You examine them, pass them, and the Company gets the money due to it from the cashier.'

'It doesn't sound very difficult.'

'No. That isn't difficult. A statement of accounts is sent to the *Tribunal de Cuentas* where they're passed and filed. Now the point is that no statement of account must ever be rejected as inaccurate.

Therefore each entry must have its voucher. And here you have the key to our accountancy: THE VOUCHER. No voucher, no money is our rule.'

'That's not difficult either, it seems to me.'

'But it is difficult. The voucher question is the most difficult of all. I'll give you an example, and you'll see why.'

Then, using as his example the issuing and accounting for rope-soled canvas shoes, he explained the complicated machinery by which the privates were made to pay for thousands of pairs of those *alpargatas* which were officially a part of their free equipment. The swindle went all the way up the line to the manufacturer who supplied the *alpargatas*. The privates knew, of course, that they were being cheated, and that the thievery began with their quartermaster sergeants, but they didn't dare to make a formal complaint about them. Having explained in detail the *alpargatas* fraud, all covered up with vouchers, 'The Parrot' said: 'And now do you see?'

'Yes, I see more or less. No wonder you've got as nervous as you are with all these complications.'

'Yes. Imagine that it is the same with every scrap of equipment and even armament. And all the accounts with their vouchers go through your hands. The only thing you've got to do is to see that every item in every account has its voucher, never mind about the other things. Now I'll tell you what to do. Take the latest statement of account, go and see Romero, the sergeant of our depot, and meet the various quartermaster sergeants of the companies. I won't give you any work to do until Monday at the horse auction. You'll have to act as secretary there, but since it is the first time I'll help you.'

In the courtyard flanked by the stables stood a big table, a comfortable armchair, and on both sides of it a row of chairs. The papers for the twelve animals to be auctioned were on the table. Civilians, who were allowed to come to the barracks on this occasion, were milling around in the canteen. The sunlight thrown back from the lime-washed walls was blindingly white. In this crude light the gypsies stood out like statuary, their short white jackets showing off wide shoulders and narrow waists, their dark corduroy trousers tight across the hips and widening around the knees. They beat a tattoo on the paving stones with their sticks, the kind of stick all cattle dealers carry, they whispered in the fashion of conspirators among each other and counted their money and shouted for wine. Horses and mules were tied up along the watering trough, plunging their noses into the water now and again more to cool off than to drink. The whole courtyard smelled of the sweat of men and horses.

People had been waiting since ten o'clock in the morning. The auction was supposed to start at eleven. At half past eleven the Colonel of the Army Service Corps arrived; he was to preside over the auction board. I felt uneasy. I was to be auctioneer and secretary; I was to take down the prices fetched, to receive the cash, to write receipts, to issue the papers for each animal to each buyer and to get his signature for them.

At last the board was assembled at the table: the Colonel of the Army Service Corps, a slow-moving, rheumy old man with a weak, shrill voice in the armchair, to his right and left the Colonel – our CO – the Major, the Veterinary Captain, the Adjutant, and two officers I did not know.

The gypsies ranged themselves in a circle round the table. The Veterinary Captain, standing in the centre, gave the order to lead in the first horse. I rose and read out:

'Fundador. Three years old. Sixteen hands. Bay with white markings on the haunches. Tuberculosis of the lungs. Fifty-five pesetas.'

Every six months the horses and mules unfit for army service were sold by public auction. The tubercular horse was a beautiful creature on fine legs, twitching nervously in the middle of the crowd. An old gypsy, hat slant-wise on his head, came forward, pulled the horse's nether lip away from the teeth and examined the gums. He patted it on the back and said, slowly:

'Seventy-five pesetas.'

A voice in the ring shouted:

'One hundred.'

The old gypsy dug his hands into the horse's flanks and waited, listening to its excited breathing. After a while he stood aside, paused, walked back into the ring and said to the second bidder:

'Yours, kid.'

'Nobody offering more?' I said.

Silence.

'Gone.'

A young gypsy stepped forward, carefully untied the string wound round his pocketbook, and put a one hundred peseta note on the table. I took it, noted his name and address, and wrote a receipt.

'You can come this afternoon at three and fetch the horse.'

The auction went on. The old gypsy bought a horse and a mule. The twelve animals sold at an average of fifty pesetas. In the end the two colonels took the officers upstairs for a drink before they went to lunch. Cárdenas and I did the same; we were back in the office at three o'clock to deal with the gypsies. It was the hour of the siesta, stifling, sultry, heavy with vapour. One of the orderlies fetched us beer from the canteen.

The first gypsy entered. Cárdenas turned round to the orderly: 'You, there, Jimenez, stand outside the door and tell the next one to come that he will have to wait until this gentleman leaves.'

This gentleman, a gypsy as greasy as though he had just handled a spluttering frying pan, pulled off his hat with a flourish, sat down on the chair waiting for him, planted his stick between his thighs and offered us fat cigars with gold bands.

'Have a smoke.'

'Let's leave them for later,' said Cárdenas. We were smoking. He pulled out a drawer and put the cigars inside.

'Well, now, I've come to settle the bill.'

The gypsy opened a pocketbook bulging with banknotes and began to count, wetting his fingers and crunching each note between them. 'Because one day, you know, it happened to me that two big notes were stuck together, and I got one back only because I was among honest folk. But you can't count on that – I beg your pardon.'

He spread notes to an amount of one thousand five hundred pesetas on the table.

'Now you sign here,' Cárdenas said.

The gypsy scratched his signature and Cárdenas handed him the papers for the horse

'Go down to the stable and they will give you the horse.'

When all the callers had gone, there were more than eight thousand pesetas in our drawer. Cárdenas took them and locked them up in the strong box.

'Let's go for a walk,' he said to me.

Outside the barrack gates I asked him:

'But tell me now, what exactly is the game?'

'The voucher, my boy, the voucher. Everything is checked and found in order. Tuberculosis of the lungs, according to the chit of a veterinary and the certificate of a veterinary inspector. Worth a hundred pesetas. This African climate is very bad for horses, they just die from one day to the next, of a hundred and one illnesses.'

'But nobody would pay one thousand five hundred pesetas for a tubercular horse.'

'Of course not. The tubercular horse is over there in the stables and will die within the next few days. We've sold a healthy brute. But in our files we've got the certificate that he was tubercular and the receipts vouching for the fact that a gypsy has paid one hundred pesetas to take him to the only place where they have any use for a tubercular horse, to the bull ring.'

Next morning, when the Major arrived, Cárdenas fetched the bundle of notes from the strong box and took it to the Major's room. He did not say a word to me when he came back.

I took charge of the Regimental Office. Those who had been clerks with me when I was a corporal were still there, still soldiers, and still scribes. They were no longer my friends. They called me 'sir' and lived their lives apart. The two orderlies were still the same; they showed me increased respect. Cárdenas was now HQ quartermaster sergeant. He treated me paternally and tried to endow me with his vast store of experience.

Again, I found myself isolated from all of them.

On many afternoons we did not work, not only because of the heat, but also because there was little to do except towards the end of each month, or when a class was discharged, or when a shipment of recruits arrived. A few steps from the barracks was the sea. I bought tackle and went fishing.

2. Face to the Sea

Fishing gave me an excuse to escape from the orbit of the barracks. The diversions Ceuta offered were taverns, brothels and gambling tables in a casino. If I went about with my own set, the other sergeants, I could be certain of landing every single evening in at least one, possibly in three of those kinds of establishment. I was by no means a puritan, but I found myself incapable of organizing my daily life after the patterns of the others.

I liked wine, women, and an occasional game of cards, but not for seven days a week in monotonous repetition. All my life I have enjoyed drinking a few glasses of wine with friends in the evenings, chatting for an hour about a hundred and one personal and impersonal matters, and then going home. I disliked having to sit before a bottle with the people whom I had seen all day long, having to empty a second bottle, and a third, and let the hours go by until we were all more or less tight. I disliked being a regular customer of a brothel, going there every day with the same people, hearing and repeating the same phrases and the same jokes. I disliked sitting down at the same gambling table every night and passing the thirty days of the month in a chain of good or bad streaks of luck, borrowing money from one or the other of my inseparable partners.

Four sergeants, one from the depot, one from the Colonel's office, one from the pay office and I, lived in a room behind the offices. There we had our beds, a table, half a dozen chairs, and our trunks. We had an orderly who cooked for us and served our meals in the sergeants' mess-room. Through our work we were in continuous contact with each other. At meal times we ate at the same table. We slept in beds six feet apart from each other. We new one another's intimate affairs and most intimate habits. As the heat compelled us to sleep naked on top of our beds, we knew each other's skin and movements. It was an astonishing fact that the friendliness of our communal life was never shattered. Yet a link was lacking.

Romero, the sergeant of the depot, was thirty-eight years old, a merry, expansive, agile Andalusian. He came from a little village in the province of Cordova, where his parents had been small holders with a flock of children, eking out a meagre existence. It was to escape from the petty misery at home that he had stayed on in the army.

Oliver, the sergeant of the pay office, was a tall Castilian of thirty-odd years, the son of an underpaid civil servant. After the death of both his parents, the boy had been taken on by an uncle in what is called reduced circumstances. At eighteen, Oliver failed in the examination for the postal service. His uncle suggested the army as the only road to a career. He joined as a volunteer, intending to enter the Officers' Training School in Cordova as soon as he became a sergeant. But he was made assistant to the Paymaster. And the atmosphere of Ceuta, combined with his strongly sensuous temperament, smothered his plans, leaving the empty shell of an ever remote project.

Fernadez, the sergeant in the Colonel's office, was only twenty-two years old, but he had lived in barracks for almost six years. He was the son of a colonel on the active list. Born and bred in Madrid, he began to study law at the university, but his pranks were so wild that his father sent him straight to the barracks 'to drive the nonsense out of his head'. First he rebelled and stayed away from barracks for a whole week; he was sentenced to two additional years of army service and sent to Africa for the period. There he was used for office work; later his sentence was lifted and in the end he was made a sergeant, thanks partly to his father's influence and partly to his education and intelligence. He had learned to work well by now, but still remained the Madrid ne'er-do-well, always wanting to paint the town red. His only worries were how to cope with his deficit at the end of each month and how to preserve his standing as the Don Juan of all the brothels in Ceuta. He was a dapper young man, exquisitely dressed. He had special protégées in three of four brothels and let them give him presents, although he was not out to exploit them, but was simply the type of man with whom prostitutes get infatuated.

Those three were my companions. I lived together with them and we got on well, but that was all. The company of ordinary rankers was prohibited to me; the Spanish Army frowned upon intimacy between sergeants and privates or even corporals. Equally, officers were not allowed to make friends with NCOs. They might favour one of them with their particular esteem, but they had to respect the class barrier.

So I went fishing to be free.

At the edge of the sea there is a fringe of rocks. The high tide covers them and at low tide they are dry. They are carpeted with a thick moss which is harsh to the touch and pale green in colour, as if bleached by the salt water. Crabs nibble at it and fish burrow in its pile for worms hidden among the roots.

You pour a few drops of vinegar on the moss, and the worms appear in legions, madly wriggling their frail bodies and craning their heads as though they were choking and fighting for a last breath of air. You pass your hand over the moss and gather them in hundreds; you put them in an old tin can half filled with mud, and they dig themselves in at once. There you have your bait. You put a worm on your hook, taking care not to squash it and to leave the tail free so that it can wriggle in the tranquil water. Sardines, cackerel and gilt-head pounce on it voraciously, and an infinite number of other fish hover near, dappling the water with blue, black, russet, silver and gold.

The ledges of the huge concrete blocks of the mole were teeming with anglers who hung out their rods between the wall of the quay and the bellies of the moored ships. I was not interested in fishing there. I explored the rocks fringing the Monte Hacho and found a stone balcony overhanging the sea.

There were three boulders: two smaller ones in front, in the form of a V, a bigger one topping them, shaped like an armchair, its seat polished, the back seamed and wrinkled. Below the V, the bottom of the sea dropped sheer to a depth of six or eight yards, forming a wide, deep, well-like pool. Farther out, a row of rocks, hardly visible above the water, acted as a breakwater so that the pool was always calm. Only during a storm were the three boulders drowned in a fountain of spray.

I would collect worms among the rocks, catch sardines or small cackerels in the deep well and use them as live bait for my lines. A line consists of fifty metres of silk cord with a leaden sinker at one end. You slip a cast carrying a large baited hook on to the cord with a running knot. You swing the lead in the air and cast the line. The sardine swims and moves freely, though held by the cast, all along your line from the pool to the open sea. Big fish, which would not come near the rocks, go for the bait, and your catch is a matter of luck.

Every day I laid out four lines, each tied to a solid rock, and sat down in the stone armchair to read, to write, or to think. If a fish was biting, the little bell fastened to the line gave the alarm.

It was a day of calm. The waters in the Straits were tranquil as a garden pool. They mirrored the blue sky and were themselves a limpid blue filled with glitter. On this mirror small streams were running in milky little ripples. Faint, outward traces of the deep currents of the two seas which met there, they gathered in a wide band, a bigger stream, which entered the port of Ceuta from the west and swept out again towards the east. At time this stream and its tiny rivulets changed direction; sometimes the Mediterranean pours its waters into the Atlantic, at others the Atlantic sends them back.

I dropped my book and submerged myself in this tide of perfect peace. I saw the coast of Spain in the far distance, and the outline of the Rock, and all was full of light and calm as though the sky were an immense glass dome with a reflector in the apex, and there were no world outside.

I had come to a crossroads in my life. I was twenty-four, I had no fortune, and I was still the son of Señora Leonor, the washerwoman, although my mother had long since ceased to break the ice of the river with her wooden beater in the grey winter dawns, or to be scorched by the noonday sun of July. In less than a year I would have finished my subjection to barracks life. I had to plan my future.

I was a sergeant in the army. If I were to re-enlist instead of taking my discharge I would have a fixed pay of 250 pesetas per month, stay on in Africa and never have my hands clean. I had come to be the office sergeant at headquarters, an enviable and envied post; I could live in peace and make money for eight or ten years, at the end of which I would become a warrant officer. I could also enter the Officers' Training School at Cordova, study for three years, and become an officer.

If I took my discharge at the end of my military term, I would have to return to civilian life and at once seek a job. There were thousands of unemployed clerical workers in Madrid. After my three years in the army, out of contact with the business world, with old testimonials, I would in all probability become just one more un-employed clerk. And even were I to find work immediately, my salary would be 150 pesetas a month at best.

And yet those were the only two practical solutions open to me, one of them – the army – certain, the other problematic. Who would support me if I were to stay in Madrid without work for six months or more?

There were two other potential careers, more in keeping with my wishes; both of them seemed so difficult to realize that they became practically impossible. And yet I would have liked to be a mechanical engineer, or I would have liked to be a writer.

My wish to be an engineer was as old as I myself. When my uncle's death had cut short my prospects and forced me to turn myself into a clerk to earn a living, I had not given up hope. The Jesuits had established a Polytechnic in Madrid which was infinitely better than the State School. The sons of the wealthiest families studied engineering there; at the end of their courses they paid matriculation fees to the State, passed the official examinations and became professional engineers by title. At the same time the Jesuits' school offered free instruction to the sons of poor families who were guaranteed to be safe Catholics. My Cordovan relatives, knowing my ambitions, had sent me an introduction to the Head of the Polytechnic when I was seventeen. I went there.

We had an endless conversation. He showed me all over the school, at that time a marvel of technical organization, and in the end put the whole issue before me with complete frankness. An in-telligent youth like myself would be able to complete all the studies for an engineering career in their school. When I had finished, the Polytechnic would give me a certificate which meant the certainty of employment in Spanish industry. Of course this certificate was not an official title, for which I would have to pay the State a matriculation fee of several thousand pesetas. It would simply be the certificate of a school testifying that its holder possessed the same knowledge as an official Engineer – or even more. Spanish industrialists accepted this certificate because they knew to what degree the School vouched for its pupils. I would not find it difficult to get a job. There were ample possibilities.

I had learned enough in my years of apprenticeship in the bank to realize the power of the Society of Jesus in Spain. I knew that the Sacred Heart had been enthroned in the factory plants of the north, and that the big shipowners had Jesuits for their father confessors, and that big banks were so intimatley bound to the Order that some of them were assumed to be its financial figureheads. I had seen that a letter of recommendation from a Jesuit opened all doors in Spanish industry and that a discreet hint from the same quarters had the power to shut those doors for good.

I would be able to work in any factory in Spain as a mechanical engineer without the legal title, but it would be tacitly understood that I was to remain in contact with the Order, confess my sins to a Jesuit, and obey his instructions unless I wanted to lose my job from one day to the next. And where would I go then with a certificate which was nothing but a scrap of paper when the *placet* of the Society of Jesus backed it no longer?

Under such conditions I did not accept the invitation to become a student in the Polytechnic of Areneros. I went back to the bank, to the figures in the ledger, and shelved my ambitions.

Later, when I was secretary to Don Ricardo Goytre in Spanish Motors at Guadalajara, he found that I could help him with the sketches of engine projects. He sent me to the evening classes the Augustines had started in the little town.

The Order had seen an opportunity for influencing the workers as soon as the big new plant was established, and had opened a technical school with classes for drawing and mathematics. I went there. A priest needed no certificate in Spain in order to conduct a school or to act as a teacher; the good Brothers of Guadalajara had embarked upon technical tuition without further preparation. After a week I saw clearly that I was only a disturbing element. With my scanty knowledge I knew more about technical drawing and mathematics than the masters. The Head sent for me:

'Would you like to help us, my son? As part of our endeavours on behalf of the poor we have opened this institute which is only an elementary school of its kind. You would need more advanced tuition than we are able to give you. Yet I do not want to tell you not to come; on the contrary, come and help us. Your assistance would be very valuable to us.'

For a time I gave lessons in elementary French and in instrumental drawing. But the only advantages for me were that I had to attend all religious functions, to dine late, and to incur the hostility of the workers. After a few weeks I deserted from the Augustines and tried to learn integral calculus from a colleague.

When I was called up for military service I signed on for the Second Railway Regiment. They accepted me as a draughtsman; I hoped to receive some training there. Then the lots were drawn for Africa, and I was sent to Morocco. I served with the Engineers, but my technical qualifications had only succeeded in turning me into a clerk.

I still had the possibility of starting as a simple mechanic after my discharge. I would have to enter a workshop as an apprentice – but could I do it? The workers' organizations did not tolerate apprentices of twenty-five years of age, and even less, apprentices who paid for their training. Adult apprentices would have meant that in times of industrial crisis workers would be taken on at low wages in the guise of apprentices; apprentices paying for their training would have robbed a worker of his job. I knew I would have been an excellent mechanic. And yet in the order of things there was no room for me either as a mechanic or as a mechanical engineer. That, road was closed, and I might as well accept it.

I might be a writer.

It had been the second ambition of my childhood. My school, the Escuela Pía, had published a children's magazine under the title *Madrileñitos*. When I was ten years old I was a contributor to every issue. They published my ingenuous stories and verses, all profoundly religious and moral. I had forgotten all but the two most important contributions: a biography of Saint Joseph of Calasanz, founder of the Order of the Escolapians, and a biography of Paul of

Tarsus, which earned me an edition of the Epistles to the Corinthians. I still had it at home.

When I was a clerk in the bank, at sixteen, I wanted to gatecrash the literary world. My colleague Alfredo Cabanillas and I encouraged each other to send our work, he his verses, I my prose, to every single literary competition organized by a number of weeklies. Neither of us ever won a prize, but they published some of his poems and two of my stories, naturally without payment. When the second of my short stories had appeared in the press, my neighbour in the old tenement house, Rafael, son of the cigarette maker, took me along to the Ateneo to introduce me to the great men of Spanish literature. Rafael was the barber of the Ateneo.

'If you've got your wits about you, you'll make your career here,' he said.

I found myself near the circle of the great intellectuals of the country, intimidated and shaken in my self-confidence in that atmosphere of ardent discussion. Somehow I was singled out by the man who bore with a swagger his self-chosen title of 'The Last Bohemian': Pedro de Répide.

He was round faced, with a big mane, a wide-brimmed soft hat, a thick scarf knotted round his neck, and the body of a farmer turned man-about-town, incessantly sucking his pipe which, at times, he filled with cigarette stubs. I felt it was an honour when he deigned to let me invite him to a glass of beer. One evening when I was in cash I suggested that we might go to Alvarez' at the corner of the Plaza de Santa Ana, a bar famous for its beer and its shellfish. He began to talk to me:

'So you want to become a writer? I'll give you a few tips. In Spain being a writer means to court starvation. The only way to earn money as a writer is to become a playwright or to produce pornography. Or rather, there is only one way to become a writer. Who's your favourite living author?'

'I don't really know. Benavente – Valle-Inclán – and a good many others too.'

'Never mind, you just choose the one you like best. Then you stick to him, flatter him, find a way of paying for a cup of coffee for him, but so that he is aware of it, and one fine day, when he's in good humour you read one of your things to him. But take care to wait until he knows who you are and that you always applaud whatever he says, even the most arrant nonsense. Then he'll give you an introduction to a newspaper and they'll print your stuff, without paying for it, of course. If you're lucky and if you really can write, you may get fifty pesetas for an article or a story in, let us say, ten or twelve years' time. It's more difficult to get a play accepted, but the technique is the same. At any rate, once you have selected your master you belong to him, unconditionally. If he's of the Right, you belong to the Right. If he's of the Left, you belong to the Left. It doesn't matter what you write. In this country you have to belong to one side or the other, right or wrong.'

He spoke well, but I resented his advice, just as I used to react against his work. Pedro de Répide had made his way in Spanish letters by specializing in the cynical short story. His tales of beggars, prostitutes, drunkards and débauchés were always built round himself as the hero who showed in his narrative that he could not only acclimatize himself to any surroundings, but also surpass them. I thought his explanation was malicious and libellous, and decided to acquire my own experiences.

In the lounge of the Ateneo grave gentlemen were discussing politics, science, and letters, but I quickly tired of playing the role of audience to discussions about Plato's political theory or the esoteric significance of Don Quixote. I possessed neither the necessary knowledge nor interest. The many literary groups gathering evening after evening in the cafés of Madrid attracted me more, and I started to explore them.

The most aristocratic circle was that of the Café de Castilla, presided over by Don Jacinto Benavente who was then at the pinnacle of his fame as a playwright. The Café de Castilla was a single room with cast-iron columns, red divans, and walls covered by mirrors and caricatures, in which no one could hide from anyone's sight, but had to see himself and others from innumerable angles through the manifold reflection of the mirrors.

One evening I went in, hesitating, clutching the red door curtain while I looked round the small room which seemed enormous to me in its reflected multiplication. Somebody waved to me from one of the tables: a young man whom I had met in the Ateneo. I joined him with all my aplomb recovered. Then I recognized Don Jacinto in the midst of a large party two tables away. He was half-reclining on the divan and looked smaller than ever; all I saw of his face was a cigar between a grey goatee and a huge bald forehead.

Don Jacinto was listening to the arguments of one of his circle who was expounding the weaknesses of an extremely successful comedy then on the Madrid stage. In support of each of his critical points he quoted a scene or a passage from one of Benavente's plays. As soon as the man had finished, amid murmurs of assent from the whole table, another started dissecting a second play, drawing a new set of comparisons with Benavente's plays. Don Jacinto stroked his little beard and listened. He looked profoundly bored. In the end he took his cigar from his mouth and said in a mellifluous voice:

'Quite so; we are all agreed, gentlemen, that I am a genius. But who is cashing in? All those others whom you have mentioned!'

'Ah, but Art . . .' somebody exclaimed, 'Art, sir, is a truly great thing. Money, on the other hand . . .'

'You have no reason to complain, Don Jacinto,' interrupted another. 'You always fill the theatre.'

'Oh, yes, I fill the theatre all right, but the theatre doesn't fill my pockets.'

And the conversation returned to the subject of Benavente's superlative prose. Don Jacinto listened and sucked his cigar.

The young man from the Ateneo nudged me and we left.

'You know,' he said, 'it's always the same story in there. The only thing you hear is frankincense for Don Jacinto. Of course, it's necessary to go there so that they get to know you, but if you want to learn something you must go to another place. Let's go to the Granja, Don Ramón is sure to be there.'

The Granja, a café with a low ceiling, its panelled walls and stout wooden pillars painted a light ochre, was overcrowded and its air fetid. Don Ramón del Valle-Inclán sat there as the centre of a gathering, to make room for which tables and chairs had been joined together so as to form a solid mass of marble, wood and people. When we entered Don Ramón was on his feet, leaning over the table, his big rabbinical beard fluttering like a pennant, his tortoise-shell glasses ceaselessly turning from one face to the other, to see whether anybody would dare to contradict him.

Nobody did dare to contradict Valle-Inclán. He waited for it when he had finished his peroration, but his whole circle broke into applause, seconded by many other people in the café. When they ceased Don Ramón banged his fist on the table:

'You're a pack of idiots!' and he sat down.

The public laughed heartily, as though the invective had been a stroke of genius. My companion said:

'That is Don Ramón's way. He would insult anybody, but always with so much charm . . .'

I felt, on the contrary, that he had done it in an overbearing and crude manner. But I went back to the Granja, fascinated, and took my place at the edge of Don Ramón's circle.

One evening I took the liberty of disagreeing with one of his statements which, like many he made, was a patent absurdity, only proffered to humiliate his hearers.

Don Ramón pounced on me, irate:

'So the young man thinks I am wrong?'

'I do not only believe you are wrong, sir, but also that you know it and that all these gentlemen here know it too.'

A murmur of disapproval rose around me. Don Ramón called for silence with a haughty gesture:

'Be quiet! Nobody asked your opinion.'

He began a dispute with me and I answered back, resentful of the disdain he showed towards all of us. But Don Ramón cut the discussion short:

'Well, now, young man, what's your profession? Do you write?'

'I would like to write.'

'Then why are you here? To learn how to write?'

'I might say, yes.'

'Then don't say it, and you'll avoid saying something idiotic. You may come here to drink coffee, preferably at the expense of somebody else, to speak evil of all the others and to ask for an introduction. But if you want to learn how to write, stay at home and study. And then you may begin to write – perhaps . . .

'Now you think I'm offending you, but you're wrong. I don't know you, but I have a better opinion of you than of many of those who are sitting here. And therefore I tell you, don't come to this kind of gathering. Stick to your work, and if you wish to write,

write. Here you won't reap any profit except perhaps a petty job in a newspaper office and the habit of swallowing insults.'

Alfredo Cabanillas took me to the old Fornos, a café frequented by toreros and by several sets of budding writers and artists. I thought they were behaving like irritated madmen. Many of them wore the traditional long hair, knotted scarf and broad-brimmed hat. They used to discuss the most recent movements in art and literature, at that time Dadaism, Futurism and Expressionism, and they recited pieces of verse and prose to each other, which I found impossible to follow.

Cabanillas played quite a role in these gatherings because he had just published a book of verse and had moreover paid for its publication himself, a unique event in this circle of hungry bohemians. His friends praised the book beyond measure, asked him for free copies and let him pay for their coffee. They all grew heated on hearing Cabanillas tell and re-tell his experiences.

First, he had sent his manuscript to one publisher after the other, only to get it back unread. He knew this for a fact because he had glued several pages together and they had come back as they had left him. When he had finished with the whole list of publishing firms, he decided to have the book printed at his own expense, that is to say, at the expense of his family. He had gone to one of the best printing and publishing firms, and the manager had given him a polite hearing.

'All right, we have no reason not to publish your book if you bear the expenses. Poetry, you say? What kind of poetry?'

'Modern poetry, of course.'

Cabanillas had launched forth with all the enthusiasm of his eighteen years: modern poetry, a revolution of poetic art, kindred to the new currents in French poetry, but in a purely Spanish sense.

'Well, then, it's revolutionary poetry, isn't it?'

'In a poetical sense, yes. As to revolutionary, I'm not an Anarchist, of course. It is romantic poetry in a modern form.'

'Well, well – and what are you?'

'I – I'm a bank clerk.'

'No, no. I don't mean that. I mean, what are your political ideas? You sound like one of those modern, advanced young men. That is so, isn't it?'

'Naturally, we must bring about a revolution in art and . . .'

'Yes, yes, I quite understand. I'm sorry, but ours is a serious firm. You are a new author. I quite understand that you want to pay for having our name on the title page when you publish your book, because the public know that we only touch serious stuff. I'm so sorry, but I'm afraid we cannot publish your work.'

Cabanillas visited other publishers. One of them was of the Left. Over his desk hung an engraving of an impressive woman with a Phrygian cap, symbolizing the Republic. But Cabanillas did not belong to the political Left; his poetry was not republican, nor even revolutionary, but simply lyrical with a slight modernistic flavour. The publisher was so sorry. He turned the book down, without even looking at it.

In the end Cabanillas had settled with a little firm which printed mainly handbills. He gained by the process, because he had to pay very little for the whole edition. Nobody bought the book, but he did not lose much money by it either. The critics took no notice of him; after all, the book had not even been printed by a serious firm and he did not belong to any of the political groups.

I began to think that Pedro de Répide had been right after all. Yet I was unable to practise wholesale adulation, and I had neither the time nor the money nor the temper to become one of the regular members of a literary set.

There existed a progressive cultural centre in Madrid, Giner de los Rios' *Institución Libre de Enseñanza*. From there and from his *Residencia de Estudiantes* issued a new generation of writers and artists: my own way of thinking might have fitted in there. But when I probed the chances of entry I was confronted with a new aristocracy hitherto unknown to me, an aristocracy of the Left. It was as expensive to get into those Institutes as to enter one of the luxury colleges of the Jesuits. There were free courses and lectures, but to follow them would have meant giving up the work I had to do for my living. I came to feel that the marvellous achievements of Giner de los Rios had a very serious defect, the basic defect of all Spanish education: the doors were closed to working people. Intellectuals of the highest standard might issue from there, as in fact they did, but all of them came from well-to-do families which could afford not only to give their sons a professional career, but also to let them study for this career in open challenge to the formidable organization of religious schooling.

There was no road for me there. I gave up writing for the time being.

And now the old problem had to be tackled anew. In the barracks I had started to write again. I felt both the urgent need and the gift of expression.

But could it give me a living? Perhaps, after years of hard work and submission to the rules of the game. Yet, it could not be a solution to the problem I would have to meet on my discharge.

Life does not consist of earning or not earning money; but I had to earn money in order to live. I would not be able to take up the fight against the hundred closed literary circles; I would not have money to invite people to have a drink on me, nor would I have time to follow café debates for nights on end. One of the things one can neither buy nor sell is one's self-esteem. But to stay on in the army would mean that I would lose my self-esteem for good. On the other hand, to take my discharge would mean misery. . . .

Above all, I had to think of my mother. I was responsible for her as long as she lived. It was my responsibility to make sure that she should not have to work anymore, neither washing in the river, nor washing dishes as a charwoman. And then I wanted to have a home and a family one day, to become a complete being through my wife. But to have this complement it was necessary to earn money; if you want a wife, a home and children, you must pay for them.

The barracks offered me the certainty of all that as long as I lived and even after my death. If I died, my mother, or my wife and children, would be saved from sheer poverty. The wife of a bank clerk has to face poverty the week after she has buried her husband.

But was it true that the barracks offered that security? Was it true that, come what might, I would always have my post and my pay and my family's bread assured?

The line you cast into the sea is never quite taut. You roll up its slack end and drop the little coiled heap beside you on the rocks.

One of my coils unfurled and the cord shot away, a snake striking to attack. The bell tied to its end tinkled madly. The line tautened and moaned, like the thick string of a violoncello, which rumbles and quivers plaintively when you pass a finger across it. An angry furrow crested with froth was tracing an arc in the quiet pool of the sea. A red-hot iron seemed to have plunged into the water.

I grasped the line and gave it a tug. A fierce tug answered from the other end, as though a runaway horse were tearing at the reins. The cord slipped from my hand and pulled furiously at the rock to which it was tied, tense and vibrating, trying to escape into the sea. I caught the line with both hands, squared myself against a boulder and hauled. The fish suddenly stopped tugging, the line went slack and I stumbled. Before I had regained my stance, the live thing on the hook out there had turned towards the open sea. The running cord scorched my hands and tore itself free once more, the angry whirlpool in the sea grew enormous. Better leave it. Better wait until the fish becomes tired, or the line breaks, or a bleeding piece of gum is left behind on the hook, or the rock topples and rolls into the water. I stood there watching the foaming trail, the quiver of the cord, and the jig of the little bell.

A fish fighting for its liberty is surely one of the most splendid beings in creation, yet no one of us is quite able to gauge its valour. There it is, a single smooth muscle gathering strength from the resistance of the water where the hardest blow of a man's fist comes to nothing, laden with the furious energy of a cornered wild boar or a cat attacked by a pack of dogs. A steel hook had dug itself deep into the curved jawbone. It would bring relief from that savage pain clawed into splitting flesh and crunching bone to slacken the cord, to cease struggling. Yet even the smallest fish twists and jumps, leaps out of the water or down into the deep, always pulling, ceaselessly pulling, at the price of maddening pain, only to get free.

I tried once more to haul in the line. The ferocious brain which animated the powerful muscle felt every movement of my hands through the wound in its flesh and rebelled against it in tireless fury. Time and again the line was torn out of my grip, leaving a damp, searing trail on my palms. At one of the pulls I managed to loop the cord once round the rock, shortening its length by something like two feet. For minutes the fish tugged at it in tearing rage; the line groaned so that I expected to see it snap at any moment. The fish seemed to be aware that it had been robbed of a few inches of freedom.

After more than an hour's battle I saw that I would never be able to overpower the beast. Two workers were just passing on the road behind me, with lunch packets in their hands and white blouses slung across their shoulders. They threw their blouses on the rocks and watched me with a supercilious air, slightly contemptuous of the lanky sergeant who wanted to fish and could not manage it. One of them started hauling in the line, then both of them, then I joined them and the three of us pulled together, panting and sweating, our arms and legs propped against the boulders. And thus we wound the line round the jutting rock in slowly growing loops.

'Whatever sort of a beast is this, in the Devil's name?' growled one of the men. The three of us rested for a while, staring at the churn of water and foam, now only some twenty metres from us. A sharp flick of the tail showed a long, blackish back mottled with silver.

The worker shouted, 'A moray – we'll never catch it!'

The moray is a kind of sea-eel, usually not more than a metre long and ten centimetres broad, with a squat head and powerful jaws bristling with triangular teeth. It fights and devours fish far bigger than itself, destroys fishing-nets and tackle and even attacks people, inflicting bites like the clean cut of an amputation. A moray's tail can break a man's arm hours after the head has been cut off. People on the coast are often reluctant to eat it, for it might have feasted on human flesh.

The moray on my hook looked about two metres long and as thick as a thigh.

One of the men went to a roadside tavern and came back with a boat-hook, accompanied by a couple of curious spectators. Between the lot of us we hauled in the cable until the moray was inside the well-like pool in front of the rocks. Incredibly enough it did not dash itself to pieces against the cliff walls. Even when we had it there at our feet we felt sure that the line would snap and the beast escape in the end. The man with the boat-hook tried to grapple the head, while we held him in a safe grip on the ledge of the cliff. Furiously, the fish turned against the new weapon and slashed at it. Then we saw that it could not close its jaws. The line passed freely from the red, bleeding hole of the throat through between the rows of teeth which tried in vain to shut on it.

The man finally pinned the hook into one of the eyes, and a stain like a swirl of mist floated on the water. The fish was now moving in spasmodic ripples. We all pulled. It fell on to the rock, contracting in mad rage, smearing the stone with viscous froth, staring at us out of its single eye, twisting on its whitish belly in search of prey. We took cover behind boulders and stoned it from there. We threw our stones so as to crush the hideous squat head, to kill it and to free ourselves from the sight of that hate-filled mask. A huge stone hit the head and turned it into a grey-white mass flecked with slime. The body jerked and then straightened.

Three of us carried it away. The two workers eagerly offered to go with me and my catch to the barracks. We would drink a bottle of wine there. Antonio, the canteen-keeper, would cut the fish into slices and fry them for us.

It weighed quite a hundred pounds and we had to walk at a slow pace, followed by a small crowd of lookers-on and urchins who touched the body of the moray with their fingers, as a daring deed. Something like a filthy rag hung where the head had been.

The body contracted in a spasm and jumped out of our hands, leaping in the road dust, a live mass of slime and mud. The man who had carried the tail end shouted a curse and doubled up. The tail had hit him in the ribs. He kicked the mass, which was rolling in the dust, and the headless body twisted and then stretched, suddenly motionless. We caught it up and walked on, smirched with sticky mud. It escaped us twice more. The boys shrieked and laughed. We must have been a dire sight, with mud dripping from our faces and hands, clutching at that mass of dirty slime which shuddered in spasms and made us stop at intervals.

When we reached the barracks we threw it into the horses' watering-trough, and it whipped the water as though in an electric discharge. The blind body hurled itself against the cement walls with all its undying strength.

Soldiers came running through the courtyard; Antonio, the canteen-keeper, came, looked and walked away to his canteen. He returned with a big knife for cutting ham. 'Catch hold of it, some of you, and put it here on the edge,' he said.

Twenty hands held the body, now clean and shining, against the edge of the trough. Antonio began to cut it into slices, which slipped back into the water, each with a drop of red blood in the centre, which slowly dissolved.

Antonio paid me thirty pesetas for it.

3. The Barracks

I learned about the races of Spain by dealing with the shipments of recuits.

It was the busiest time at HQ. First we would receive a list of the raw recruits detailed to the Engineers in Africa from all the recruitment centres in the country. Then the ships with what, in the language of the barracks, were called 'the sheep', began to arrive. The recruits came in groups of five hundred to a thousand, guided by a sergeant and a few corporals from the military region which sent them. The moment they reached port they were taken over by sergeants of the various units and sorted out according to their destination.

The ship moored, the gang-plank was fixed, and they began to stream out of the boat, mostly land workers and labourers from all parts of Spain. There were the Andalusians in their short, light jackets, white or khaki, often in shirt sleeves, their trousers held in place by string or a sash. Most of them were slim and straight, dark, sallow, gypsy-like, with black eyes opening in mingled apprehension and curiosity, talking quickly in a torrent of obscene swear words.

There were the men from the Castilian plains and sierras, taciturn, small, bony, tanned by sun, wind, frost and snow, the legs of their corduroy trousers fastened with twine over their bulging pants, which in their turn were tied with tape over thick, blue or red, home-knitted socks. Every now and again the whole formation would be upset because a man's tape ends had come untied.

Basques, Gallegos and Asturians usually came in a mixed lot on the same ship, and their discrepancies were astounding. The huge Basques, in blue blouses, with the inevitable beret on the crown of their small heads, were serious and silent, and if they spoke in that incomprehensible language of theirs, they measured their words. You felt the strength of their individual being and of their self-contained culture. The Gallegos came mostly from poor, forlorn villages; they used to be incredibly dirty, often barefoot, and they faced this new affliction, worse than the familiar penury at home, with a bovine resignation. The Asturians from the mountains were strong and agile, great gluttons and bawdy merrymakers, and they mocked at the wretchedness of the people from Galicia, as well as at the gravity of the Basques.

Then there arrived pot-bellied, old transatlantic steamers with a load of recruits from the Mediterranean provinces, from Catalonia, parts of Aragon, Valencia and Alicante. The mountain people from Aragon and northern Catalonia differed in language, but they were much alike, primitive, harsh, and almost savage. The Catalans from the ports, in contact with all the Mediterranean civilization, were a world apart from their own countrymen of the mountains. The people of the Levante, in black blouses and laced *alpargatas*, rather handsome, but lymphatic and flabby with promise of an early paunch, were a group by themselves.

And it seemed to me that a Madrileño is less of a stranger to the New Yorker than a Basque is to a Gallego, with their villages a bare hundred miles apart.

Along the motley stream of recruits the sergeants began to shout:

'Regiment of Ceuta! Regiment of Africa! Chasseurs! Commissariat! Engineers! . . .'

Some of the newcomers would catch the meaning of the shouts at once and range themselves in a double file beside their sergeant. Yet the great majority were thoroughly confused, after having seen strange cities and made their first sea journey, shaken by seasickness and with the fear of the army in their bones. They drifted hither and thither, helpless and bewildered, so that we had to pull them by their sleeve and round them up, one by one, like frightened sheep.

'Hallo, lad, where do you belong?'

The doltish eyes looked at you filled with fear.

'I don't know.'

'What are you, infantry – or cavalry – or what?'

'I don't know. They told me I'd be artillery. I don't know.'

You shouted for the artillery sergeant: 'You there, here's another one of yours.'

Thus we went on shunting the men about until nobody was left on the mole but the three or four of the dumbest, out of whom we had patiently to drag their own name and the name of their village, so as to be able to find them in our lists. In the end, one or two would always be missing. We would find them in a dark corner of the ship, dozing or monotonously moaning, tumbled in their own filth.

The Commandant of Ceuta, General Alvarez del Manzano, used to come down to the mole whenever big troopships from Catalonia or the North arrived. Heavy and paternal, he liked to speak to the most scared-looking recuits and to give them gentle little pats on the back. One day he tackled a peasant from Galicia, whom we had had to track down in the remotest corner of the ship and to drag out, frightened, like a whipped dog.

'What's your name, my boy?'

'Juan – Juan.'

'All right. And where do you come from?' And the General patted his shoulder.

The peasant swung round like a startled beast:

'Don't touch me, God damn you!'

'Why, what's the matter with you, my boy?'

'You won't touch me. I've sworn by this' – he kissed his crossed thumbs – 'to bash in the head of the first whoreson sergeant who lays hands on me!'

'But my man, this isn't hitting you. Nobody will hit you here.'

'Nobody, huh? And all the kicks they gave my father and grandfather? I told them. I said if they lay hands on me I'll kill someone.'

'Well, listen: I'm the General here. If anyone hits you, just come and tell me about it.'

'Pooh – the General! That's a good joke, that is. D'you think I'm one of those silly sheep?'

When we had taken them to barracks, we let them come into the office one by one to make entries in our files.

'What's your name?'

'My name? The Rabbit.'

'Yes, that's all right for your village. They call you the Rabbit there, don't they?'

'Of course. Everyone's got a name. My grandmother had twenty children and they called her the Doe, and then they called our whole family the Rabbits. And that's our name now.'

'All right, but you've got a Christian name as well, haven't you? Antonio, or Juan, or Pedro?'

'Yes, sir, Antonio.'

'And then you'll have a surname as well, Perez or Fernandez?'

'Yes, sir, Martinez.'

'There, we've got it. Nobody will call you the Rabbit here. Here you're Antonio Martinez, and when they sing out "Antonio Martinez" at roll call, you must answer, "Present". Do you understand? You're called Antonio Martinez. And your father and mother?'

'They're all right, thank you, sir. And how's your family?'

When they had been listed they were given their first meal in barracks. The Engineers were privileged; our kitchen provided copious and substantial meals. Many of the recruits had never eaten so well in their lives.

One day a recruit who came straight from one of the poorest districts in the province of Cáceres refused to eat.

'Why don't you eat?' I asked him.

'I won't touch mess food.'

'Why not?' I knew well that deep-rooted resistance which had its origins in the stories the men had heard about the food in Spanish barracks, food, which until the year after the Great War, had indeed been sickening refuse.

'Because it's filthy.'

'Now, look here, you must eat something. Take the stuff and try it. If you don't like it you can always throw it away. But you must take your share and eat at least something of it. In barracks you can't just say: "I don't want to".'

The recruit filled his mess tin. That day the soldiers had rice boiled with scraps of mutton. He tasted it, and his face was transfigured.

'You like it?'

'Do I! I've never eaten anything like it before.'

'All right, if you want more, go to the cauldron there, and they'll fill your tin. Eat as much as you like.'

After the meal the recruits walked about the courtyard waiting to be called to the depot to be given their clothing and equipment. My recruit drifted nearer to me, timid but determined. It was so obvious that he wanted to speak to me that I called him:

'Do you want something?'

He whipped his greasy cap from his head and twisted it round and round in his hands.

'Yes, sir . . . I wanted to ask whether we'll always get a meal like that here.'

'Yes, you will, and sometimes better meals than today. On Sundays they often give you cutlets and fried potatoes. In the evenings, beans cooked with pigs' trotters. And at dinner, mostly a *cocido* with meat and sausage and soup paste. You'll see.'

'You're pulling my leg, sir.'

'Oh, no, my boy, you'll see for yourself.'

The cap was gyrating more quickly in his hands. He stood there, chin on his chest, thinking strenuously. Suddenly, he straightened himself and said:

'Well, if we get meals like that I won't ever leave.'

'What kind of meals did you get in your village?'

'Well, it was all right in the summer because we had tomatoes and lettuce and onions. The autumn was best, then we had work in the oak woods knocking down the acorns for the pigs; they let us eat as many of them as we wanted to. But in winter we hadn't anything, you see. Just a piece of hard bread with garlic or a dry onion.'

'But didn't you get any *cocido*?'

'No, sir, never. When we'd earned something picking acorns, mother cooked stew for supper with a piece of bacon in it. But when we were out of work. . . . Well, I'll tell you the truth, we *did* lay snares for rabbits and sometimes we caught one, and we stole acorns from the pigs. But it was risky. If the Civil Guard caught you they beat you up. They beat me up twice, but they didn't mark me. The son of Mother Curra was crippled for life. The doctor in Cáceres said they'd broken one of his ribs and it got stuck to another rib and now he can't get straightened out ever. He's lucky, though. They haven't called him up. Well – perhaps not so lucky. If he knew how they fed us here, as you say, he would join up like a streak, crooked back and all.'

The hunger of so many of the recruits was what impressed me most deeply, but next to it their illiteracy. Among the men of some regions over 80 per cent were completely illiterate. Of the remaining 20 per cent, some were able to read and write – badly though – but many more just managed to decipher print letter by letter and to draw the letters of their own signature. The completely illiterate men were usually sent to the Chasseurs and the remainder carefully sifted to find men for special duties. We were lucky if, in a group of four hundred recruits sent in replacement of discharged soldiers, we found twenty who could enter the signalling school at once to be taught morse, and fifty more who could be trained for signalling after an intensive course in reading and writing. We would hardly ever discover more than two or three men qualified for office work, but we usually found a certain number of skilled workers who could be detailed to the various units as barbers, shoemakers, masons, carpenters and blacksmiths. There was always an acute shortage of personnel for any service requiring more than the most elementary schooling.

This state of affairs involved me in difficulties not very long after my appointment to the regimental office.

In 1922 radio telegraphy was still in its heroic stage. In a small room of the pavilion opposite our barracks there was a Marconi transmitter of the early type, with an oscillator between points, a helmet with earphones for reception by sound, and a carbon filament lamp for reception by sight. Listening, you would occasionally receive an electric shock in your ear. This station was run by a sergeant, two corporals, and a number of soldiers who had been trained in transmitting and receiving morse by ear. The only person, however, who understood anything of the installation was the captain of the Telecommunications Company.

During Captain Sancho's brief visits to our office and in our occasional conversations, I had become aware of a current of mutual sympathy. Once he came to Ceuta to carry out repairs in the radio station, and I hinted that I would like to see it. He invited me to go with him. We began to discuss the installation, but as soon as he saw that I was not completely ignorant of its problems, he plied me with questions. We were soon enmeshed in a technical conversation. In the end he asked:

'Do you know morse?'

'No, sir.'

'What a pity. But after all, you would learn it in a fortnight. I'll speak to Don José. I want to have you here with me.'

'I don't think the transfer would be at all easy.'

'We'll see. I need people who understand about these things, and they simply don't exist. But clerks for office work are found quite easily.'

Captain Sancho spoke to Don José. He met with a blank refusal. Shortly afterwards the Captain took me along to the Colonel's office. The Colonel was a kindly old man who had attained his post exclusively through the merits of seniority.

Captain Sancho plunged straight into the question. 'Sir, this is the sergeant I spoke to you about. You realize the importance of the station. I've a few men under my command who can transmit morse, but they don't understand the least thing about the set. You know yourself that every time something goes wrong I'm forced to come down to Ceuta, which means leaving the Company and the field stations alone. And while we're engaged in operations this station here is out of order for days the moment anything happens to the apparatus.'

'*Caramba* – you didn't tell me it was Barea you were thinking of! Have you spoken to Major Tabasco?'

'Why yes, sir, but he doesn't agree, otherwise I wouldn't have bothered you.'

The old man turned livid:

'That's to say, if the Major had agreed to your suggestion, it would not have been necessary to tell me anything? You gentlemen have got into the habit of doing whatever pleases you, without reckoning with the CO. That has got to end.'

'Sir . . .?'

'I beg your pardon. I've not yet finished my say and I don't like being interrupted.'

He pushed the bell button and told the orderly to call in the Major.

'I believe you know what the Captain wants. What is your opinion?'

The Major hedged: 'My opinion? It's up to Barea. If he wants to leave . . .'

And so I found myself between the three of them. Captain Sancho gave me a look and said, smiling:

'What do you say about it, Barea?'

'I – I'll stay in this office, sir.'

Captain Sancho walked up to me, took my hand and shook it:

'I understand. You're clever. I assume you won't be so dumb as to stay on in barracks when your term is over.' He stood at rigid attention in front of the Colonel: 'Any orders, sir?' He swung round and stood at attention in front of the Major: 'Any orders for me, sir?'

The Colonel stiffened behind his desk and his face grew apoplectic. 'What does this attitude of yours imply?'

'Nothing, sir. We carry the insignia of rank on our sleeves, but we carry the insignia of talent somewhere else. The former is visible and commands respect by complusion, the latter is invisible and earns respect by conviction alone.'

'I don't understand all this rhetoric.'

'Quite so, sir, and I hardly think I ought to make it any clearer. You place before the sergeant the alternative of making enemies either of you both or of me, but you don't give him a chance to choose what he thinks best. He's intelligent, but after all he is only a sergeant and naturally he prefers making an enemy of me. Only, I don't take it amiss. I shook his hand because I understand his position, and for the same reason I told him that I hoped he would continue to be intelligent and not stay in this place for good.'

'You'll oblige me by withdrawing. This is an impertinence.'

The Captain[1] left the room and I was left there, face to face with the two lords and masters of the regiment. The Colonel scratched his white beard.

'So, so. A nice scene. Very nice indeed. How is it that you've applied for a transfer?'

'I haven't applied for any transfer, sir.' I explained how events had developed. The Colonel said to the Major:

'It's always the same story. That man steals the best boys from us because Telecommunications is a technical unit.'

---

[1] Years after this scene, Captain Sancho became one of the victims of the fascist-reactionary movement in Spain. His name belongs to the history of the Spanish Republic, as one of its heroes. – Author's note.

'I can understand that he wants to get the men with the best education, but the devil take it, in this case it was the sergeant of the Regimental Office!'

'Quite my own opinion! Never mind, the affair is closed now.'

The Major beat a retreat and I followed. Suddenly the Colonel called out:

'Just wait a moment, sergeant.'

When he was alone with me the Colonel dropped his stern rigidity.

'So you know something about radio telegraphy?'

'Not much, sir, but something.'

'And so you would have liked to be on duty at the station, eh?'

He said it with so fatherly a smile that I felt I had to tell the truth.

'Well, yes, sir – frankly I'd prefer it to the office.'

He changed at once to fury:

'You're a disgraceful lot, all of you. Here we pull you out of the front line, offer you a post which means safety for your whole future, and this is how you reward us! Out of my sight – quick!'

When the recruits were fully equipped, they were distributed among the companies attached to Ceuta or Tetuan, for a few months' training. The clash between the veteran soldiers and the newcomers was always violent, all the more so since the veterans had the same background as the newcomers. Their barrack life of one, two, or three years had not made them less primitive, but only helped to build up their defences against their surroundings and often to bring out their worst qualities.

There were the brutal but ageless jokes of initiation. During one of the first nights in our barracks the inspecting corporal would wake up each of the recruits, with a list in his hand.

'You there – get up.'

The recruit, in his first sleep of exhaustion after the drill under the African sun, would open bewildered eyes.

'What's your name?'

'Juan Perez.'

The corporal would search the list.

'You've forgotten to make water before going to bed. Quick, get out and make water!'

He would force fifty recruits to go down to the other end of the courtyard in their pants. A corporal of the First Company of Sappers had invented the procedure and it had become a tradition. So was the schoolboy practice of putting a pail of water on the equipment chest at the head of the bed, placed so that the man would bring the water down on himself as soon as he lay down. Inevitably, he would play the same trick on the dumbest among the next batch of newcomers. But these were the innocent jokes.

Normally, the training period lasted four or five months. Yet in that particular year men were needed in the front line. The recruits were given a summary training and sent out to the field, wedged in between the experienced soldiers. And that mass of illiterate peasants commanded by irresponsible officers was the backbone of Spain's Moroccan field armies. So-called expeditionary regiments had been sent over from the Peninsula, seen off with patriotic speeches and music, and landed in the three zones of Morocco to the accompaniment of the same speeches and the same music. They had filled the front pages and the society columns of all the papers; sons of good families were among the ordinary rankers, and sons of the noblest families of the realm among the "auxiliary officers". Yet those units were nothing but a liability; the stories about them which reached HQ were legion.

An artillery regiment sent over from the Canary Islands became famous for its marksmanship: whenever our advanced posts set up their signals to inform the range finders of their position, the batteries from the Canaries showered their shells on the signals with unfailing mastery. An infantry regiment from Madrid had scattered in wild disorder in the middle of an operation, leaving a company of the *Tercio* exposed; that night men of the *Tercio* and of the Madrid regiment fought with daggers against each other in a canteen on the beach of Tiguisas.

The soldiers who had bought themselves out originally and now had been called up demanded privileges over the ordinary soldiers of the line. This led to general discontent, not only among the men, but also among the officers. Among the arrivals were young men with letters of recommendation from deputies, bishops, or even cardinals. In the rooms where the regimental colours were kept officers competed in feasting the son of some grandee or other, who, in acknowledgement of favours received – they let him pay for the champagne but saved him from going to the front – would send his father a list of candidates for promotion for merit in battle, or at least for a decoration.

The old African campaigners had the worst of it. They felt it, and resented it. They knew that, since the arrival of the reinforcements, their own share of work, of forced marches and dangerous operations had increased. Even the *Tercio* showed signs of insubordination.

One day a company of the *Tercio* refused to eat the rotten food of their mess. The first man in the queue shouted something like:

'Those sons of bitches of the Expeditionary get chicken and champagne in the officers' mess, while we have to eat stinking muck.'

He took the mess tin and shoved it back. The officer on duty shot him clean through the head. The next man refused the filled tin. The officer shot him. The third wavered, carried his mess tin away from the field kitchen and smashed it on the ground. The officer shot him. The others ate their portions.

A few days later three officers of that Company were killed in action at Akarrat, shot in the back.

Yet this kind of violent reaction was rare. Generally, the men adopted an attitude of passive resistance, evasion and listlessness, which made the handling of the forces in the field most difficult. When the officers tried to tighten up the discipline, matters only grew worse. The recruits suffered more than all the others through the violence from above and through the violence of their own comrades, which cowed them for good or else turned them into undisciplined, restless soldiers prone to any kind of rebellion.

These soldiers, the class of 1900, the echo of whose training I heard in Ceuta at that time, were to bear the whole brunt of the withdrawal of 1924, a disaster infinitely greater than the disaster of Melilla in 1921.

The attacks of the rebel Moors were growing in intensity. This was the period of Abd-el-Krim's victories; even the zone of Ceuta was under the shadow of his threat. All men fit for field service were at the front, with the exception of the 'indispensable services'. Not more than thirty of us remained stationed in Ceuta. At night the

Engineers' barracks were almost empty. During the day a corporal mounted guard with four men; by night, one of the four sergeants took over the command of the guard and slept in the guardroom. The Major lived in a little house a hundred yards from the barracks, so that it was easy to call him in when necessity arose. All those not on guard duty had passes which allowed them to be out at night or even to sleep elsewhere. Other regiments had similar arrangements. Thus we all knew each other and each other's whereabouts. The barracks with their regular inmates formed a single clan with set sympathies and antipathies. When a company came from field operations to rest for a week in the garrison, we saw little of them. The unit was then lodged in one of the big halls, the officers disappeared immediately, the sergeants followed suit, and we closed both our eyes to the doings of the men. They wallowed for a week in their short-lived freedom and sought amusement as best they could. This little world of ours seemed settled in its grooves, even while the fighting was going on not too far from us.

It was an upheaval when our Colonel reached the age limit and was pensioned off. The new Colonel came from the 30th Sappers Regiment of Valencia. Immediately on setting foot on land, he turned up at the barracks, at the unusual hour of half past nine in the morning.

At the gate he was met by the corporal on mess duty, a short fat young man, his uniform greasy from kitchen work, and by two equally untidy soldiers.

'Where is the officer on guard?' bellowed the new Colonel.

'There is no officer on guard, sir.'

'What, no officer? Fetch him at once. How is it that you're all so dirty? And why are there only two men? Where are the other men on guard? In the canteen, I suppose, what!'

'Sir, we're alone . . .'

'Shut up. You're all under arrest. Wait, one of you will come with me.'

The corporal took him to the office. There I was, alone, working at some accounts.

'You, what are you doing here?'

'I'm the sergeant in the regimental office, sir.'

'I suppose you're something because otherwise you wouldn't be here. I'm not a fool. Where is the senior Major?'

'I think in his house, sir. He usually comes at eleven.'

'And there's no officer here?'

'No, sir.'

'When the Major arrives send him to me immediately. How does your coat come to be unbuttoned?'

'Because I was alone here, sir. And it is so hot here that most of us work in shirt sleeves.'

'Well, that won't happen again. You're under arrest. That will teach you how to present yourself to your superior.'

When the Major came he had an interview with the new Colonel behind closed doors, but all of us, down to the office orderlies, found a stragetical position for eavesdropping. The site of the Colonel's room made it easy. And the Colonel roared:

'This is a disgrace! No officer on guard, a filthy-looking corporal and two even filthier soldiers at the gate! Not a single officer on the premises! And you asleep, what! All this must finish. Do you understand?'

There was a pause; it was impossible to catch the Major's reply. Then came another bellow:

'I see. Here you're all accustomed to grab as much as you can, what! That's got to end. From today onwards all accounts will go through my hands. And I don't want to see any more dirty soldiers!'

The Major came out of the room with purple ears. By afternoon, nearly everybody in the barracks was under arrest.

That night the First Sappers Company arrived, sent to garrison after a year in the field. Probably not one of the men realized that there was a new CO, for an hour after their arrival they were scattered all over the taverns and brothels of the town. I went to town for supper and returned to the barracks at eleven, to take over the night guard. But I arrived at five minutes past eleven. The corporal on stable duty met me:

'Nothing to report. The only thing is that Captain Jimenez' – the officer in command of the First Company of Sappers – 'is in the officers' room and you have to present yourself to him.'

There was nothing unusual in the fact that the Captain was in the officers' room; it often served as headquarters for officers passing through Ceuta, since there were three dormitories and a bathroom behind it. It was also quite normal for a strange officer to call in the

sergeant on guard and ask him about something or other. I knocked
and entered.

'At your orders, sir.'

'Do you know the time?'

'Five minutes past eleven, sir.'

'Be quiet. If a superior speaks to you, you have to keep quiet.
What time of day is this for a sergeant to come in? The sergeants
must be here at eleven sharp. You're under arrest.'

'But . . .'

'Shut up, I told you. And be off with you.'

'Sir . . .'

'Shut up!' He jumped up from his chair like a man possessed and
seemed about to pounce on me. I lost my self-control.

'You shut up. Here it's I who am in command of the guard. And
while I'm in command I won't allow such treatment.'

The absurdity of the situation must have paralyzed him. He sat
down again.

'So you're in command of the guard? Let's sort that out. Then
you're in command of the guard like myself, without knowing it.
Where have you come from just now?'

'From my supper. I've a pass for sleeping out of barracks – all of
us sergeants in barracks take turns at guard duty on certain nights,
from eleven onwards.'

'I understand less and less . . . All right. You're under arrest.
Take over the guard and tomorrow we'll clear up the muddle. By the
way, I'd forgotten to tell you: I'm Captain in command of the
guard.'

That night all four of us sergeants were put under arrest; there
followed all the men of the First Sappers Company with the exception of about a dozen, each being put under arrest on his belated
arrival in barracks; and finally all those on special duty in barracks.
Reveille was sounded at seven in the morning. At five minutes to
seven the Colonel appeared. Fortunately I was awake, because the
sergeant on guard had to supervise the distribution of the morning
coffee and to prepare the report for the Command to be submitted at
eight. Captain Jimenez was lying fast asleep on his bed, stark naked,
having forgotten all about the guard duty. To sleep in a real bed with
a real mattress after a year in the front line must have been

irresistible. I had no time to wake him, and thus had to report to the Colonel myself.

'Where is the Captain on guard?'

'I think he's asleep, sir.'

The Colonel hurtled himself into the officers' room. Five minutes later he came out with the Captain whose face was red from sleep and who was fumbling at his buttons. The signal for breakfast sounded, but the only persons to appear were a dozen soldiers. The Colonel emitted another of his roars:

'Where are all those rascals? Asleep, what! That's why I've come. This is a disgrace.' He marched towards one of the dormitories, the Captain behind him, and I following them. It was empty. The Colonel stood there in the middle of the huge room, staring bewildered at the heaps of equipment on the beds.

'Where are all those men?'

The Captain swallowed.

'Under arrest, sir. In quod.'

The explanation followed. When the Captain had finished, the Colonel put him under arrest as well. We sergeants decided to stay in our room under arrest and not go to our various offices, where work was waiting. They came to fetch us later in the morning. Our arrest was called off. Yet from that morning there was an open war between the Colonel and the Regiment. The most important share in the battle fell upon the senior Major and myself. The rigour of military discipline may make a subaltern's life unbearable, but the same rigour, applied by a whole regiment, can make the Colonel's life a misery. Occasionally I enjoyed that warfare.

But I learned another lesson. I knew the limits of security in barracks. A sergeant was just a sergeant. The troubled liver of any officer might turn him into an ordinary ranker from one day to the next, after three or after twenty years of service.

4. Dictator in the Making

My friend Sanchiz had come back to the Ceuta office of the Legion and took me once again to the tavern of the Licentiate. I went along with him, struggling against my ingrown aversion, but my nightmare was laid. The entrance had lost its colour of a bleeding gash and was painted a clear pink. Instead of the oil lamps hanging from their hooks there was plain electric light; the red walls were now a deep cream and the bar table was just like that of thousands of taverns in Spain, an oak slab with taps and a zinc running board. The Licentiate himself looked a prosperous tradesman in his green-and-black striped apron.

The main customers were still soldiers of the *Tercio* and prostitutes, but the gallows-birds and the old hags with the markings of syphilis and scab on their faces had disappeared. Men from other units entered freely to drink a bottle of wine and to eat dried tunny. The fish were still hanging from the big cross beam over the bar table, but now the beam was clean, the tunny no longer tasted of oily soot.

'My word, it has changed,' I said to Sanchiz.

'Nothing changes things so much as having money. When *El Licenciado* started here with his few old packing cases and his vitriolic wine, he hadn't a bean. The only thing he had was the courage to set up a tavern for the *Tercio*, when no one in Ceuta wanted to sell us so much as a glass of wine. He's made a lot of money by now, and he picks his customers. Just wait, in a couple of years he'll set up a modern bar in this place and stand as town councillor.'

Sanchiz paused and looked moody.

'Do you know that of all of us who formed the First Standard of the *Tercio* there's almost nobody left? The Betrothed of Death – do you remember? – have married. I'm one of the very few who have not yet met the Bride, and it seems to me that I'll have to wait a long time yet. It's a pity.'

'Don't think about it. You'll die like all of us when your hour has come, and you won't change it, even if you have got it into your obstinate head that you want to kill yourself or to get somebody to kill you. Do tell me instead what you've been doing with yourself all the time.'

'I've changed a lot, my boy. D'you know that it's a year since we met in Beni-Aros? In that year I've seen more than in all the thirty-eight years of my life. I've gone white.' He pulled off his cap, and I saw that his fair hair had turned silver.

'All right then, tell me about it.'

But on that day Sanchiz did not feel like talking of the war and the *Tercio*. He talked ramblingly of the events which had driven him to Morocco when he was thirty-six years old, a man who had never been a soldier and who seemed predestined to work in an office all his life.

Sanchiz came of a wealthy, middle-class family. His parents had given him a solid education; he had studied for a commercial career at a time when such studies seemed a novel and preposterous thing in Spain, and he had also obtained the title of lawyer. Before he was thirty he had become the manager of the Spanish branch of a big American manufacturing firm. Then he married. It was a perfect marriage. After a year the woman expected a child, but it was never born. She had to be operated on and became unfit to conceive any more children. Sanchiz resigned himself to their childlessness and devoted his whole energy to making his wife happy. He loved her blindly. After a few years she began to languish. The physical sensitiveness caused by the operation sharpened. It was at that stage that I came to know Sanchiz. He was taking her from one specialist to the other, but she was only getting worse. Then the doctors passed sentence: they could no longer live together as man and wife. She had cancer in the matrix. An operation was possible, but the doctors were extremely pessimistic about it. The invalid refused to be operated on.

I saw something of what happened to Sanchiz then. For months the physical contact which to him was both need and happiness had hurt the woman he loved and had thus turned into intimate torture for him. And then even that was past. He, who was a healthy, normal male, lived close to his wife whom he desired ceaselessly and hopelessly. He tried to escape from the bodily strain by going with other women, but it was impossible for him. He loved her. Then he started to drink. Her illness ate up his savings. His drunkenness lost him his job. After a period of acute poverty Sanchiz found employment in an office as an accountant at two hundred pesetas a month. What were two hundred pesetas to him who had a sick wife in need of daily morphine injections?

When his wife died I went to see Sanchiz in his flat. She has died wrapped in an old blanket, on a spring mattress barely covered with straw-filled sacking. He had neither furniture nor clothes. All had gone to the pawnshops.

After they carried away the dead body Sanchiz locked the door of his flat and gave the key to the concierge. He never came back. The few who knew him at all thought he had committed suicide. Yet he had not been able to bring himself to it. He wandered round Madrid, begging for a pittance, and slept on the benches in the avenues. When the Foreign Legion was formed he enlisted at once.

The age limit set by the *Tercio* was far too low for Sanchiz, but he passed for younger. He was fair, with milk-white skin, fresh, rosy cheeks and a scanty beard, a type rarely found in Spain. He met with no difficulty in joining. The Legion did not insist on papers or even on the names of its recruits.

He joined so as to be killed. But when the Legion's offices were set up he was picked out from the ranks and sent there. The risk of the front line had eluded him. He got drunk and disorderly, in an effort to be kicked out of office. But his superiors had grown fond of him, and all they did was to put him under arrest in barracks for days on end.

He tried to provoke the violence of the worst gangsters of the First Standard. But in a place where brawls were often decided by a bullet or the knife, the men simply grinned at Sanchiz and bought him a bottle of wine to get rid of his blues.

Finally, he succeeded in being sent to the front for two months as instructor to the South American Standard. That was meant as a punishment. After the first engagements, the disaster of Melilla intervened. Sanchiz was sent to Melilla. There were companies of the *Tercio* of which not a single man escaped unscathed. More than half their number were killed. Sanchiz did not receive a scratch.

And then he was called back to office work.

We saw much of each other. Whenever Sanchiz came to think of his own history he would drink himself unconscious. When he came out of his drunken fit he was repentant. Then he used to send for me, or come and fetch me for a walk. We would stroll along the West Mole to its farthest end, two miles away from the town, and sit down among the rocks facing the sea.

'We got fifty new recruits today,' he said one evening. 'They've no idea what they've bargained for. These people don't come for the same reasons as the old gang. They just come because they want to show off.'

He threw flat stones into the sea and watched them ricocheting.

'You know, barbarism is surely one of the most contagious things in life. When the First Standard went to Melilla, we attuned ourselves to the bestiality of the Moors. They cut off the genitals of Spanish soldiers and stuffed them into their dead mouths and left the corpses rotting in the sun. You've seen it yourself. Then we cut off the heads of the Moors and put them on the parapet of our position in the mornings. Well, you've seen that too. Anyhow, that's what the *Tercio* was like from the beginning. And there is no remedy. But I don't know whether you've seen that we've got a new form of enlistment for the Legion now. People sign on just for the period of the reconquest of Morocco. They're different from us. Hundreds of them have come already, many of them from good families, educated men with university degrees. There was a big clash between them and us old campaigners, and some couldn't stick it out. But most of them are staying on, and do you know, they're more savage than any of us.'

'I believe it depends mostly on the officers.'

'Yes, of course, it all depends on the officers. But don't you see, the same thing happened to the officers as happened to us. I remember perfectly well that when the *Tercio* was organized, our officers were just like any other officers, with the only difference that they'd gambled away the funds of their company and had no choice but to join the *Tercio*, or else that they were really brave and wanted to get promotion by risking their skins. But then they had to tackle the First Standard – you remember, the first thing we did in Ceuta was to bump off three or four people, and then they had to send us posthaste to Riffien! – and the officers changed at once.

'I believe that at bottom it was only fear. They were afraid of us. But they were in command, and most of us hadn't even a name to ourselves. They imposed the brutal discipline we've got now. If a man refused to obey an order he got two bullets in his head. If a man overstepped his rights – a knapsack filled with sand and two hours' running in the noon sun. What I mean to say is, we infected one another, and by now the officers have become savage barbarians, not only against us, but against everything and everybody. Of the First Standard there's not a single officer left unhurt. At least, Major Franco is the only one who got through it without a hole in his skin.'

'Tell me about him. I've heard a lot of stories. For instance, is it true that Millán Astray hates him?'

'Of course. Listen, Millán Astray is a braggart. I've seen it for myself by now. When he starts shouting, "To me, my brave lions!" or something of that kind, we can be sure that we'll soon be in the thick of a fight. We march forward in an avalanche while he makes his horse caracole and turns round to the General Staff: "How do you like my boys?" Of course, the General Staff and the Generals are never at the head of the troops when we make a real attack. And so nobody sees through his tricks. He's got the fame of a hero and no one will take it away from him. The only man who could do it is Franco. Only that's a bit difficult to explain.'

He began to throw stones into the sea again, and became engrossed in the game until I urged him:

'Leave that and go on with your story.'

'You see, Franco . . . No, look. The *Tercio*'s rather like being in a penitentiary. The most courageous brute is the master of the jail. And something of this sort has happened to that man. He's hated, just as the convicts hate the bravest killer in their jail, and he's obeyed and respected – he imposes himself on all the others – just as the big killer imposes himself on the whole jail. You know how many officers of the Legion have been killed by a shot in the back during an attack. Now, there are many who would wish to shoot Franco in the back, but not one of them has the courage to do it. They're afraid that he might turn his head and see them just when they have taken aim at him.'

'But surely it is the same story with Millán Astray.'

'Oh, no. One couldn't take a pot-shot at Millán Astray, he takes too good care of himself. But it wouldn't be difficult to fire at Franco. He takes the lead in an advance, and—well, if somebody's got guts, you just have to admit it. I've seen him walk upright in front of all the others, while they hardly dared to lift their heads from the ground, the bullets fell so thick. And who would shoot him in the back then? You just stay there with your mouth open, half-hoping that the Moors'll get him at any moment, and half-afraid of it, because if they did, you would run away. There's another thing too: he's much more intelligent than Millán Astray. He knows what he's after. And that's another reason why Millán Astray can't stand him.'

'And how did he behave in Melilla?'

'Franco? Believe me, it's sticky going with Franco. You'll get whatever's due to you, and he knows where he's taking you, but as to the treatment you get . . . He simply looks blankly at a fellow, with very big and very serious eyes, and says: "Execute him", and walks away, just like that. I've seen murderers go white in the face because Franco had looked at them out of the corner of his eye. And he's fussy! God save you if anything's missing from your equipment, or if your rifle isn't clean, or you've been lazy. You know, that man's not quite human and he hasn't got any nerves. And then, he's quite isolated. I believe all the officers detest him because he treats them just as he treats us and isn't friends with any of them. They go on the loose and get drunk – I ask you, what else should they do after two months in the firing line? – and he stays alone in the tent or in barracks, just like one of those old clerks who simply must go to the office, even on Sundays. It's difficult to make him out and it's funny because he's still so young.'

In the year 1922, events developed quickly in Morocco and in Spain. More than 60,000 men had been sent over from the Peninsula under the title of reinforcements, but the disorder and disorganization among these troops was such that commanding officers with any experience in the African campaign refused to employ them anywhere but in the rear. The discontent spread. In Spain the public protest against the disaster of Annual and the demand for an investigation into the responsibility for it had first been centred on the King and on the dead General Silvestre; now they became focused on the High Commissioner for Morocco, General Berenguer. In the zone of Melilla, nearly all the territory lost to the Moors in the catastrophe of the previous year had been taken back in a spectacular reconquest. Yet the situation remained critical. Abd-el-Krim had made contact with different political groups in various countries of Europe and his forces under the command of his brother had filtered into the zone of Ceuta, menacing Xauen. The Raisuni had allied himself with Abd-el-Krim whose thrust towards Xauen promised to smash the ring of encirclement in which the Raisuni's men were still held. It also threatened to provoke a rising in the zone of Ceuta.

The number of casualties grew incessantly. General Berenguer began to speak of resigning as soon as the Raisuni was overcome. It was a matter of public gossip that General Sanjurjo, in command of the zone of Melilla, was the real High Commissioner. In Madrid governments succeeded each other after holding office a few weeks; each one left the problem of Morocco to the next as a dire legacy.

The Chancelleries of Europe envisaged the possibility of Spain having to resign from the Moroccan Protectorate and France taking over the heritage. No one doubted the fact that Abd-el-Krim was receiving war material and technical support from across the French frontier.

We were all aware of cross currents which affected us, but which we could not gauge. The only things we knew for certain were the changes in personnel. Thus, Lieut.-Col. Millán Astray had been made colonel and had resigned from the command of the Legion on the plea of physical incapacity, owing to his many and terrible wounds.

I asked Sanchiz one day:

'Who's going to succeed Millán Astray? Franco?'

'Pooh, Franco – this time they've pulled one on him. They're going to appoint Lieut.-Col. Valenzuela. You see, there are only three possible successors among our officers here: Gonzalez Tablas, Valenzuela, and Franco. But Franco is only a major and the other two are Lieutenant-Colonels. Before making Franco Chief of the

Legion, they would have to make him a Lieutenant-Colonel too. Apparently Sanjurjo has put him forward for promotion twice, but all the greybeards say that it would be too much to promote him and to give him the command of the *Tercio* into the bargain. So they're going to give it to Valenzuela. But Franco has been given a medal.'

In the spring of 1923 General Berenguer launched the operations against the Raisuni's last place of refuge, Tazarut. Towards the end of May the troops entered there. Lieut.-Col. Gonzalez Tablas was killed during this action. Berenguer handed in his resignation; the Government in Madrid decreed that operations were to be suspended and a great number of troops discharged. For a few days it looked as though the war in Morocco was coming to an end. Negotiations with Abd-el-Krim had been started, in an effort to make peace with the tribes of the Riff. In the zone of Melilla the Spanish Army had stopped its advance and lay in front of Beni-Urraguiel, waiting for the result of the negotiations. Yet Abd-el-Krim wanted the recognition of the Riff as an autonomous State, as the Republic of the Riff; to give weight to his pressure, his troops continued attacking the Spanish outposts by day and night.

Early one morning the rumour spread all over Ceuta that a second disaster had occurred in the zone of Melilla. The Legionaries stationed in Larache had been sent over to Melilla at breakneck speed. There was no reference to it in the press, and the officers who were informed of the happenings kept silent.

Major Tabasco was rung up from the General Command in Tetuan every half hour. He had a conference with the Colonel and when he left the room his face was very grave. In the end he told me:

'Things are going badly again, Barea.'

'Something's happening in Melilla, sir, isn't it?'

'Yes. Apparently, the Moors have surrounded Tizzi-Azza, and if they take it there will be a second Annual. Don't go out for a walk this afternoon, because we may have to organize a relief column in Ceuta.'

I had often heard about the fortified position of Tizzi-Azza. It lay on the top of a hill and had to be supplied periodically with water, food and ammunition. The supply convoy had to pass through a narrow defile, and every passage had to be forced by fighting. Now the Moors had cut the road. The last convoy had entered, but not left, and the outpost was encircled.

A huge relief column was organized and the ring round Tizzi-Azza was shattered. But during the attack the new commander of the *Tercio*, Lieut.-Col. Valenzuela, was killed.

'Now Franco is the Chief of the Legion,' said Sanchiz, when he heard the news.

'But they haven't made him a Lieutenant-Colonel yet,' I quoted back at him.

'They'll promote him now, whether Millán Astray likes it or not. Whom else should they put there? Of all the officers we've not got one who would take the post, even if they gave it him on a platter. They're all afraid of it.'

Sanchiz was right. In the Cortes Franco's promotion was passed. He was made Chief of the Legion.

Major Tabasco's only comment was: 'Well, it's his funeral.'

At the beginning of July, General Berenguer ceased to be High Commissioner in Morocco; he was succeeded by General Burguete. Ceuta prepared a parade for his reception. On the day before his arrival the Major sent for me:

'There will be a review tomorrow in honour of General Burguete. I'm sorry, but we haven't anybody but yourself to lead the *gastadores*.'

In the Spanish Army, in front of any regiment in full formation there marches a so-called squadron of *gastadores* – eight soldiers, chosen for their height and bearing, in two files of four each, and at their head a corporal who acts as the guide of the regiment and executes all the motions to be followed by the rank and file.

We had no corporal who could have gone through the intricate movements without disgracing the unit. I had to take off my sergeant's stripes for a day, to sew on the insignia of a corporal and to select the best-looking eight soldiers in barracks. By dint of a series of manipulations we were able to muster something like two companies, with our senior Major on horseback as Chief of the force. Luckily, the Colonel happened to be away in Tetuan. The other units in Ceuta were equally short of ordinary rankers and consisted mainly of men on special duties; they all had to make shift in a similar manner. There were quite a number of sergeants converted into corporals and quartermaster sergeants converted into lieutenants.

We had to dress in our 'semi-gala' uniform, dark-blue cloth, unbearably hot in a Moroccan July. But we were confident that the review would not last more than half an hour and consoled ourselves with the thought that the ship was due at half past nine in the morning.

As the Engineers are considered an *élite* corps, we were detailed to the quay where the ship was to be moored. We were lined up at eight o'clock. It was a radiant day and the sea was perfectly smooth. For an hour we waited, smoking cigarettes and drinking the refreshments offered by the street vendors. Shortly after nine the ship moored and the regimental bands began to play. The High Commissioner received the same honours as the King – in the King's absence. All the officers had to present themselves to pay homage. Afterwards the General reviewed the troops.

General Burguete was a tall, slightly pot-bellied man, with an enormous black Kaiser moustache. He showed at once that his inclination towards Prussianism was not confined to his style of whiskers and kept us there in the broiling sun, motionless, while he scrutinized the exterior of every single private.

The dark-blue cloth uniform was hardly ever used in Morocco; most of the men had been given theirs in the various depots at the very last moment before the parade. Thus, the General had occasion to find fault with every detail of every part of the uniforms. Soon he was indignantly shouting; the commanding officers of each unit shouted at their subalterns with equal indignation, and so on down to the men in the ranks. Eighty to a hundred men were put under arrest then and there on the mole. The review lasted until eleven o'clock. When it seemed impossible to prolong it any more and we began to hope that our sweat and toil would soon be over, the General decided that the troops had to render the traditional homage to the statue of Our Lady of Africa, to whom he was to offer his baton of command.

We stood lined up in front of the church for another hour. Then the General went to the *Comandancia General* and from the balcony of the building reviewed the troops marching past. We were back in barracks at two o'clock. We had two cases of sunstroke and five of illness. It was the same with other regiments. The new High Commissioner had started his career well.

Yet General Burguete had come to put Morocco in order. That same afternoon he walked round the streets and put soldiers under arrest. They arrived in droves to report for arrest in the barracks. Officers followed suit. The Colonial Army had created its own code for dressing and behaving in the streets, which was obviously different from the military rules applied in the Capital. But General Burguete intended that the soldiers of Morocco, with their uniforms bleached by the sun and marked by campaign life, should look like soldiers of the Madrid garrison on a Sunday afternoon.

One of the men answered him back sharply:

'I've no other clothing, sir. I've got these rags – and they're full of lice! – because they don't give me any others.'

'Any man who's without a decent uniform will have to stay in barracks. You'll present yourself to the officer on guard in your regiment.'

'Now, Franco could be his brother,' said Sanchiz to me when I told him the story. 'You'll see when he comes to Ceuta.'

Burguete at once opened peace talks with the Raisuni. From one day to the other, the Raisuni, who had been encircled in Tazarut and at the mercy of the Spanish Government, became an important personage; his princely honours were restored to him, he received a large amount in cash and our troops were withdrawn from the Jebel-Alam. Then he made suggestions as to which officers, native or Spanish, should be discharged because he disapproved of them. The Engineers were not affected by these intrigues, but the repercussions on other units were very grave.

'Things are getting serious, my boy,' said Sanchiz to me one day. He heard more than I did, through his post in the Central Office of the *Tercio*.

'You know that our officers are very friendly with the officers of the *Regulares*. After all, many of them served with the Moorish troops before they joined with us. Like Franco himself. Now Burguete is discharging people, and they say that he does it according to a list he's got from the Raisuni. And some of our people want to organize a rising. You know, I think it's a dirty trick myself, to put that old rascal, the Raisuni, in cotton wool, after the thousands of dead he's cost us. I don't know what Franco is going to do. They say he's very angry and has made a protest. But I can tell you one thing: if he decides to raise the Legion in rebellion, we'll all go with him. And there'll be hell to pay.'

Yet what was happening was not Burguete's personal policy, it was the policy of the Government. They wanted to get rid of the Raisuni so as to have their hands free against Abd-el-Krim and to put an end to the conflict in one way or the other. Peace negotiations with Abd-el-Krim were still going on, and so were negotiations for the release of the prisoners in his hands.

It was a renewal of the old Spanish policy in Morocco, the policy of suborning those tribal chiefs who were powerful enough to stand up against the army. The Raisuni was being bribed, and there were hopes of doing the same with Abd-el-Krim. The expeditionary forces were being sent home. The country was left in the dark about all the moves; yet we in Morocco sensed them, and among the troops factions began to form.

There were three big parties within the army. Leaving aside the few who were against the Moroccan venture by reason of their general outlook, the Government's part was taken openly by all those who were pining for the ease and tranquillity of their provincial garrison. Then there were the old 'Moroccans', interested only in the return of the times when profiteering and racketeering were possible without much risk. And thirdly there were the 'warriors' who spoke of the honour of the Spanish Army and the honour of the monarchy and the honour of the country, and who demanded war at any price.

Among the 'warrior' party was the new Chief of the Foreign Legion. And the Legion grew quickly into a state within the State, a cancer within the army. Franco was not content with his promotion and his brilliant career. He needed war. Now he held the *Tercio* in his hands, as an instrument for war.

Even the last soldiers in the ranks of the *Tercio* had their share in it and felt independent from the remainder of the Spanish Army, as though set apart. They would draw themselves up, recall their deeds and express their contempt of the others.

'We saved Melilla,' they said. And it was true.

But from being a hero of this kind to being a rebel – and a Fascist – there is only one step.

5. Farewell

Major Tabasco called me to his room and gave me a batch of handwritten pages.

'Will you please type this for me, with as many copies as possible? It's confidential stuff. The best thing would be to do it in the evenings.'

I copied long lists of 'members' and 'proposed members', of motions and resolutions. It took me some time until I realized that Don José was something like the Secretary General of the Officers' Juntas in Ceuta. A big meeting of all the Military Juntas of Spain was apparently planned for the second half of the year 1923 in Madrid, 'pending unforseen events', and Don José was to go there as a delegate. It would be easy to organize the conference during the summer leave period, and representatives of all arms, units and military zones would meet:

'We cannot shut our eyes to the course events are taking in the country. We of the Armed Forces have the obligation to serve the Nation. The country must not go further along the present disastrous road. We are in the hands of revolutionaries. How else could it happen that a Parliament should attack the Supreme Chief of the Nation, or that one part of the country should intend to declare itself independent? It is our clear duty to cut short these developments.' And so on.

I had heard of the Juntas – what Spaniard could have failed to hear of them? – but I had never to my knowledge met any of their members. Eager to find out more, I asked the Major as ingenuously as I could:

'Are the Juntas run by the Government, then, Don José?'

'That would just about suit the Government! No, the Juntas are independent. They are the bedrock of the nation.'

I made a vacant, foolish face, and Don José laughed.

'You don't know anything about what's happening round you, I can see that. Now listen, my boy. Spain was on the brink of perdition once before, in 1917, during the Great War. The French and the English weren't pleased with our neutrality and tried to embroil us in the war, by making friends with all the enemies of the country, the Anarchists, the Socialists and the Republicans, and even with the Liberals. They managed to win over Romanones, who was Premier then. The Socialists and the Anarchists organized a strike – but you must remember it, you weren't as young as all that.'

'Of course I remember, sir. But the General Strike started because of the increase in prices, and because the people said that all the commodities were being sent abroad. The workers demanded a reduction in the price of bread, or an increase in their wages.'

'Pooh, that was only the pretext. The truth was that they wanted to make a revolution like the one that was just beginning in Russia then.'

'But – the Allies were against the Russian Revolution, sir!'

'You just don't understand the whole story. The Allies turned against the Russian Revolution later, when the Russians refused to go on fighting for them. It served them right, too, because the revolution was manufactured by the English and the French themselves. What happened was simply that their child turned out to be a changeling. Remember how the Allies fomented the revolution in Germany.'

'So you think the Allies made the German Revolution?'

'Of course, my boy. Who else? Certainly not the Germans. They were too wretched, poor devils, to involve themselves in new complications. The Allies did it because they wanted to destroy Germany for good. But never mind, that's another story. Anyhow, in Spain, Romanones wanted to drag us into the war, and because he alone was too weak, he and his friends incited the Republicans and the workers so that they could pretend that the whole country wanted to help to defend the Allies. One had to show the rabble they had reckoned without their host. A great patriot called together all the officers with a sense of honour, and the Government got some plain speaking: "Either you break with the mob, or the army will march!" Fortunately, it wasn't necessary. But the Juntas continued functioning. After all; we had had a sample of the sort of things bad

Spaniards are capable of, and we didn't want to be caught unprepared the next time.'

'I seemed to remember that in 1917 the army was not all united. Millán Astray set himself against the Juntas, didn't he, sir?'

'Oh, yes, and he even wanted to shoot us all! But Millán Astray isn't a military man, he's a maniac. Do you know his history?'

'No, sir.'

'Well, some time in the 1890s, his father was the Director of the Model Prison in Madrid. When the prisoners wanted to go on a spree, they tipped the Director and he let them gad about in Madrid all night long. It so happened that a prisoner by the name of Varela went out one night and bashed in his mother's head and stole her belongings in complicity with a servant girl. When the police found out how the crime had happened, they sent Millán Astray, father, to jail himself. And the son, who was only a child then, went quite mad. He said his father was innocent, and that he himself would have to restore the family's honour. Then in the Philippine wars he became famous. He was promoted and his father was set free, but it didn't cure the son. In 1917 he machine-gunned the strikers, and he would have liked to machine-gun us as well.'

'And now the Juntas want to prevent a rising of Millán Astray's?'

'No, the Juntas don't deal with small matters. What we want to prevent is things going on as they are at present. We are on the brink of a revolution. The rabble has managed to make the King responsible for every muddle in Morocco. They intend to proclaim the Republic and to make us leave the Protectorate. The English would like that very much indeed. Then they would establish themselves here in Ceuta and be able to wave across the Straits to their people there. But they won't get it all their own way.'

'Then you believe, sir, that General Picasso[1] is in league with all those people?'

'General Picasso is a poor old fool who can't see beyond the tip of his own nose. They've pulled wool over his eyes and he believes that everything he's been told is gospel truth. As if the kind of papers

---

[1] The Judge Advocate who was entrusted with the investigation into the causes of the disaster of Melilla, and who in 1922–3 was preparing the so-called *Expediente Picasso*, a documented account inculpating the King.

he's supposed to have found in Silvestre's desk would have been left lying about for everybody to see! Never mind, all those tricks won't get them anywhere, because we're here. And if a rising is necesssary, we shall rise.'

I found that difficult to understand. A military rising? Against whom? For what? For a return of the times of Ferdinand VII or Isabella II, when Generals ruled the country?

I talked to Sanchiz about it, and he grinned.

'It's all very well for those people to talk, but they haven't counted with Franco – nor with us. Everything will happen just as the Legion wants it to, you'll see.'

I felt muddled and uneasy. A few days later I spoke to Captain Barberan, our paymaster, whom I knew to be different from the others.

There was an odd kind of fellowship between the Captain and myself, ever since he had found me trying to draw a map of Morocco, in my early days as a corporal on office duty. Captain Barberan used to shut himself into his room every evening to study, to make notes and calculations. Once he came to my desk, looked at my sketch, criticized it and then proceeded to teach me topography. Occasionally he took me to the quarries at Benzu for surveying practice and carried on his own experiments with strange electrical apparatus, while I sketched away under his guidance. After a time he explained to me what he was doing. He was a pilot and he was doing research. There was a new method of taking one's bearings in the air, which was known to not more than half a dozen people in Spain; it was too complicated to explain, but roughly speaking it meant steering by radio-telegraphic waves. And now he was working at it:

'A few friends and I, we have a project, we want to fly to America.'

He was obsessed with flying: I presume that he talked to me simply because I never tired of listening to his technical dissertations. Captain Barberan was a small, nervous man with feverish eyes behind his glasses, prematurely bald, silent and self-contained. His relations with the other officers were scanty; he never took part in their amusements, but lived the life of a single-minded recluse. He looked like an ascetic monk in uniform.

I would hardly have dared to speak to Captain Barberan about political problems. But a few days after I had come across the Juntas within the narrow circle of our garrison life, he gave me the chance, beginning as always with his obsession:

'Of course you risk your life, flying. But at least you risk it for something great.' He laughed a nervous little laugh. 'I'm an ambitious man, really. There have been Transatlantic flights already, but we as Spaniards have the obligation to fly to South America. We have many obligations . . .'

We were standing on the terrace of the barracks, which dominates the whole Straits of Gibraltar. Captain Barberan went to the telemeter and adjusted the screws. There he remained for a while, stooping, looking through the lenses. When he straightened up, he said:

'That is another of the things we must do. The Rock is a bit of Spanish soil which we must redeem . . . What do you think of this war?'

'It's not for me to have an opinion, sir.'

'Everybody has an opinion. Forget for a moment that I'm your Captain.'

'Well – Morocco is quite simply a despicable affair, in my opinion.'

'*Caramba* – despicable – you're very outspoken. And whose fault do you think it is?'

'The fault of very many people. Firstly, of those who made the Treaty of Algeciras. On one side the Spanish leaders wanted something which would permit the army to wipe out its defeats in Cuba and the Philippines, and give our generals a living. On the other side there was England, interested in having no other power facing Gibraltar, not even France. And Germany, too, not wanting France either. Between them they've brought it on us. While we were wrestling with this damnable problem of Morocco, we had no chance to become a power in Europe. Perhaps it saved us from the Great War, but certainly it has ruined us as a nation.'

'Hm – you've got hold of a nice set of theories. There's a grain of truth in them, though. Do you know that England won't allow us to fortify Ceuta or the Sierra Carbonera? We've still got our old batteries from the year 1868, and in a few places even bronze guns.'

'But who has been keeping the Moors supplied with munitions ever since the attack began in Melilla, twenty years ago? The rifles are French and the cartridges too. But this trafficking suited many of our own people down to the ground, sir. Why not admit it? They didn't want things to be settled. Once, in Kudia Tahar, I overheard a telephone conversation between General Berenguer and General Marzo. Marzo had carried through an operation with the aim of setting up a few blockhouses and a fortified position. I happened to be with the soldier on telephone duty who made connection with HQ. General Berenguer asked: "Well, what was it like?" "Very bad, old man," said Marzo. "Why, what happened? Did you run into heavy fire?" "No, what happened was that those sons of bitches did not fire a single shot against us – you can't get anywhere that way!"

'And now we've made a pact with the Raisuni, given him every honour and a peace treaty, and are trying to do the same with Abd-el-Krim, simply because things are getting too hot. A real war doesn't suit certain people, because it could only end with a complete conquest and a final settlement with the chieftains. And then the goose which laid the golden eggs would be dead.'

'Then in your opinion we should either conquer or evacuate Morocco?'

'Yes, evacuate it. I think we ought to address ourselves to the Powers who gave us the task to tackle, and say to them: "Gentlemen, here you have it back; settle it between yourselves as you like." And I believe that three quarters of the Spanish people think the same. Except the professional soldiers, of course.'

'Well, quite a few men in the army would agree with you. We shall see how things work out.'

Suddenly, a new personage was featured on the front pages of the Spanish press: Horacio Echevarrieta, one of the Spanish mining magnates. He was a friend of Abd-el-Krim and offered to seek him out in the heart of the Riff to negotiate the release of Spanish prisoners. The public enthusiastically acclaimed the idea. Echevarrieta appeared as a saviour. The officers of the Moroccan Army protested: it would be an intolerable disgrace – the prisoners had to be freed at the point of the bayonet. But the Government backed the undertaking and Echevarrieta obtained the release of the prisoners, at the price of some four million pesetas.

Major Tabasco raged up and down in our office.

'It's a dirty shame! They didn't even let the army intervene. The army counts for nothing. Of course, Echevarrieta is a good friend of the Mannesmanns, and wolves always understand one another.'

I was honestly puzzled by Tabasco's outbreak. To me it seemed an excellent thing that somebody had ransomed hundreds of Spaniards from a slavery worthy of the Middle Ages. I knew, however, that I could not discuss this problem with my chief and that it would be best to pretend to be deaf and dumb. But Tabasco needed a responsive audience:

'Why are you making faces? Perhaps you don't even know who Echevarrieta is?'

'I know just as much as everybody knows, sir, that he's a wealthy man from Bilbao who knows Abd-el-Krim from the time when they studied together at the school for mining engineers.'

'Yes, yes, very nice. He's a trickster and a rogue. A friend of Prieto, the socialist millionaire, you know. A rogue, that's what he is. Don't you realize that Abd-el-Krim has some extremely rich mines in the Riff, and that those mines really belong to Echevarrieta? Here you have the reason for their so-called friendship.'

'That's the first I've heard of it, sir.'

'It doesn't surprise me. These are things the people who want to get rid of Morocco won't tell you – those people who want us to make Abd-el-Krim Sultan of the Riff Republic! Now listen. A couple of Germans, the brothers Mannesmann, found out that there are iron ore mines in the Riff and something else, manganese, or whatever it is. And when Abd-el-Krim's father was chief of Beni-Urraguiel they talked him round and got a concession from him. That happened twenty years ago. Of course, we couldn't agree to this kind of plunder. Then the brothers Mannesmann engineered the war of 1909 against us, and Abd-el-Krim, the father, wanted to destroy our mines. We had to let them all feel a heavy hand. We even had to put one of Abd-el-Krim's own sons in jail – a good-for-nothing who had established himself in Melilla and was editing a newspaper. When the Germans saw that their business was coming to nothing, they arranged things with Echevarrieta. He bought up their concession for a pittance and then he made a deal with his little friend Abd-el-Krim, the son. Together, they demanded from the

Sultan his official signature for this concession. Yes, my boy, people say that we in the army are responsible for everything that happened. But nobody tells you that in 1920 the Sultan decided the concession was not valid – and that that is what we're paying for now. It's the height of impudence that one of those men who provoked the whole thing should now visit his accomplice and bring him four million, paid by the Spanish people, as a gift! I can well imagine how the two rascals enjoyed sharing the money. Quite a rich mine they've struck there! Well, it won't last them long.'

When I told Sanchiz about this explosion, he said:

'He's only forgotten to tell you that the man who's after the mines now is Count Romanones. He's the owner of all the Riff mines.'

'So the papers say.'

'And I believe it. The generals and the millionaires always come to an agreement. The generals because they don't want to lose their revenues, and the millionaires because they want to increase theirs. It's all the same to me. A clean bullet for me – and all the politicians can go to hell.'

'It may be all the same to you, but it isn't to me,' I told him. 'I believe we ought to finish with Morocco one way or the other. Then at least they won't kill those people who don't want to die. If you like, they can leave you and your *Tercio* here all by yourselves.'

'Well, that wouldn't be such a bad idea, either! But what would all the generals do then, and all the people who get their graft out here? Would you put them into the Legion with us? Don't be a fool. The day the Moroccan business is over, you'll have to find another war for our generals or they'll make one. If the worst comes to the worst, they can always make war among themselves, as they did for a hundred years.'

In the meantime the day drew near when my term of service was coming to an end and I would have the right to ask for my discharge. Financially, my family's situation had become more troublesome. My brother Rafael was out of work, the liquidation of the bread factory being completed. His letters spoke of the impossibility of finding a job; not only were there few vacancies, but the mass of unemployed office workers had lowered the level of salaries. The best paid clerks earned no more than 125 pesetas monthly. My mother, my sister and he were living on a few savings and the earnings from the fruiterer's shop. Yet if things went on as they were, he wrote, the shop would have to close down.

Obviously I had not the right to come home as an additional burden on them.

And yet I felt that I had to leave the army. The decision had grown in me, or else it had been there all the time. I found the atmosphere of the barracks unbearable, even more so now when it was charged with tension. I felt that I could not keep up my equivocal position much longer. It had become too much like tight-rope walking. So far, I had been able to avoid being enmeshed in any deals, without antagonizing the others, because Cárdenas had continued to liquidate the monthly accounts. He had found it irksome to lose his extra income from the Regimental Office all at once and had signed vouchers and papers as before, first with the excuse that he had to keep things going until I was run in, and later on the plea that the new colonel with his interfering, fussy and grabbing ways created difficulties with which only an old hand could deal.

But now he began to think that it was time for me to become part of the system, and repeatedly said:

'I'll leave the whole thing to you in future, because the truth is that I'm not letting you profit from the opportunity.'

'Don't worry,' I would tell him. 'I've got plenty of time. I should hate to mess things up and come a cropper, just for the sake of earning a little more.'

So far, Cárdenas had paid me five hundred pesetas a month out of his pocket. I never knew how much he kept for himself, nor did I find out the secrets of the accountancy which he and the Major managed between themselves. Yet even though the Major was patently loath to lose the man who had been his partner for eight years, Cárdenas could not go on forever. I knew that sooner or later I would have to sign an account or a receipt with an obscure history behind it. Both the Major and Cárdenas were confident that I would re-enlist and stay in the profitable job, otherwise they would never have taken me on, and I had said nothing to cause them qualms. But now I was trapped in a blind alley. There were only the two clear alternatives which had worried me all along: either I could take my discharge and risk starvation, or I could stay and say goodbye to any life of my own.

I started writing letters to almost everybody I knew in Spain. The answers were most discouraging; relatives and friends told me I should not be a fool, but should stay on in the army. There I had my future career assured – what more did I want?

I wrote to my mother, explained my situation and asked for her advice. 'Do what you like,' she wrote back. 'Things are going badly here, but where three eat, four can eat as well. I would be glad to see you rid of the barracks. And I feel sure you will get on, even if the beginning is hard.'

So I made up my mind. After my discharge I would have money enough to carry me through three or four months, and in that time many things might happen. I racked my brains to find the least offensive form in which I could tell the Major of my intentions, but my difficulty was settled by pure chance, as so often happens.

I fell ill of acute rheumatic fever. My experience in Tetuan had made me fight shy of military hospitals and I persuaded the Medical Officer to let me stay in barracks. He was a young captain, friendly and loquacious, but not very much interested in his profession, and he filled my body with salicylate and morphine. One day he sat down at the head of my bed.

'Well now, you're getting on much better. Still a bit weak, aren't you? You're not strong anyhow. It's the fault of the climate. This hot, damp climate doesn't suit you. You ought to go back to Spain and live in a high, dry place.'

I seized my opportunity.

'To tell you the truth, it's given me a scare. In a month's time I'll have to decide whether I'm going to take my discharge or re-enlist. Naturally I thought of re-enlisting, because I've got my living assured here, but I must say, I'm even more interested in my skin. Only, I wonder what the Major would say.'

'Think it over and don't worry about the Major. I advise you to take your discharge. Your heart isn't strong, and these attacks always lead to complications of that kind. It's quite possible that you won't be fit for service. I'll speak to the Major about it.'

He did speak to him. Tabasco came to see me:

'How are you getting on?'

'Much better, sir. I hope to get out of bed in two or three days.'

'Fine. But don't hurry. The doctor told me that you're not really strong enough for this climate. What do you intend to do about it?'

'To tell you the truth, sir, I'm thinking of getting my discharge now, because it wouldn't suit me to ask for a transfer to a unit in the Peninsula. You know, sir, that I've no real vocation for the army, and a sergeant's pay over there is less than I could earn on my own. . . . Of course, I would stay here as long as you needed me, until you'd found somebody else.'

'I don't like to lose you, personally, but I can see that there's no other way out. It won't be necessary for you to stay beyond your time, we've got Surribas who knows all the ropes.'

And that was all. It was astonishingly easy.

6. Coup d'Etat

I had been to my old tailor, I had selected some dark cloth and had my measure taken for a new suit. Before I could wear this civilian uniform in place of my army uniform there was nothing for me to do. I went to the Puerta del Sol, for no other reason than to have a look at it and see whether I would not meet someone I knew. Everybody in Madrid sooner or later passes through the Puerta del Sol.

'*Caramba*, Barea, back in Madrid? I thought you were in Morocco?'

'I came back from there today, Don Agustín.'

'I'm glad to hear it. Are you on leave?'

'No, my term is over.'

'So much the better. And what are you going to do now?'

'Office work, I suppose. That's to say, if I find a job, which seems to be difficult.'

'Yes, rather. . . . I tell you what, look me up in my office. I can't offer you much, but there's always room for you.'

Thus I entered the firm of Don Agustín Ungría as a clerk on the very day I arrived in Madrid.

In the Plaza de Encarnación, Don Agustín had an office with fifty-odd employees, housed in two huge rooms with iron pillars and a maze of tables of every description. There were tall old writing desks with sloping flaps, ministerial tables, which had lost their varnish, two or three roll top desks, each of a different colour, and a host of big, small, square, round, polygonal and oval tables. There were chairs with seats of plaited straw and curved legs, chairs with square, massive oak seats, wooden armchairs of monkish aspect, round stools, square stools and even benches. The firm had been in these rooms for thirty years, and it had started with six clerks. For every new employee up to the fifty who made up the full strength, a new table and a new chair had been bought in a second-hand furniture shop.

The staff was like the furniture, all second-hand. Only four of the employees were expected to know more than is necessary to fill in forms and to add up figures. The salaries were miserably small. There was a core of ancient clerks who had nowhere to go and clung, rheumy and coughing, to their old table and chair. Then there was a group of young people who were noisy and troublesome and disappeared from one day to the next, to be replaced by others of their ilk. Jobs in this firm were only taken to fill in the gap before a better job came along.

The business activities of the firm were as checkered as its furniture and its staff. Don Agustín Ungría was a business agent. He provided commercial information, collected debts for private individuals and for the State, registered patents, conducted proceedings, and altogether undertook everything which meant coping with papers and forms in the hundreds of official departments.

Don Agustín himself, the head of the firm, was sixty-five and looked like a portrait by El Greco. His hair, purest white, swept back in long, curly waves from a high, open forehead; his long face with fine, waxy skin was made longer by a small pointed beard, as white as his hair and his moustache. But the arch of his eyebrows over the very bright eyes was heavy and hard, his wide mouth sensuous, and his nose strong and arrogantly curved. His body seemed to belong to another person, a man of mighty bone without an ounce of fat. It was the body of a peasant from Aragon. He was still able to work for thirty hours on end, to eat a fried chicken after a three-course meal and to empty half a dozen bottles of wine. No one knew the exact number of his illegitimate children.

He came to Valencia from an Aragonese village when he was twenty years old. Until then he had worked on the land. In the city he learned to read and write. He worked as a labourer and lived among the people of the port. The story was that he earned his first little capital by deals in smuggled silk and tobacco. Anyhow, he invested his savings in the orange trade, lending money to small growers to whom the customary delay in payments caused great trouble. He established a little office in Valencia. In his dealings with the orange merchants he had noticed that foreign exporters were eager to get commercial information; he turned his office into an information agency, exploiting his intimate knowledge of all the local people. Later he paid the deposit required to become a fully-fledged business agent. There were few competitors. Don Agustín prospered and transferred his business to Madrid.

He treated his family and his staff in the manner of a patriarchal despot, and with all his worldly success he never lost the standards of his youth in the village near Saragossa, where a silver coin meant wealth. Honours and decorations had an irresistible attraction for him. For some service to the State during the reign of Alfonso XII he had been granted the Order of Isabella the Catholic, and it was his greatest pleasure to go to every banquet clad according to the most rigorous etiquette, with his Order pinned to his frock coat. It was of enamel ringed with small diamonds and his staff used to call it the 'Fried Egg'.

He was not miserly. If he paid miserable salaries, he did it because his instincts were still those of a poor peasant to whom one hundred pesetas are an exhorbitant sum. 'When I was your age,' he shouted at one of the clerks, 'I earned three pesetas a day, had a wife and children and a mistress on top of it, and I was putting money by!' But then he loaned a hundred pesetas to the man to get him out of a tight spot, and never collected the debt. Once he showed me a thick old ledger:

'Do you know how much my employees owe me in debts they've never paid back, ever since I started having clerks forty years ago? Over one hundred thousand pesetas. It's all entered in this book. And yet they're not satisfied! Every day I see new faces in the office. The only people who stay on are the old clerks who are no good for anything any more. But still, I can't throw them out into the street.'

I myself had passed through the office for a few months years before and got on well with the old man. Now he offered me a position of trust. I was to work with his son Alfonso who 'had ideas in his head', as the father put it, and wanted to build up a patent agency business with foreign firms. He already had an English secretary and wanted me because I knew some French and would be able to deal with Spanish customers in technical matters. Don Alfonso himself had an oddly limited mind. He learned with great ease and remembered everything, but was incapable of the smallest creative effort. He was a lawyer and quoted from memory intricate paragraphs out of any legal code, but he was not able to give a legal opinion based on those same paragraphs; his French was perfect and his translations from Spanish into French excellent, but he could neither dictate an ordinary business letter, nor keep up a normal conversation in that language. He was deeply interested in industrial organization and knew Ford's system in all its details, but he was unable to organize his own office.

This gave me my chance. I had accepted the job as a stop-gap, but very soon I became absorbed in the problems of industrial patents. They led me back to mechanics. The Spanish patent laws require no more than a simple registration, but the firm began to deal with countries abroad where patents involve a meticulous technical and legal preparation. No one in Ungría's office was qualified for this kind of work. For my private satisfaction I started studying the technical and theoretical side of every patent which came our way. Soon I specialized in this. My salary was small – 150 pesetas a month – but patent translations were paid according to the number of words and thus there were months when I doubled and tripled my salary, though at the price of working fifteen hours or more.

This gave me financial independence as well as independence in my work, and it earned me the confidence of the oldest clerks.

Señor Laguna – old, or rather aged, thin, his trousers hanging loose on his shins, his cheek bones protruding and his hair lank, earning seventy pesetas a month for eight daily hours of silent, humble work – accosted me when we left the office:

'Could you spare a little time for me?'

We went out together and for a long while he said nothing. Suddenly he stopped walking:

'Do you think that Don Agustín would lend me a hundred pesetas?'

'Well, it all depends on his mood. Probably it will be no at first, but if you're insistent, it'll be yes in the end.'

After another long silence he stopped again:

'Do you think he would take my boy into the office? It would be our salvation.'

'It's the same thing again. First he'll say no and in the end he'll say yes. Especially if you speak of his kindness. Are things going so badly, then, Laguna?'

He gave a deep sigh and walked on. I began to get tired of his spells of silence, of his slow pace and of his wistful countenance.

'Let's have a drink. Come with me.'

We entered a bar and they served us with two pints of beer and potato crisps. When Laguna put the first chip into his mouth I saw that he was hungry. A second glass of beer and a ham sandwich broke through his shyness.

'You wouldn't know,' he said, 'but we're five at home, my wife, the two girls, the boy and myself. And I'm the only wage earner. Just imagine.'

'Your girls are still very young?'

'No, but they're so delicate, poor kids. Our room is very damp. Of course it's cheap. Fifteen pesetas per month. But it's six feet below street level. . . and we can't give them much to eat, they're still growing . . .'

He was so pitiful that I spoke to Don Agustín the following day. He took the boy in as clerk and raised the father's salary to one hundred pesetas, for it would not have been right for the son to earn almost as much as the father. The lowest salary was fifty pesetas. Between the two of them they were earning 150 pesetas now. Laguna brought me the fattest and biggest cigar he could find in the tobacco shops of Madrid.

Within twenty-four hours after Pepito Laguna started working he had a nickname: Charlie.

He had huge, feverish eyes in a small, pale, pinched face, curly hair, and a thin neck which emerged from an outsize shirt and padded shoulders as the hook of a clothes hanger emerges from a heavy tweed coat. His too big and too long trousers fell over boots in which his small feet must have had room to dance.

Marquez, the accountant, looked at the boy, produced a small bamboo walking stick from somewhere and presented it to him:

'Here's your stick, Charlie.'

The lad blushed violently and his eyes filled with water. There he stood, amid general laughter, with the little stick balancing in his fingers. Marquez snickered and tried to cap his own triumph:

'Just look at him, boys. Charlie Chaplin in person!'

Laguna invited me to lunch one Sunday. They lived in the Calle de Embajadores in a big stone building, three centuries old. From the flagged doorway I had to feel my way down a small, dark staircase, as to a medieval dungeon. There in the basement was a square room with cemented walls: two iron bedsteads behind a curtain of bleached flowers on a yellowed ground; a table with a frayed oilcloth, surrounded by half a dozen battered chairs; an old chest of drawers, and a leather covered, worm eaten trunk; a plaster Virgin and a bunch of paper flowers on the chest of drawers. The room smelled of sour milk.

'Fortunately we can cook outside in the courtyard,' Laguna said. 'There's a little room with a cooking stove. Only it has no door and in the winter my wife gets simply frozen.'

Steps sounded overhead. Through the iron bars of the window, which was one foot high and three feet wide, just overlooking the pavement stones, we saw the shadows of the passers-by and half their legs.

It hurt to be in that room.

Charlie lasted no more than a couple of months. He caught a cold and died. Laguna became a little more wistful and silent. Sometimes he said to me: 'Just now, when we could afford a meal every day . . .' and stopped. Charlie had died of hunger.

I hated that terrible, hidden, shame-faced hunger of the office workers, which then ruled so many hundreds of homes in Madrid.

One day I met my old companion Antonio Calzada. He was gaunt and sallow, his suit had carefully mended cuffs. He was out of work. What he told me about himself was the old story of war prosperity and post-war crisis. During the Great War he had been given a promising job as manager of the newly founded Puente de Vallecas branch of the Banco Hispano. His salary was only 250 pesetas, but he had a flat on the floor above the office premises free of rent and including lighting and heating. He married and had three children. The branch flourished; he soon had an accountant, two clerks and an office boy, a steel safe, and the right to sign. If his business continued to prosper, he could count on promotion to a bigger and more important branch in the city. Then the War came to an end and the bank began to dismiss its staff. His branch was left with only the office boy, and then even he disappeared. Calzada remained as manager, clerk, and errand boy in one, living in constant dread of a sudden dismissal.

All the bank clerks, he said, seemd to feel the same dread and they tried to get together so as to be strong enough for collective resistance. First, the banks gave all those the sack who were known to belong to a trade union. Then the "Free Syndicate of Banking and the Stock Exchange" appeared on the scene. Its organizers came from Barcelona with the reputation of settling all social questions by direct action; they would solve the problems of the employees, if necessary by machine-gunning the directors. 'I thought they were different fellows from your old fuss-pots of the UGT, and I didn't believe, then, that Martinez Anido and his gunmen and the banks themselves were behind them. I joined too,' said Calzada. Thousands of bank clerks had joined the organization, which then demanded the cessation of dismissals and the fixing of minimum salaries. They started a strike and the strike was lost. The organizers of the "Free Syndicate" left the strikers in the lurch; many hundreds got the sack. Calzada went on strike and lost his job. 'Up till now I've managed on our savings, what there was of them, and by pawning everything of any value at home. Now I'm at my wits' end. I've just got what I'm wearing now, I owe two months' rent – and God knows how we're getting our meals.'

Don Agustín took him on at 100 pesetas per month, and he was privileged among the thousands of poor wretches looking for jobs in that summer of 1923. At the time, assaults, robberies, and murders began to occur in Madrid, such as Barcelona had known on a much larger scale. Governments came and went, and the chaos only seemed to grow worse.

I met Major Tabasco in the streets one evening. He greeted me affectionately and wanted to hear all about my way of life. I knew why he had come to town, but it would have been an impertinence to make a direct allusion.

'Are you here on holiday, Don José?' I asked.

'Quite, on holiday – you're as sly as ever! A pity you didn't stay in the army, you would have been useful to us. You know quite well why I've come here. If you'd been in Ceuta now I would have brought you with me. I'm dead-tired and could do with a secretary.'

'But things are going well, aren't they?'

'Oh, yes, everything's settled. Within two or three months there will be a complete upheaval. They've come to a dead end with all their intrigues. We must show the rabble that there exists a Fatherland and that Spain is not just a foreign colony. Look what happened in Italy' – in Italy Mussolini had snatched the political power – 'and then think: we're in just the same situation. Either there will be a Russian Revolution here, or the Spaniards, the real Spaniards, must take matters in hand. It's high time.'

'Frankly, I can't make out what's happening in politics. In the few months since I've left Morocco I've worked and worked, and nothing else. And then, life here is so different from the barracks, I can't say I've disentangled all the problems. Nobody agrees with anybody else here. And it seems to me that things in Morocco aren't going well.'

Don José grew excited: 'How can things go well, the devil take it, when they don't let the army settle them? There they are, sending us civilians to negotiate with Abd-el-Krim – what do they know of Morocco? That scoundrel wants an independent Republic, supported by the French Bolshies and our own Reds of the "People's House". What we need is to shoot a few hundred of them and to raze the Riff to the ground. Oh well, it will all come in due course, and sooner than people think!'

That night I wanted to be among people and to talk. I went to the little tavern in the Calle de Preciados (a German bomb wiped it out in November 1936), where clerks from the innumerable offices round the Puerta del Sol met after work. I joined some of my cronies and told them the gist of my conversation with the Major.

'What we need is a Republic,' exploded Antonio, a small sickly youth whose pockets were always bulging with Anarchist and Socialist pamphlets.

'No, what's needed here is a man with guts to teach all those people discipline,' retorted Señor Pradas, a short-sighted accountant with thick-lensed glasses balancing on the bridge of his nose.

'That's it,' applauded Manuel, prosperous first salesman of a big shop.

'I have nothing against it,' said Antonio, 'as long as the man really has guts and is a Socialist – a real Socialist – a Lenin. Yes, that's what we need, a Lenin and a revolution.'

Señor Pradas put both his elbows on the table: 'Look here, you're just crazy. Well, now, not crazy, but just a raw boy. The misfortune of this country is that we haven't got another Espartero – a general who's as great a fighter as he was and wipes the floor with all the politicians. We need a grand fellow who will go into the Cortes, bang his fist on the table and chuck them all out into the street. I'm not in favour of killing, but I can tell you, a few dozen executions, and everything would be settled. And about your Socialists – a bullet for Prieto and Besteiro and company, that's what they need.'

Antonio rose, white in the face:

'You're a dirty swine and the son of a bitch!'

In the little tavern no conversation was ever private. Half a minute later a hundred people, crowded together in a room of thirty square yards, were shouting and shaking their fists. Five minutes later the first blow sounded, and shortly afterwards Antonio and four others were taken to the police station between a pair of policemen. There was broken glass and spilt wine on the floor, and Miguelillo, the brightest of the tavern boys, was bathing the bruise on the forehead of an old customer with eau-de-vie. Señor Pradas, red in the face and his eyes unseeing behind their lenses, perorated:

'Anarchists, gentlemen, Anarchists, that's what they are! And all this because somebody dares to tell the truth as an honest man. I'm an honest man. Forty years I've been working like a beaver, and now that young boy wants to lecture me! What we need here is a man like General Espartero, a man with guts to teach everybody discipline. Long live Spain!'

A second incipient row was drowned in wine. The tavern keeper, an energetic man with the philosophy of his profession, cut it short:

'All right, gentlemen, that's that. No more politics. If anybody wants to talk politics he can do it outside in the street. Here, people come to drink and have a good time. Miguelillo, bring these gentlemen a glass of wine each, on the house.'

I did not feel like talking any more.

General Picasso had finished his investigation into the Disaster of Melilla in 1921. His report was in the hands of the Parliamentary Committee: the announcement of the date for the debate in the Cortes was expected any day. The Socialist minority had copied and printed the report; a few copies were already circulating in Madrid. Among the papers left in General Silvestre's headquarters, General Picasso had found a number of documents which revealed Alfonso XIII's personal interference in the course of military operations. But none of the short-lived governments of those days dared to tackle the question in the Cortes. The Opposition formed a bloc and demanded with increasing energy a public inquiry into the responsibility for the Moroccan catastrophe. Something was going to happen.

If you want to hypnotize a hen put her on a table covered with a black cloth and force her beak down until it touches the dark surface. Then place a piece of white chalk just in front of the hen's beak, close to her eyes. At the psychological moment you move the chalk slowly away, drawing a white line on the black cloth. Then you loosen your grasp. And the bird will stay there motionless in its precarious equilibrium on two legs and the beak, following the growth of the white line with staring eyes.

It seems to me now that something very similar happened to us in those days of September 1923, when General Primo de Rivera made himself the Dictator of Spain by a *coup d'état*.

We were all waiting for something to happen, something very grave and very violent: the overthrow of the King – an Army insurrection – a rising of the Socialists or the Anarchists – somebody's revolution. Something had to happen, for the life of the nation had come to an impasse.

I was in the Café Negresco in the night from the 12th to the 13th September. My old friend Cabanillas used to come there when his work on the editorial staff of *El Liberal* was over. I had joined his circle of journalists and half-baked writers because I wanted to hear the stop-press news from him. He arrived at two in the morning, excited and pale, his hair in wild disorder.

'Have you been to the première – what's the matter with you?' I asked.

'Nothing's the matter with me. But do you know the latest?'

'What?'

'The garrison in Barcelona has revolted, with Miguel Primo de Rivera at their head.'

'Alfredito, you're not quite all there,' someone shouted. 'Have a brandy.'

'But look here, it's true. Primo has proclaimed a state of siege in Barcelona and has assumed all power in the city. Now they say he's put an ultimatum to the Government.'

The news spread through the café, as it must have spread through all the crowded cafés of Madrid at the same time. When we left, the

Puerta del Sol was a milling ant heap. People asked each other: 'What's going to happen here?'

Nothing happened. My brother and I stayed in the Puerta del Sol taking part in the shouted disputes until the first tram with early workers arrived from the outskirts of the city and the street cleaners began to sweep and spray the square. When the newspapers came out with huge headlines above the General's proclamation and the announcement that the King had sent for him, nothing happened. Most of the papers unconditionally welcomed the military dictatorship, a few reserved their judgement. The two most important dailies of the Left, *El Sol* and *El Liberal*, manoeuvered skillfully, neither criticizing the jump to power nor offering full support. The man in the street stared at the facts, as the hypnotized hen stares at the piece of chalk, and when he tried to recover his stance events had forestalled him.

The Government had resigned, some of its members fled abroad, the King had given his approval to the accomplished fact and Spain had a new government called the Directorium which suspended all constitutional rights.

'Hallo, Luis, how are things?' I said.

Plá's pig-like eyes tried to place me somewhere in the direction of my voice.

'Sit down, have something with me.'

'Are you still in the bank? How have you survived the strike?'

'I was lucky, my boy. Two weeks before the strike started I caught pneumonia, and when I went back to work everything was over. Otherwise I would have got the sack, I'm sure. I'm not in favour of those rascals of the "Free Syndicate", but I would have gone on strike with the others. As it is, they've raised my salary. I get 250 pesetas now. It's true that I've been in the bank for nearly twenty-five years . . .'

'Don't exaggerate.'

'Well, since 1906, that's seventeen. Anyhow, all my life.'

'Tell me, what do you think of Primo?'

'To tell you the truth, I like him. He's got guts. And he's got a sense of humour. Have you read his latest manifesto? It's very Spanish to tell people that he is where he is through his "attributes of masculinity". I like him. Of course, I can't quite imagine how it will all develop. Apparently he wants to collaborate with everybody, even with the Socialists. He's invited Largo Caballero and a few others to settle labour problems. And the gunmen in Barcelona are piping a different tune now. He has declared that he'll shoot the first of them who gets caught, even if he's one of Martinez Anido's own gang.'

A flock of newspaper boys came running down the street with shrill cries. Two of them entered the tavern, shouting:

'Mail crime in Andalusia!'

Every customer bought a copy. Giant letters announced the latest murder and robbery: a mail coach of the Madrid-Seville line had been assaulted, the postal official murdered, and the post bags robbed.

'Primo won't have an easy time after all. Here they are, the gunmen, alive and kicking, and he thought he'd finished with them!'

'It's the Anarchists,' said somebody.

'You'll see, those fellows won't ever get caught,' grumbled Plá.

This crime was a serious test for General Primo de Rivera. The Spanish public is inclined to feel entertained by any attack against a ruling power and to look on at the spectacle, with a certain bias in favour of the rebel against authority. Robbery by armed violence had almost disappeared at the time, and the feeling of general danger and uneasiness resulting from the wave of crime had subsided. Now this new assault, though it provoked the natural recoil from brutal murder, also held the thrill of a challenge to the new Dictator.

The press of the Right exploited this opportunity for a violent, indiscriminate campaign against the 'unleashed forces of Freemasonary, Bolshevism, Socialism, Anarchism, and so forth, still rampant in a most Catholic country ruled by a patriotic general.' Now was the time to set a stern example and to give short shrift to all the guilty men, so as to save law and order in the country.

The mail robbers were caught. The assasins were two young men from wealthy middle-class families, vicious degenerates, with a homosexual of the effeminate kind as their accomplice. The two murderers were hanged and their associate sentenced to hard labour for life. It would have been impossible to let them escape capital punishment after the intense campaign carried on while the criminals were assumed to belong to a political group. Yet even though that myth was exploded, the full rigour of the dictatorship hit all Left-wing associations. Some were dissolved, others subjected to close control and curtailment; the workers' right to strike was suppressed. At the same time, special tribunals were set up to decide on social matters. The Directorium launched large-scale public works. Unemployment figures sank rapidly. The new régime seemed to be consolidating itself on the home front.

But there was still the struggle in Morocco.

The Duke of Hornachuelos came to the office one day and wished to register a number of patents for cigarette cartons. Told that this was not a matter for patents, he said: 'You just apply for the patents and the Patent Office will grant them.' The Head of the Patent Office refused to accept the registration because these were not inventions of any kind, but a friendly letter from the new lord and master of Spain made him change his mind. Our office carried through the proceedings, which brought me into frequent contact with the Duke.

I was interested in him and he seemed interested in me. On my side this interest went back to a childhood memory. On one of my holidays in Cordova I had heard a tale about the young heir of the avaricious old Duke of Hornachuelos. At a carnival he had been exposed to ridicule because his father gave him no more than fifty *céntimos* a week as pocket money, and had exclaimed furiously: 'How I wish that my papa would die, so that I could spend five pesetas!' When I came to know him, he had kept his word. He had spent the family fortune and was over his ears in debt, but as one of the boon-companions of Alfonso XIII he was a privileged person. Now, under the Dictatorship, he counted on getting the monopoly for cigarette and match packings, protected by his worthless patents. It would be easy for him to find somebody to finance him. And he spoke about Morocco:

'I was there as a lieutenant, and I know the country. That's where Spain's future lies. But now Primo's talking of abandoning Morocco – it's intolerable cowardice, and so I told him to his face. Morocco is Spanish by right, it is our inheritance from the Catholic kings, it is our sacred duty. The last thing we want is for old Miguel to kick over the traces and play the fool about Morocco. It would mean that the English would establish themselves there within a fortnight, and then the fishermen from Malaga would have to ask permission to go fishing in the waters of Cadiz. It would cut Spain in two. No, if Primo seriously intends to abandon Morocco we would have to kick him out.'

The second of our clients who spoke to me about Morocco at that time was Major Marín, a swarthy, cynical, easy-going little man. He worked for a condensed milk company and acted as its go-between in matters referring to army contracts for Morocco. Now, some of the Dictator's protégés had set up a factory for condensed milk, counting on orders for the army in Morocco as the mainstay of their business. They had registered a series of trade marks which encroached on the trade marks of Marín's firm. The Agency Ungría was to conduct legal proceedings in the case, and Marín frequently visited us to discuss matters. Thus he came to tell me one day:

'What a business! That man Primo will drive us all crazy. There he is dishing out favours to his friends and giving away monopolies right and left, and in the meantime he has quite forgotten that Morocco is the only place where we can keep our army fed. There are more than a hundred thousand men in Africa at present. So now is the time of the fat kine. Those rogues who've set up the milk factory know it only too well. If we give them time to do it, they'll sell more condensed milk in a year than we've sold in ten years. And that man has got it into his thick skull that the country wants him to clear out of Morocco, and that he only wants to serve the country! I tell you, the old fellow may be honest, but he's a fool, nothing but a poor fool. He hasn't the faintest idea of how to govern the country.'

My brother and I were living alone with our mother since my sister had married and set up her own home. Whenever Rafael and I hotly discussed the present and future of the country, my mother showed neither excitement nor apprehension. She had shown none when she had heard of Primo de Rivera's *coup d'état*.

'It was bound to come to this,' she said. 'It's just as it was in my childhood and later, when I was a young girl and served as a maid in the house of the Duke of Montpensier. There were people who wanted to make the Duke King of Spain instead of Isabella II. That was all before the Republic, and General Prim himself came to Cadiz all the way from England to take the Duke's part. I was a child then, but I remember that there were mutinies every day until the Queen was dethroned and the Republic came. But then the Generals had nothing to do, and they began to seek for a king everywhere. Some wanted to make the Duke king again. In those days, some General or other was always making an insurrection with two or three regiments, and either he was shot or he became the Leader of the Nation. When I was there, the Duke's palace was always full of generals, and one of them was the father of this Primo de Rivera – a man who at times was fighting the Carlists and at others trying to find a king to get rid of the Republicans. In the end they got hold of Alfonso XII, and he married the Duke's daughter. A pity she died that summer. And from then onwards till now there has always been a General to make a rising in protest against something, but none of them ever put the country in order. This one won't do it either.'

'What do you think would put Spain in order, then?' I asked her.

'What do you expect me to say? I don't know. If your father were alive, he could explain it to you better than I. He was a Republican all his life and I think he was right.'

I knew my mother's secret weakness for the one historic incident in my father's life. 'Come on, tell us the story again,' I said.

'Well, it happened in '83 when they wanted to get the Republic back, a short time after Alfonso XII became King. And your father saved his skin only because he always slept like a log. In Badajoz the sergeants had made a Junta, and your father was its secretary. They were going to lead the troops out into the streets at daybreak. And your father lay down to sleep in the sergeants' room and told the others to wake him. I don't know whether they forgot or he didn't hear them. But General Martinez Campos, who was then in power, had got wind of the story, and when they opened the gates of the barracks to march the men out into the street all the sergeants were taken prisoner and shot. And your father went on sleeping in his bed like a blessed baby. Nothing happened to him, because his comrades didn't give him away. But the General who was at the head of the rising was hanged . . . I think your father had too many illusions about it all, though, because if things had turned out well for them, the Republic would have been a Generals' Republic, and then they might as well have stuck to the King.'

We were well off in those days. I was earning, and Rafael had also found a post as accountant with a Catalan contractor who had come to Madrid to get a share of the contracts for the projected public works. His chief had already obtained a few road-building orders, but he was after the fat contracts for building estates of cheap dwelling houses, planned in the suburbs of Madrid.

Then Rafael came home from work with the news that his chief had been given the contract for two of these building estates:

'If all the business deals of the Directorium are the same as this, it's going to be a nice kettle of fish. You know, my chief had friends in the Ministry who kept him informed of the other tenders. At the last moment they told him bluntly that he could have the contracts, but only if he was willing to pay a tip of a million pesetas, cash down. Of course he hasn't got a million at his disposal to pay out in banknotes; he's working on the credit he gets from the Urquijo Bank. So he went to his bankers, first of all to settle about the million in cash, and secondly to find out whether they were willing to give him a loan for the work until the State pays him. And everything's in order. Now he's got the two contracts and the bank has given him a loan for the total expenses, on the condition that the contracts will be taken over by the bank's nominee if he doesn't pay back the loan and the interest. Just a trifle – ten million pesetas.'

'But after all it's a good thing that poor people should get homes of their own, even it is costs a lot of money,' said my mother.

Rafael gave her a scornful glance: 'But do you imagine, then, that those so-called cheap houses are built for poor people? They're going to build two housing estates of little houses, each with its garden and its fence, and they'll be let at 150 to 350 pesetas per month. The cheapest as much as my monthly salary.'

'I'm sorry it's another swindle. Do you know that our old garret for which we paid nine pesetas a month is let for twenty-five pesetas now? I told you those Generals only make things worse.'

She paused thoughtfully, and added:

'If at least that man would finish the war in Morocco – but how could a General finish with wars?'

7. Villa Rosa

The year 1924 marks a deep incision in my life. If the later evolution of my country had not had the effect of a catalysis on me, as on twenty million other Spaniards, the course of my inward and outward existence might have been fixed then.

I married and I changed my social status in that year.

My family, and above all my mother, cherished the conviction that I could find a wife with every quality which goes into the making of a so-called 'good match'. I had a girl friend, just as had every young man of my age in Spain, because it would have been humiliating not to have one. My family did not expect this girl to become my wife, and neither did I; so far, I had not been thinking seriously of marriage. Other relationships satisfied my sexual needs, and 'my girl' meant simply an exhibition of my manliness. I pushed the thought of matrimony away until the time when my financial position would be better. Yet apparently other people began to think that I had reached the marrying age.

Old Ungría called me to his room while his daughter, an attractive girl of about twenty-three, was with him. He began to dictate a few notes to me and she left us alone. When he had finished, he took off his glasses and asked:

'What do you think of Conchita?'

'She's very nice – and she's very pretty.' I said what I thought, and he was shrewd enough to note it.

'She's the kind of girl that makes a good home and she ought to get a good husband. But she hasn't found him yet.'

'Isn't she engaged?'

'She has several admiriers, yes – Señoritos. But I want a husband for her who knows the meaning of work, and if possible somebody who understands this business of ours. I'm getting old – don't grin, I've still got twenty years of life before me, or perhaps I haven't.

Well, anyhow, the best thing for Concha would be a husband like you. Have you got a girl?'

'Yes.'

'Tell me who she is. Is she of good family?'

'If you mean, is she of a well-to-do family, then she isn't, she's very poor. And if you call a "good family" a family of distinction, hers isn't that either.'

'But, my boy, they you're being very foolish. What you need is a marriage which definitely puts you on a decent level. You need a wife such as Conchita. After all, she has her dowry, and as her husband your future in our firm would be secure. You'll understand that there's nothing against taking one's son-in-law into partnership.'

'Do you mean this as a suggestion, Don Agustín?'

'Take it as you like. We old people haven't much to consider, but you ought to think of what's best for you. Then you would no longer be a Sir Nobody.'

'But supposing I don't please Conchita?'

'The girl does what I want her to. And anyhow, women don't know which man they like or not so long as they haven't been to bed with their first.'

And there the conversation ended. I never could make out whether the initiative came from the father, the daughter, or the mother, who used to show a great liking for me.

But I had near me a living example of the consequences of Don Agustín's marrying zeal in the person of his son-in-law Domingo. He used to say that his father was an engine driver on express trains, but the statements which he let fall made it obvious that his father had been a stoker in the station yard at Albacete. They were a large family. Domingo, who had a good head for figures and beautiful handwriting, was sent by his father to Madrid to seek his living. The young man turned from one thing to another, always hungry and never finding his way to a career. When he was thirty, he came to work for Ungría, like so many others, accepting a miserable existence to escape starvation. Don Agustín's eldest daughter found the clerk attractive and greeted him warmly from her balcony which overlooked the office rooms. She was a plain woman of thirty-odd years, but he had gone hungry for a long time. They married. Don

Agustín set up house for them, assigned him a salary of 250 pesetas, which was quite a lot at that time, and made him his proxy. The couple was prolific. Don Agustín gave Domingo a rise of 25 pesetas per child.

Sometimes he would call him to his room: 'You're a silly brute. If you weren't my son, I would chuck you out this very instant. Be grateful to your wife, who's a saint, and to your children – my grandchildren – if I keep you at all. I'll put you on to copying accounts. You're supposed to be my proxy? You're a complete idiot.'

The whole staff heard these rows. Don Agustín enjoyed making them in public, and Don Domingo's defence was to curse, also in public, the hour in which he had tried to escape from his misery by marriage.

Don Agustín's offer did not appeal to me. But I told my mother about it.

'And what did you answer him?'

'Nothing. The girl doesn't interest me, but that's something I couldn't very well tell her father. It would have been too rude.'

'And what are you going to do?'

'Nothing. I told you that the whole affair doesn't interest me in the least. I've only got to look at Don Domingo to see the consequences of that kind of thing.'

'But you're much more intelligent than Don Domingo.'

'So what? Perhaps the old man wouldn't tell me that I'm a stupid brute, as he tells Don Domingo, but some day or other he would tell me that he lifted me out of poverty.'

She thought for a while and then said:

'You know, you'll be very unhappy if you don't marry for love, and that's a very rare thing.'

Though my mother did not follow up this discussion, she told some of her friends and relatives of it. As a result, I had to listen for days on end to well-intentioned advice that I should not spoil my chance. At the same time, the general opposition against the girl with whom I went about became very outspoken. It came also from her own family. Her parents and her sister considered that, as I would not decide either to marry or to leave her, she was wasting her time with me. I resented both attitudes. One day I announced that I was going to marry her. And we married.

Almost simultaneously one of the heads of the best-known patent agency in Spain died unexpectedly. I knew that it was difficult to find a replacement for him, because his work needed highly specialized qualifications, and went to see the Director of the firm. He knew me, as we all knew each other within the narrow circle of the profession, and we came to an agreement. I would be technical manager of the firm, with a salary of 500 pesetas and a commission. My married life started under good financial auguries. Though I realized that there was little in common between my wife's mind and my own, I was confident that a few months of living together would convert her to my ideas about relations between man and wife.

Within a few months I had mastered my new task and had failed in my marriage.

Her father came to seek me out.

'I want to speak seriously with you,' he said. 'The girl has told me how things are. You've got a lot of modern ideas in your head and want to change the world, that's what it is. But now look here. A woman is either married, and in that case she's got to keep the house clean and feed the kids, or else she's a bitch and a street walker. So don't you set your mind on something different. The man must support his home and children, that's his business. And if you've got an itch to amuse yourself . . . well, you go and find a woman somewhere, amuse yourself without a scandal, and that's all there is to it. Listen to what I'm telling you, I'm getting on for sixty and I know what I'm talking about. If you go on as you are, things will come to a bad end.'

'All right. But I think that only a fool would marry just to have a woman in his bed. What I want is that my wife should be my best friend, besides being my bedfellow.'

'Pooh, that's just romantic nonsense. Look here, a man marries to have a home of his own and woman to nurse him when he's ill and to look after his children. And everything else is just modern claptrap.'

I tried not to want more from my wife than she wanted to give. Our marriage was soon destroyed and consisted of nothing but the physical relationship. But if one's own wife differs from other women only by the colour of her hair, the cut of her face and the shape of her body, she becomes one among the many women who are attractive to the man, with the disadvantage of being at hand day and night and having her attraction submitted to the relentless test of proximity without tenderness.

Señor Latre was a man of seventy years, so perfectly conserved that no one would have taken him for more than fifty. He spoke three languages fluently and knew the world outside Spain. As the owner of one of Madrid's few novelty shops, he had travelled widely and frequently, in addition to having studied at a German university. He had remained a bachelor and was now retired from his business. Groping in my isolation, I thought that I could not bear the reaction of most of my countrymen to my problems, which would only have been a repetition of my father-in-law's counsel on a different level. I spoke to Latre.

'I don't know what to do. I can't formulate any concrete complaint against my wife. Physically she pleases me and I think I please her. Anyhow, I'm sexually satisfied and I've no kind of jealously. But apart from that we are as complete strangers to each other as if she were the woman on the nearest street corner and I a regular customer of hers. My life and my person do not interest her, and whenever I try to take an interest in her I come up against an unsurmountable barrier. She usually says: "Those are matters for women." I can't call it incompatibility. We aren't imcompatible and not even antagonistic, I should say. We simply live in different worlds and there is no communication between them.'

'After that, what can I tell you? You're a patient who's given his own diagnosis. But there's no remedy I know of for the disease. The problem doesn't lie in you or in her – or rather, if anything, it does lie in you. But in any case, one can't do anything about it.'

'I don't quite see what you're driving at.'

'The problem is complicated in detail, but simple in its general outline. You see, in Spain boys and girls grow up in two separate, water-tight compartments. The boy is told that he mustn't go near the girls or play with them, and if he does it all the same, he's called a cissy. The girls are taught that boys are brutal and beastly, and a girl who likes playing with them is not a "little woman" but a tomboy, which is considered something very bad. Later, the school teachers get busy teaching the boys that Woman is a vessel of impurity and teaching girls that Man is the incarnation of the Evil Spirit, created only for the perdition of women. So the boys form their masculine society and the girls form their feminine society, and when sex awakens, the young man goes to a brothel to learn about it and the young woman sits and waits until one of the men who come glutted from the brothels invites her to go to bed with him. Then some agree to do it through matrimony and others without it, and the first become so-called decent women, and the others whores. How do you expect real, complete marriages to grow from this soil?'

'I know all that, but I still don't understand why, after marriage, the two people can't adapt themselves to each other.'

'Well, do you adapt yourself to your wife, or don't you rather think she ought to adapt herself to you? But apart from your case, they can't do it because the whole weight of the society of their own sex is against them. I'll describe to you what happens in daily life, and you will admit that you have seen it for yourself countless times.

'Two young people marry because they're more or less in love with each other. During the first two months they go everywhere together arm in arm, kiss each other in public, and people say: "How charming, how much they're in love!" But after the honeymoon, the great offensive begins and it's very effective even while it is unconscious. One day when he's finished working, the young husband's friends will say to him: "Come along with us to So-and-so's house and drink a bottle of wine." "No," he'll say, "I'm going home." "What, still in love? Your wife won't run away from you. Partridge every day grows boring." The man may fence them off, but they will renew their attack, and it will be more direct. "Well, well, you seem to be pinned to your wife's petticoats. A man mustn't be ruled by women." If the husband doesn't give in, his male friends will drop away, he'll be left alone and people will say of him that in his house it's the woman who wears the trousers.

'And it's the same with the young wife. If she shows her fondness for her husband too openly, her friends and even her mother will begin to criticize her. They will say: "What, your honeymoon isn't over yet?" And in the end they'll say to her: "My dear girl, you're behaving like a bitch, always running after him." So she won't dare to show that she's really fond of him, because she's afraid of the strictures of the other women, and she will become convinced that he's right if he keeps to his male society and his amusements, and that he's not a real man if he doesn't. It will end as most marriages in our country are doomed to end, with a great emptiness. As things are, anything else would be a miracle.'

There was no remedy. I tried to form part of a male society. I did not want to be shut up in loneliness. For a short time I frequented the little tavern of the clerks in the Calle de Preciados. But quickly all the customers knew of my new job and I lost my old companions. A discussion would start, but almost at once whoever was holding forth would interrupt himself:

'Of course, Don Arturo' – now I was "Don" Arturo to them – 'won't be able to agree with me. I quite understand. He's in a different position from us now. He's become a *bourgeois* and there are certain things he can't see as we see them. . . .'

On other occasions the talk would take a more aggresive turn:

'What we need is a revolution. We must make a clean sweep and execute all the generals and all the priests. And we must burn down the churches and . . .'

'In the end you'll be the only one left, isn't that so?'

'Of course, you're a *bourgeois*. They've bought you already. You've sold yourself for a mess of pottage. My dear friend, you'll get fat and you'll buy a diamond ring and you'll attend Mass with the Jesuits. I've seen only too many like you.'

One Sunday after a bullfight in which a famous and much disputed *torero* had taken part, we were sitting in the tavern discussing his feats. One of his enthusiastic supporters made a statement which I contradicted.

'Of course,' he said, 'you've seen him from nearby. As Don Arturo belongs to the upper class, he can afford to sit in the front row and see what we others can't see from far up under the roof.'

In this manner our discussion sank to a ridicuous level. If somebody said that it was cold and I answered that I didn't think so, I was told that I didn't feel the cold bcause I could afford a good great-coat. Sometimes I reacted sharply, at other times I turned it into a joke. And in the end I went there no longer.

I took refuge in the tavern of The Portuguese, in the company of Luis Plá. He had known me as a boy and as a man, he would not misunderstand me. After a few months, Plá was the only one in the circle to defend me, and even his defence was sometimes fainthearted. My membership card of the UGT had become a double-edged weapon. To those above me it seemed a disgrace that I, the manager of a big firm, should mix with the 'mob' of the People's House. To the workers, including the white-collar workers, I seemed an intruder.

I buried myself in work, and it had much to attract me. I had not been able to become either a mechanical engineer or a mechanic, but I was now the adviser of inventors. Often I helped them in their research work, as an escape for myself. I wrote juridical and technical articles for two professional magazines, and my chief let me start a technical review as a propaganda organ for his firm. My work brought me into the realm of big industry and my journeys to the two industrial centres of Spain – Catalonia and the North country – became more frequent. And all the time I was more and more losing the habit of personal contact with people.

Yet I liked being among people. I became a regular customer in two widely different places, in the Villa Rosa and in Serafin's bar.

The Villa Rosa was one of the best-known night establishments of Madrid, a *Colmado* – an Andalusian winehouse – with extensive basements in the Plaza de Santa Ana. I used to go there when I was eighteen, with money in my pockets and a predilection for Andalusian wine. Nothing was left of that period to link me with the Villa Rosa but my friendship with the old waiter Manolo. He had scolded me or even manoeuvred me out of the place when I had more wine than was good for me, like an old retainer. He had given me advice about life with the picaresque humour of an old rake and with an honesty seldom found in Spain except among rogues and cynics with a code of conduct of their own. Now I met him in the street by chance and we dug out reminiscences. He looked half like the dignified steward of an aristocratic house and half like a buffoon grown aged and wise, with an infinitely sagacious face under his grey hair.

'I'm still at the Villa Rosa,' he said. 'Do come and visit us there.'

'I'll be there tomorrow night, I promise you.'

And I went. To those young and old men-about-town Manolo the waiter vouched for my quality as a gentleman.

About the same time I passed by the tavern of Señor Fernando in the Calle de la Huerta. In that tiny bar, frequented by workers from Avapiés, by the tarts of the Plaza de Antón Martín and by their pimps,

I had drunk my first glass of wine in public. When Rafael and I were boys, we were sometimes sent there to fetch a bottle of wine. Then the owner, Señor Fernando, would give us a glass of lemonade or a few coppers for sweets, and we would play with his plump little son Serafin when he was not too busy rinsing glasses and bottles under the tap. Now, a strong, plump young man in a black-and-green striped apron was standing at the door when I went by and stared at me. He made a step forward.

'You're – I beg your pardon, are you Arturo?'

'And are you Serafin?'

He dragged me into the empty bar. The hacking dry cough of Señor Fernando sounded from the back room. I sat down with them and told them about my life. Their own had not changed; they had their business and their old customers, grown a little older, and a few new ones to replace those who had died. 'Come and visit us,' said old Fernando, 'that's to say, if you're not too proud for us.'

'I'm still the son of Señora Leonor, thank God. I'll come.'

When I did not go to the Villa Rosa to exchange jokes with Manolo I went to Fernando's bar, or rather to Serafin's, for his father died soon after I had met them again. There they accepted me as a proletarian because Serafin had played with me, and because Señor Fernando had known my mother when she still took her bundle of washing down to the river.

Manolo came to my table, wiped it with his napkin and asked: 'What's yours today? The usual? And a little glass for me, please, because I'm thirsty.'

'Bring half a dozen.'

'We've got a merry party in there today. I'll tell you about it later.'

He brought me a tray with six small glasses filled with Manzanilla and raised one of them:

'Your good health!' He leaned over to me: 'Do you know who's in the Patio?'

The Villa Rosa had a glass-covered courtyard imitating an Andalusian Patio, filled with flower pots, its arches and walls covered with arabesques in plaster of Paris.

'Well, who is it?'

'Don Miguelito.'

'What Don Miguelito?'

'Good gracious, how stupid you are! Whom do you think I mean? The king of Spain! Primo de Rivera. And I bet he's out on a spree tonight. He's got *La Caoba* with him and some flamenco singers, and they want to paint the town red. After the rush hour, we're going to close to the general public.'

'So that's why I've seen some funny figures outside.'

'Of course, the detectives. He doesn't want police protection, but they follow him and stay outside.'

Manolo went away to look after his own customers, but soon he came back and hovered around.

'What do you think of Don Miguel, Manolo?'

'Hm, what do you want me to say? I don't meddle in politics. He's a man with guts. That's why I like him. But you see, those Señoritos who are always with him, they're ne'er-do-wells and can't carry their wine. Between you and me, he'll come to a bad end. All that crowd are simply sponging on him and making up to him: "Don Miguel, do drink a little glass . . ." and another, and another. In the end – I've seen it myself – they get him to give a road-making contract to a little friend of theirs, or a job in a Ministry, or a letter of recommendation. And when the cow won't give any more milk, they'll send it to the butcher's. Wait and see.'

Manolo winked like a wise old gypsy soothsayer.

'I would like to see him from close to,' I said.

'Haven't you ever met him, then?'

'I haven't even seen him, except in photos.'

'Then wait a bit, I'll present you.'

He disappeared for a while, only to come back and whisper into my ear: 'Come along.'

He stuck his head through the door of the Patio: 'If Your Excellency will give me permission . . .'

'Come in, Manolo.'

'Well sir, I've got that young gentleman with me who's an old friend of mine and would like to pay his respects to you.'

'Let him come in.'

Somewhat excited and confused I entered the Patio, met by the stare of the whole party. General Primo de Rivera was lolling in a wicker armchair and a dark, gypsy-like woman was at his side. In the opposite corner was a group of gypsies with guitars and two girls with wide, swinging skirts. The small tables were pushed together to form a single big one, covered with glasses and bottles, and around it sat a crowd of men and women, the men of all ages, the women all young except for two who looked like procuresses.

'How do you do? Have something,' said the General.

'Thank you very much, sir.'

It was an embarrassing situation. What could I say to this man, and for that matter, what was he to say to me? I took a glass of wine. What the devil was I going to say? To toast the dictatorship was something I could not do. To say 'Your health', or something like it, seemed ridiculous to me. The General saved me from my difficulty.

'If you want a really first-class Manzanilla, gentlemen, go to Montillano's in Ceuta. That man knows what wine is.'

'You're quite right, sir,' I said boldly.

'*Caramba*, you know Montillano?'

'I've been a sergeant in Ceuta, sir, and General Serrano took me there a few times.'

'Those were good times! When did you leave Morocco?'

'Almost a year ago, sir.'

'Good, good. And what's your opinion about Morocco?'

'Well, sir, it's difficult to say. I was there as a soldier, but it wasn't too bad. Others have gone through worse, not to speak of those who died there.'

'That's not what I'm asking you. I'm speaking of Morocco. Ought we to give it up or not?'

'These matters are too high for me, sir.'

'All right, but I want to know what you think. You've been there – what would you do in my place? Be honest.'

'Well then, frankly,' – fleetingly I wondered whether I was so courageous because of the wine – 'I've served there in the ranks and I've seen much misery, and worse things than misery. I believe, sir, that the man who wants to rule Spain must give up Morocco, because it is nothing but a slaughterhouse.'

In the background Manolo echoed me with a single gypsy exclamation: '*Éle*!'

'General Primo de Rivera believes the same, my boy. And if he can, he'll do it. And he can, the Devil take it!'

The General had half risen from his wicker chair to say that, but now he slumped back heavily against the curved back. His fatherly mien changed to sullenness. He said nothing more.

'My apologies for having distubed you, gentlemen. Have you any orders, *mi general*?' Suddenly the automatic routine of the army came to my support. I felt sorry for the old man in his chair who had a beaten look at that moment.

'It's all right, my boy. Thank you.'

Manolo accompanied me back to my table. 'What do you think of the General?' he asked. 'He's a good fellow, isn't he?'

'Manolo, do you realize that I could get a thousand pesetas for telling what the General said in there?' I visualized my impromptu interview on the front page of the papers. Manolo turned very grave:

'By your mother's life, Don Arturo, don't be silly and don't do things which would compromise us all and only land you in prison for so many years that you would get grey hair. Listen to an old man who has never yet deceived you. And I think you'd better go now.'

Up to the time when I joined the circle in Serafin's bar, Señor Paco had lorded it there. Then I did. He might have resented my taking from him a right acquired in twenty years of political discussion round the marble table in the right-hand corner. But with all his revolutionary aplomb, Señor Paco was a simple man who felt stupefied by everything he did not know.

What he knew well were the four walls of his carpenter's shop, the thousand-and-one sorts of wood he used for his work, the information contained in the more vehement papers of the Left, particularly in the satirical reviews, the topography of the whole quarter of Avapiés, and the River Jarama where he liked to fish and in the summer to bathe.

'Nowadays trade has gone to the dogs. Give me a massive walnut table, and that poor stuff made of pine wood with mahogany strips on top as a veneer is simply nowhere. Or oak. Oak is the finest wood in the world. But you must know how to work it, or the tools slip off it as if it were a piece of iron. My master who taught me the trade, Señor Juan – God rest his soul – kept me sawing oak for a whole year. I was fed up and one day I threw the saw on the bench. He tweaked my neck – that's what an apprentice got in those days, and sometimes even a journeyman – and said: "You believe you know all about it, don't you? All right, then, you'll work with the plane." And he gave me a jack plane and an oak board, and I had to smooth it. I should like to see one of you do it. That damned tool gets stuck in the wood and doesn't cut, even if you sweat your guts out. It took me two years to learn how to plane oak and make my shavings as thin as paper. But now . . . you saw with a machine, you plane with a machine, and you burnish with a machine. At the most you cut pine and stick a few thin sheets of mahogany varnished with a pulverizer on top of it!'

'But, Señor Paco, machines mean progress. Now which is it to be? You're always talking big of Socialism and Progress and then you start cursing the machines!'

'Man alive, I'm not saying anything, but it's a fact that there are no real workmen nowadays. I can work wood but people now can't work as much as this,' and he made the nail of his thumb crack. 'Everything is mechanical nowadays. And what happens is that they manufacture things in big heaps, like buns, and then, of course, when the workers ask the master for a rise he tells them: "Get out of here. I can get anybody to work the saw, even women".'

'And what's wrong with a woman working a saw?'

'Women are here to wash dishes and suckle children.'

'And you call yourself a Socialist?'

Señor Paco was helpless when, mockingly and cruelly enough, I exposed the contradictions in his emotional socialism.

There was a night when the papers contained the information that Abd-el-Krim had cut the communication lines between Tetuan and Xauen. They did not say it in so many words; they only spoke of a few engagements and the loss of certain positions whose names meant nothing to the common reader, although they spelled disaster to those who knew the battleground. Not only had the insurgents cut off Tetuan from Xauen, but they also threatened to cut it off from Ceuta. They had captured several points of the Gorgues massif, the mountain which dominates Tetuan, and from there they had the choice of attacking the city or overrunning the railway line and the road of Ceuta. The *kabila* of Anyera, whose ramifications cover the whole stretch of coast between Tangier and Ceuta, gave signs of insubordination. Apparently the tribesmen had been given arms as a political measure and were now inclined to use those same arms for an assault on Ceuta and Tetuan, in league with Abd-el-Krim.

I spread the newspaper out on the marble table in the right-hand corner at Serafin's. Señor Paco took it out of my hand and read the headlines.

'Just the same old story all over again! They'll never finish in Morocco. That henpecked old fellow, Primo de Rivera – always promising that Morocco will be finished with, and all the time tricking us just as we were tricked while I was there.'

'It's serious this time, Paco. Abd-el-Krim has got under our skin.'

'Rubbish! Just the old tricks of the Generals. I know them by heart. A pity they don't kick us out from there once and for all. Let it cost ten thousand men, but at least it will be over. It's a slow blood-letting process going on and on as it is now.'

'I'll tell you something.' I put my elbows on the table in an impressive pose. Serafin shut the glass door. 'A few weeks ago I spoke to Primo.'

'What the Hell!' cried Señor Paco.

'Well, believe it or not. But Primo wants to clear out of Morocco.'

The circle of friends waited in suspense to see whether this would turn out to be one of my usual jokes. Señor Paco became grave.

'I'm not swallowing it this time, Don Arturo. You make a joke of a fellow because he's not an intellectual like you, but it isn't right to mock at us. For less than this I've given a man a lot bigger than you two slaps in the face. I'm not too old to have my leg pulled.'

'I was talking seriously, Paco.'

'And I tell you that it's finished with our friendship.'

I stood up: 'All right. I'll keep the peace. Serafin, a round of wine for the party.'

We drank in sulky silence. Señor Paco suddenly dumped his glass on the table.

'Primo de Rivera is a son of a bitch like all generals, past, present, and future, but . . . Well, you've been pulling our legs and I won't forgive you for it. But joke or no joke, if Old Whiskers really clears out of Morocco, Paco the cabinmaker will stand up in the middle of the Plaza de Antón Martín and tell the world that he's the greatest fellow ever born in Spain. I've said it; and now, Serafin, another round. I don't want this to finish with a bump.'

A few days later the operations for the liberation of besieged Xauen started. In a speech in Malaga, General Primo de Rivera announced that he intended to withdraw the army to the so-called 'sovereign places', Ceuta, Melilla and Larache, which did not form part of the Moroccan Protectorate but were directly under Spanish sovereignty. At once the *kabila* of Anyera revolted and communications between Ceuta and Tangier as well as Tetuan were cut. Thousands of men were poured into Morocco. The press published nothing but war news.

Señor Paco devoured the papers and commented in his way:

'Now you can see how it's going to finish. Another disaster of Melilla and another fifty thousand dead. And in the end, Abd-el-Krim will make peace and get a nice post and a lot of money. Then things will go on until the next chieftain makes a rising.'

'This time it's different, Paco.'

'What's different? I wish it were. Everything's a racket. That's why they made the dictatorship. First, so that it should not become known what the King has done – where have those papers of Picasso's gone to, eh? And secondly, so that they can make another dirty deal and get profits by the million. Cannon fodder is cheap. You go on having children so that they can be killed. God damn it all!'

Señor Paco wiped his brow; the summer of 1924 was very hot. He added:

'And don't tell me any more damned fool stories. Morocco hasn't been settled and it never will be. It's Spain's evil spirit, and all our misfortune will always come from there. You'll see in time, all of you.'

Primo de Rivera went to Morocco to take over the Supreme Command. The withdrawal was carried through. It was a strategic victory and a catastrophe. All the Moorish *kabilas* in the zone of Ceuta had joined the insurrection. Primo de Rivera's tactical method was to extricate the garrisons of the isolated positions and blockhouses as best he could, some by battle, others by bribery with money or munitions. Many garrisons were rescued at the price of surrendering their armament to the Moors who, in addition, received as much armament again in bribes; that is to say, they gained two rifles per rescued man. The Spanish forces flocked into the Zoco del Arbaa, disarmed and demoralized. From there they still had to reach Ceuta, passing through hostile forces which closed in on them. Twenty thousand men and an incalculable amount of war material were lost.

I knew that terrain step by step, and thus I could follow the catastrophe step by step. I used to buy the evening papers and sit down in the Villa Rosa to read them. I felt unable to discuss matters with Señor Paco any more.

Towards the end of 1924 the greater part of the Spanish forces had been discharged. Strong garrisons were left in Ceuta, Melilla, and Larache. The insurrection had swept the whole Spanish Protectorate. Primo de Rivera decreed the blockade of the territory. Press and public opinion acclaimed him as the saviour of Morocco.

8. The Endless Track

One night at the end of 1924, a sergeant of the Engineers came into the Villa Rosa. I was sitting at my little table in the corner and saw nothing but his back while he leaned over the bar. There was something familiar about him which made me go on watching. I wanted him to be somebody I knew. I was alone, and among people ignorant of that Morocco which still obsessed me.

The sergeant turned sideways and I saw his profile. It was Córcoles.   Friendship between people who have been in a war together is an odd thing. The army forces strangers to share the same tent or to peel potatoes for the same bucket, and turns them into so-called comrades-in-arms. War catches them together and imposes a solidarity which is not that of men, but rather that of animals in a common danger; this solidarity becomes a friendship. The day the army service ends, each of the friends goes home to his own place to be swallowed by the mass of the people. Each of them, telling stories to his intimates, will occasionally recall the other and turn him into a figure in a tale. And sometimes he will exclaim: 'That was the best friend I ever had!' Yet this friend has dissolved into thin air, has ceased to exist: he counts for nothing in the new life. Then one day the two meet face to face, and in a flash a piece of life is resuscitated which is unforgettable, however hard you may have tried to bury it.

The two slap one another's backs, babble, speak, talk, and then they separate, perhaps forever. But every such encounter stirs the sediments dormant in the mind of anyone who has been a soldier and tries to forget it.

Córcoles and I hugged each other so boisterously that we drowned the noise of the crowded bar. We would have silenced the chatter in the most crowded café in Europe. Córcoles had escaped from the slaughter, he had gone through the retreat from Xauen, and now, when he was on leave in Madrid, every nerve in his feline body was unleashed.

I had never realized that I was fond of the man. Now I felt like crying. I shouted:

'Manzanilla – Manolo – Manzanilla – one bottle or two, as many as you like! Come and drink with us, it's on us, it's on me. Wine, quick, we must get drunk. Look at him, he's got out of it safe. You can't kill a wildcat!'

When Córcoles was in the grip of emotion, he used to stutter and his vowels came out like a hen's cackle:

'Wi-i-ne, o-o-old man!'

'Who's an old man here, you shaver? I could still leave your mother with a child!'

'Manolo, don't be a brute!'

'I'll split this fellow's lip, Don Arturo.'

'You'll damned well show respect to this fellow, you braggart.'

'All right, all right. Now, let's see. Are you a friend of Don Arturo, or what?'

'Manolo, don't be a damn fool. This is the best friend I had in Africa. Can't you see his face?'

'Well then, what's all the shouting about? The bottle is on me and you can both shut up. Wine, wine! You just come and tell Manolo: "I'm Don Arturo's friend", and true as gold, Manolo will be here for you. But no talk about grey hair, eh? The stoutest fellow here is me, and then it's me again. And now let me ask you – didn't they bump you off in Morocco?'

'What the devil d'you mean? Don't you see I'm here?'

'Oh no, you're just a ghost, with those bones of yours and those clothes. I'll get you a snack, some nice little sausages, and you'll get fatter at once.'

'He's got me, that old fellow, he's got me.'

Manolo and Córcoles took to each other with a sudden affection that might have made me jealous. Manolo showed it by surrounding Córcoles with enticing dishes, more than enough for a full meal, instead of the little tit-bits usually served with the wine. He stood by and watched him eating, with his white napkin over his shoulder:

'You eat and drink. You're thinner than a piece of mending

cotton. And don't look at that tart. What you need is food and drink; you keep your oil in your oil-skin.'

Indeed, if you had shorn off Córcoles mop of unruly curls, which made his head twice its size and peeled off his uniform, he would have been nothing but a frame of bones in a coffee-coloured skin. His Adam's apple protruded from his collar, his eyes were sunk in his skull, and his hands were like five shaven dogs' tails. But his wit was more biting and more cynical than ever. He had the insolence of a man who has taken the measure of Death.

'How are you here?'

'As you see me – all bones. When we arrived in Ceuta they had to send me to hospital in bits and pieces because I'd fallen apart. And then the doctor said to me: "Two months' sick leave – where d'you want to go?" I'm a Ceuta man, and you can imagine I didn't want a summer holiday there. "To Madrid," I said. "But haven't you got your family here?" "Yes, sir," I said, "but – do you want me to leave the hospital and go home so that my mother and sisters can nurse me? They'd be saying all day long: 'Be quiet – Don't move – Go out in the sun – Here's a nice cup of something that'll help you – Keep warm – and so on'." The doctor had to laugh and he gave me a free voucher to go bathing in the Manzanares.'

He turned round to stare after a girl.

'You've got some damn fine women! Manolo, get me more ham, I'll raise your tip. I'm spending half the budget of the road from Tetuan to Xauen here . . .'

Hardly any business is done in the week between Christmas and New Year. I asked for a few days off and devoted my time to acting as Cicerone for Córcoles who did not know Madrid. And bit by bit he told me about his experiences.

'You see, old man, it was fine in Xauen. You didn't know it as it was then. Even Luisa has set up a branch of her house there, and there is a tavern at every street corner. Well – there was. Because now there's nothing left there, not even the rats. It was the same old story as always. The Moors attacked one or the other convoy and killed a man or two, but in Xauen it was quieter than it is here with all these trams – I can't get used to their noise. And then one day we heard that they had attacked Uad Lau, and the next day had attacked Miscrela, and the third – well, it went on like that. But we didn't bother about it. Then suddenly they told us things had gone wrong. We couldn't go to Tetuan any more. And there we were, running round in circles, and the Moors pulling long faces, and nobody coming to market any more. We hadn't anything to eat then. They wouldn't sell us food, and so we took it. We cleared up every corner in Xauen, my lad. Well, in the meantime they were peppering us with bullets. We had plenty of ammunition, otherwise we wouldn't have got out of it alive. They started throwing stones at us. Then the *Tercio* came and they said at once: "It's over, we're going." Going where? "Yes," they said, "we're all going back to Spain and the war is over." The war may have been over all right, but not even the devil could have stayed on in Xauen. They were plastering us with bullets by day and by night. Well, the Legion stayed there; they got reinforcements and Franco had come along. Then the Peninsula troops were evacuated and marched to the Zoco del Arbaa in the daytime. There was a bit of shooting on the way, but we were well covered and nothing much happened.

'You know the Zoco. I took you there first, remember? Well, it was bad when we got there. Thousands of men coming up from every side, all hungry, eaten by lice, dying of thirst, without arms, and half-naked. We all looked as if we were only fit to go begging for alms in the street. And all the brass-hats were there in the Zoco: Millán Astray, Serrano, Marzo, Castro Girona – well, all the first lot. Nobody knew what to do. The canteens had no water left. And two days after that, the Legion arrived at midnight. They had been stuffing uniforms with straw all day long and then they had got out of Xauen by night and joined us in the Zoco. They'd left the puppets leaning on the parapets, with sticks at their sides as if they were rifles. I suppose the Moors must have torn their hair next morning. But the Legionaries made us hurry: "Get off before they find out".'

Córcoles finished his glass of wine and drew lines on the table with his finger.

'You must remember the site of the Zoco. It's on the top of a hill, and if you go from there to Tetuan, at first there's a steep slope with a wood on the right. You remember a burned lorry lying there when you first came to join the Company? The Moors had ambushed a convoy just before. Well, about that slope. You go down and pass through a gully all overgrown with trees – that's where the wood begins – and then you climb up another slope. Afterwards the road goes straight to Ben-Karrick. Well, when we were going down the slope we ran into a hail of bullets. The Legion pushed on down the gully and the rest of us threw ourselves down in the ditches. The Moors got all those who didn't duck quickly enough. It took us four hours to get to the bottom of that ravine, and two hours to climb the other slope until we were in open country. It was the worst butchery I've ever seen, my lad. They killed nearly all the officers of the *Tercio*, they killed General Serrano, they wounded Millán Astray again. And you can imagine that the men were falling in hundreds if that's what happened to the big bugs. You couldn't see a thing in the bottom of the gully, what with the dust and the smoke, and the shrieks and the curses, and you kept treading on people who'd fallen. It was worse in Ben-Karrick. They were firing at us from the hills by day and night. Well, then we arrived in Tetuan, half of us, or a little less. And in Tetuan those dirty swine kept on firing from Mount Gorgues all day and all night long.'

Córcoles drank another glass of wine.

'Yes. But now listen. I can't stomach those fellows in the *Tercio*. Every one of them has either killed his own father or something like it, or else he's fit for the madhouse. But the truth is that without them the rest of us would never have got out alive. That fellow Franco is madder than the rest. I saw him in that gully, as cool as cucumber, shouting his orders: "You there, duck your head, you idiot! . . . Two men to that stone on the right . . ." A soldier would stand up and – boum – down he would go. An officer would come up to him to report – boum – down he would go. But Franco didn't get a scratch. He frightened me more than the bullets.'

He finished another glass and changed the subject:

'D'you remember the camp where the tortoises invaded us during the night and you had two little green ones in your shirt when you woke up? And you remember the camp where we had to clear out because of the fleas?'

Then came a night when we touched upon the political problems which at that time centred round Morocco.

'I don't understand a word of all the muddle over here,' said Córcoles, 'but in Morocco things are boiling over.'

We were in the Villa Rosa. Manolo brought a tray laden with little wine glasses and stayed leaning against the back of a chair. Córcoles shut up like an oyster.

'Go on,' I said.

'All right, then, I'll go on. In Morocco people are saying that we're going to clear out from there for good.'

'And we are clearing out,' stated Manolo, 'and you'll have to go on with your racket somewhere else.'

Córcoles said: 'I thought I should have shut up!'

'You go on,' I said. 'But you let other people speak too for once, Manolo.'

'All right, I won't say anything. But I won't go away.'

'You can stay, then,' said Córcoles. 'You didn't like what I said? Well, my dear friend, you'll hear a bit more. Morocco is a disgrace.'

Some of the customers turned round. Córcoles, inspired by his public, raised his voice:

'Yes, sir, a disgrace. We Spaniards have no right to abandon Morocco. What they've done to us is a dirty trick. They let thousands of our men be killed, just because the politicians thought it would be nice to get rid of Morocco. But we in the army have got our honour, and things can't go on as they are now. They won't go on, I tell you, even if Primo de Rivera himself wants them to.'

A man came up to Córcoles:

'You keep quiet – General Primo de Rivera is the Head of the State.'

Another man came after the first and pulled him by the sleeve:

'It's you who ought to keep quiet. The sergeant here's quite right. What's this – letting our men be killed and then giving up what they've paid for with blood? And using the Treaties as toilet paper, eh? You're a cad.'

Manolo stiffened:

'You little playboy, you pansy, shut up. Go on, Sergeant.'

A large crowd had gathered round our table. Most of the men vociferated that we ought to clear out of Morocco, but there was a minority which insisted on the opposite. Suddenly, the newspaper seller shouted:

'Hell – the gentlemen don't want to clear out? Long live the Republic!'

The shout was so absurdly unexpected that there was silence for a moment. Then glasses and bottles and stools were flying about. Manolo got hold of the two of us and pushed us into the corridor. He opened the private door into the Calle del Gato:

'Get out of here. You know nothing about what happened. I'm going back, I must see if I can't box the ears of one of those young fellows in there.'

The street called the 'Street of the Cat' is three yards wide and paved with large old flagstones. It is one of those odd little alleys you find in the heart of every big city: you enter there, and life is different. No vehicles pass, and hardly any people; the noise of cars and trams sounds very distant. The houses are tightly shut and shuttered. There is a tavern whose door is always closed; a shop for rubber goods; a café with waitresses and a few old hags, swollen with syphilis and gin, sitting in the entrance to wait for customers who never come. Cats walk serenely in the street, making love and snarling at the stray passers-by. Some of the street lamps on the house fronts are dark, but even those which are lighted give no light from their trembling flame, they only fill the darkness with shadows.

Córcoles and I pushed through the door of the tavern just in front of us and dived into the fumes of fried fish, spilled wine, and stale tobacco smoke. We sat down at a table and ordered fish and a couple of glasses.

'What a mess,' said Córcoles. 'I wouldn't have liked to sleep in a police station, especially while I'm in uniform.'

'Well, that's that. Now tell me what you really think, but without patriotic attacks. I know you.'

'The patriotism was for the gallery. But to tell you the truth, lad – where should we go to? If it's all over with Morocco, I can see myself stranded with 150 pesetas just now when I've got a girl I'd like to marry. And if I leave the army what can I do? It's the same for all of us. Take one of the Colonels with a pay of 999 pesetas 99 centimos, take him away from his pastures in Morocco, bring him here, with Mrs Colonel accustomed to have a party every week-end, and what do you think will happen to him? Primo has got a swollen head from his almightiness. But I can tell you now, this Morocco business will have a sting in its tail. Our people out there are prepared to rebel for better or for worse if they get orders to embark for Spain.

'And there's another thing. It's easy to say that Spain will keep Ceuta and Melilla, but have you any idea of what's happening out there now? Nowadays you can't even go on the mole by night, because the Moors of Anyera cut your throat, empty your pockets and throw you into the sea. If things go on like this, on the day we expect it least they'll pour into Ceuta and chase us into the sea. It's as much as your life is worth to travel from Ceuta to Tangier, because we hold only the narrow lane of the road and the railway line, and on both sides the Moors fire at you as they please. Primo wants something which is simply impossible: to stay there and not to be there – to have the cake and eat it.'

'Well,' I said, 'I don't know things as they are now over there, but I do know that everybody here is convinced we're going to leave Morocco. Primo de Rivera has undertaken to do it, he's promised it publicly to the country.'

'You can't make wheat grow by preaching. Neither the generals nor we – the sergeants – want to leave. If necessary, Sanjurjo will rise against Primo, and Franco with him, and the *Tercio*, and the *Regulares*. And then there's another factor.'

Córcoles had his mouth full of fried fish and let me wait.

'What other factor? The King?'

'No, sir. Bigger than that. Now look here. In Africa people talk a lot and they tell a lot of stories. Half of them are just talk. But this seems to be serious. By our retreat we've left the French with their bottoms bare. Firstly, they've lost their business of selling rifles to the Moors, and secondly, they're having the hell of a lot of bother with Abd-el-Krim. But the worst thing for them is that if we clear out of Morocco, the Germans or the English or the Italians will get hold of it, and that's something the French won't stand for. To cut a long story short, they've told Primo in all friendliness that he's got to honour the Treaties and that if he doesn't he'll have to bear the consequences. And apparently they've negotiated with Sanjurjo. They've been well in with Franco ever since he was in Paris for his studies under old man Pétain, and it looks as if everything was settled. So that in a few months we'll begin the reconquest.'

'The whole story sounds like a thriller. You must write me a letter when you get back and tell me the next instalments,' I said.

We went out into the dark little street and back into the lights and the noises a hundred steps further away.

Various things happened between January and June 1925.

The troops of Abd-el-Krim and the Raisuni had joined forces to throw the Spanish garrison out of Xauen, but when it came to sharing the spoils they quarrelled. Xauen belonged to the territory of the Jebala, the domain of the Raisuni, but the Riff warriors established themselves there as the lords and masters. The Raisuni, himself immobilized by dropsy in his mountain of Jebel Alam, sent out his supporters; the two chiefs waged war on each other. But the Raisuni was powerless against the machine guns and the artillery at the disposal of Abd-el-Krim. The war lasted not more than a few days. Then Abd-el-Krim captured the Lord of the Mountain in his castle at Tazarut, took his treasure, many millions' worth, and carried him as a prisoner to the Riff, where he died in April of the same year.

While the Chief won this victory, his brother Mohammed went to London, made a series of visits and published sensational statements in which he promised peace as soon as the European nations recognized the independence of the Riff. Simultaneously, the raids and thrusts into the French zone grew more frequent. In April, French troops sent to Morocco from the motherland launched an offensive. In May, Primo de Rivera took the most daring step of his career: he negotiated an armistice of three months with Abd-el-Krim.

The French forces suffered defeat after defeat at the hands of the Riff tribes; riotous clashes in the Chamber had their repercussions in the streets; Jacques Doriot, the Communist leader, issued a manifesto in which he branded the French Empire as the aggressor and demanded the recognition of the independence of the Riff as well as the withdrawal of France from the Moroccan Protectorate. The sending of expeditionary forces for a colonial war roused resentment and discontent in the French masses, still aching with the fresh memories of the Great War. By the end of May there were daily turbulent scenes in the Chamber and the French Government seemed powerless in its efforts to lessen the tension.

In that period I was trying to follow and to understand the development of the two great opposing ideas, Fascism and Socialism – or Communism – outside Spain. In my own country I found it difficult to fit the political movements into the orthodox pattern. The workers' movement, to which I felt I belonged, had small and articulate but uninfluential parties, and big, stirring, inarticulate masses driven by forces and feelings which defied organized expression. Primo de Rivera's dictatorship borrowed openly from the political system which Mussolini had erected; it established the 'Single Party' and Corporations. And yet few of us called Primo de Rivera a Fascist. I myself hated and distrusted the rule of generals, and still I hoped that the old man, honestly blundering, would rid Spain of the Moroccan incubus and of the wave of frightening violence. Even then I was afraid of the other forces gathering strength behind the scene; I had seen them in the making over there in Morocco, but I hardly understood what I had sensed. This vague dread made me turn to the scanty information in the press, as though by realizing what was happening outside my own country I would discover the right angle, the right perspective to gauge what was happening to us.

Doriot's action perturbed and puzzled me. It seemed to me obvious that a revolt of the French masses, led by the Communist Party under a flag borrowed for Abd-el-Krim, would inevitably provoke counter measures from all the Powers which had signed the Treaty of Algeciras. It would drive the French military caste to an immediate and effective activity. In fact, the immediate effect of Doriot's manifesto was that M. Malvy visited Primo de Rivera in Madrid and that, willy-nilly, the two Governments decided to crush Abd-el-Krim by joint action. At the time I thought that Doriot's tactics were so blatantly stupid as to equal those of an *agent provocateur*. His later career makes it possible to question whether he was not less of a clumsy demagogue than an efficient servant of his masters.

It was in the early summer of 1925 that I received a letter from Córcoles. He wrote:

'We can't know what will happen, but I think that Primo won't last long. You will have heard that Franco offered his resignation as Chief of the Legion. There is a story going round here which ought to amuse you. When Primo came to Melilla, Franco and the officers of the *Tercio* and the *Regulares* invited him to a big banquet in their mess and played a nice little joke on him. All courses were just egg dishes, fried, poached, boiled, omelettes and so on. He asked – so they say – why there was such a surfeit of eggs, and got the answer that those who wanted to get out of Morocco had no further need of their eggs – they were only needed by those who wanted to stay.[1] There was a terrible row and one of the officers is said to have drawn his revolver against Primo. Franco sent in his resignation and all officers here have declared their solidarity with him. The sergeants of the Engineers sent him a declaration of loyalty, too, and nearly all signed it. I have signed it myself.'

The kings of Spain built a great road which leads from Madrid to the North. Philip II was the first, he built it when he erected the huge stone pile of El Escorial. Later kings constructed their places of refuge nearer to their palace, at La Granja and El Pardo, but always on the road to the Guadarrama range. It became the road of King Alfonso XIII when he visited his castles or when he drove his fast car to the Cantabrian coast. And it is a road fit for kings. Thousand-year-old trees grow to its right and left, survivors from the primeval forests that once surrounded Madrid. For a stretch of the way the river Manzanares runs alongside, and there are sandy inlets, reeds and willows. A chain of hillocks covered with elms, poplars, pines and horse-chestnut trees lines up to the right until, near El Pardo, it is followed by a dense, wild, oak forest, once the property of the King.

On Sundays I used to take a book with me and walk along the North Road to the pines. Someimes I did not plunge into the woods before I had entered the chapel of Saint Anthony, at the very beginning of the road, and looked at the ceiling painted by Goya.

In the early mornings only a few old women would be at prayer, lost in the shadow of the chapel, but the stout, hearty priest would sit in the doorway of his house or in the shade of the thick, spreading trees. He knew that I had not come to pray. He would fold up his newspaper, or shut his breviary, and greet me as an old friend. Then he would take me to the sanctuary and turn on the lighting of the

[1] This joke turns on an untranslatable pun: 'eggs' is one of the Spanish slang synonyms for testicles and thus for the 'attributes of masculinity', of which Primo de Rivera himself had spoken in his manifesto. – Author's Note.

dome so that I could see the frescoes, bright behind the film of a century of candle smoke. The old women would turn their heads, stare at us and then look upwards. The priest and I used to discuss details of the painting in a church whisper. He found pleasure in pointing out the figure which is called *La Maja de Goya* and is supposed to be the Duchess of Alba, a girl in a red dress by the side of the holy hermit.

'Friend,' he would say, 'those were different times. The kings stopped here and the church was crowded. Now, the only people who come here are washerwomen who light a candle to the Saint because he's saved one of their children, or young girls who want a husband and pray on their knees to the Saint for this miracle.'

One Sunday when we came out on to the sun-dappled terrace I saw a newspaper spread on the stone seat. It was *El Debate*. Big black headlines announced an attack on the Riff coastline, in the Bay of Alhucemas. The war in Morocco had broken out afresh. The landing had been made by Colonel Franco at the head of his Legionaries.

I went into the pine woods of the Moncloa and threw myself down on the carpet of slippery needles. While I watched the Sunday antics of the crowd at the foot of the slope, I thought of Morocco; and the road of the kings running through the trees down there made me think of the road I had helped to build.

I saw the track of the road from Tetuan to Xauen, pushing onwards between the hills; I saw the men slowly digging the ground and crushing the stones.

There was something that had happened before the track had quite reached the fig tree, which was then still the crossroad between the mountain paths the Moors used on their way to the Zoco on Thursdays.

A blind Moor came slowly downhill, beating his stick against the rocks and testing them so as not to lose the thin trail on its meanderings through the thorn bushes. Suddenly the footpath came to an end and the blind man's stick tapped in the void. There was no firm ground in front of him. The Moors and the soldiers had stopped work and watched the blind man, jesting. I left my place under the fig tree and took the man by the arm to guide him down the cut in the ground. He grunted something in Arabic, which I did not understand.

'Are you going to the Zoco, old man?' I said. 'If you are, come along here. We're building a road and there is no footpath any more.'

At my words he lifted his seamy, sun-bitten face. He had a dirty white beard and red eye sockets, with rheumy lids folded back in the hollows.

'A road?'

'A road, yes, up to Xauen. It will be an even road, grandfather, where you can walk without stumbling.'

The blind man broke out into sharp, convulsive laughter. He hit the heaped soil and the trunk of the fig tree with his stick. Then he extended his arms as though to outline the wide horizon, and shrieked:

'An even road? I'll always walk on the path, always, always! I don't want my sandals to slip in blood, and this road is full of blood, all of it. I see it. And it will fill with blood again and yet again and a hundred times again!'

The mad, blind Moor climbed back on the trail, which had brought him, and for a long time we could see his dark shape on the hills, fleeing from that luckless road which pushed forward to the city.

I had forgotten him. Now I remembered. Twice already that road had been soaked with Spanish blood.

Yet in those days many thousands of men were building the tracks of new roads through all Spain.

Arturo Barea

The Forging of a Rebel

The Forge	£2.95
The Track	£2.95
The Clash	£3.50

'One of the key statements of that "desperate hope" by which modern political decency has kept going. It helped educate a generation to the necessity of radical illusions.'

George Steiner

'There is no book in any language which more vividly recreates the years of poverty, political corruption and social violence which finally erupted into the Spanish Civil War.'

Paul Preston, University of London

'Anyone who reads all three novels will end up *understanding* the Spain of Barea's day far better than by reading a dozen works of academic history.'

Martin Blinkhorn, University of Lancaster

FLAMINGO

FLAMINGO

Flamingo is a quality imprint publishing both fiction and non-fiction. Below are some recent titles.

Fiction
☐ Troubles *J. G. Farrell* £2.95
☐ Rumours of Rain *André Brink* £2.95
☐ The Murderer *Roy Heath* £1.95
☐ A Legacy *Sybille Bedford* £2.50
☐ The Old Jest *Jennifer Johnston* £1.95
☐ Dr Zhivago *Boris Pasternak* £3.50
☐ The Leopard *Giuseppe di Lampedusa* £2.50
☐ The Mandarins *Simone de Beauvoir* £3.95

Non-fiction
☐ On the Perimeter *Caroline Blackwood* £1.95
☐ A Journey in Ladakh *Andrew Harvey* £2.50
☐ The French *Theodore Zeldin* £3.95
☐ The Practice of History *Geoffrey Elton* £2.50
☐ Camera Lucida *Roland Barthes* £2.50
☐ Image Music Text *Roland Barthes* £2.95
☐ A Ragged Schooling *Robert Roberts* £2.50

You can buy Flaming paperbacks at your local bookshop or newsagent. Or you can order them from Fontana Paperbacks, Cash Sales Department, Box 29, Douglas, Isle of Man. Please send a cheque, postal or money order (not currency) worth the purchase price plus 15p per book (maximum postal charge is £3.00 for orders within the UK).

NAME (Block letters) _____

ADDRESS_____

_____

_____